New Concepts

in

Psychoanalytic Psychotherapy

New Concepts

in

Psychoanalytic Psychotherapy

Edited by

John Munder Ross, Ph.D.

Wayne A. Myers, M.D.

American Psychiatric Press, Inc.
1400 K Street, N.W.
Washington, DC 20005

Copyright © 1988 American Psychiatric Press, Inc.

ALL RIGHTS RESERVED

Manufactured in the United States of America

First Edition

92 91 90 89 88 5 4 3 2 1

The paper used in this publication meets the minimum requirements of American National Standard for Information Sciences—Permanence of Paper for Printed Library Materials, ANSI Z39.48-1984.   ∞™

Library of Congress Cataloging-in-Publication Data

New concepts in psychoanalytic psychotherapy.

Includes bibliographies and index.
1. Psychotherapy. 2. Psychoanalysis. I. Ross, John Munder.
II. Myers, Wayne A. [ENLM: 1. Personality Disorders—therapy.
2. Psychoanalytic Theory. 3. Psychoanalytic Therapy—methods. WM 460.6 N532]
RC480.5.N397   1988   616.89′14   87-33421
ISBN 0-88048-287-7

Contents

Section 1

Developmental Deficits:
Their Origin and Treatments

Edited by Samuel Wagonfeld, M.D.

Section 2

Consultation and Supervision:
The Teaching and Uses of
Psychoanalytic Developmental Theory

Edited by Wayne A. Myers, M.D., and Eugene Goldberg, M.D.

SECTION 3

Conflict and Deficit: The Kernberg/Kohut Controversy in Theory and Practice

Edited by John Munder Ross, Ph.D.

About the Editors

John Munder Ross, Ph.D.

Clinical Associate Professor of Psychology in Psychiatry at Cornell Medical Center; Faculty of The Psychoanalytic Institute at New York University Medical Center. Co-editor with George Pollock of *The Oedipus Papers* (International Universities Press, 1988); co-author with Sudhir Kakar of *Tales of Love, Sex and Danger* (Basil Blackwell, 1987); co-editor of *Father and Child* (Little, Brown, 1982), winner of the American Association of Publishers Award for the Outstanding Book in the Behavioral and Social Sciences, 1982.

Wayne A. Myers, M.D.

Clinical Professor of Psychiatry, Cornell University Medical Center; Attending Psychiatrist, New York Hospital; Training and Supervising and Admitting Psychoanalyst, Columbia University Center for Psychoanalytic Training and Research; Lecturer, Columbia University College of Physicians and Surgeons in the Department of Psychiatry. Author of *Dynamic Therapy of the Older Patient* (Jason Aronson, 1984).

Contributors

Salman Akhtar, M.D.
Professor of Psychiatry; Director, Adult Outpatient Service, Jefferson Medical College.

Maria V. Bergmann, Ph.D.
Faculty and Training Analyst Emeritus, New York Freudian Society; Member, American Psychoanalytic Association Study Group of the Effects of the Holocaust on the Second Generation; Member, American Psychological Association, Division of Psychoanalysis.

Emanuel Berman, Ph.D.
Faculty, Israel Psychoanalytic Institute; Professor, Department of Psychology, University of Haifa; Postgraduate Department of Psychotherapy, Tel Aviv University; Secretary, Israel Psychoanalytic Society; Past Chair, Clinical Division, Israel Psychological Association.

Steven A. Cohen-Cole, M.D.
Associate Professor of Psychiatry, Director of Division of Consultation-Liaison Psychiatry, Emory University School of Medicine.

Bertram J. Cohler, Ph.D.
William Rainey Harper Professor of Social Sciences in The College and Professor, Departments of Behavioral Sciences (The Committee on Human Development), Education and Psychiatry, and The Divinity School, University of Chicago.

Calvin A. Colarusso, M.D.
Training and Supervising Analyst in Child and Adult Analysis, Director, Child Psychoanalytic Training Program, San Diego Psychoanalytic Institute; Clinical Professor of Psychiatry, Director, Child Psychiatry Fellowship Program, University of California at San Diego; Faculty, Center for Advanced Psychoanalytic Studies, Princeton; Member, American College of Psychoanalysts; Secretary, Association for Child Psychoanalysts.

Robert Galatzer-Levy, M.D.
Faculty, Chicago Institute for Psychoanalysis; Lecturer, Department of Psychiatry, University of Chicago.

Eugene Goldberg, M.D.
Supervising and Training Analyst, Columbia University Center for Psychoanalytic Training and Research; Assistant Clinical Professor of Psychiatry, Albert Einstein College of Medicine.

William N. Goldstein, M.D.
Teaching Analyst, Co-Director of Extension Division, Baltimore–Washington Institute for Psychoanalysis; Associate Clinical Professor of Psychiatry and Behavioral Sciences, George Washington University School of Medicine.

John F. Kelly, M.D.
Associate Clinical Professor, University of Colorado Medical Center; Training and Supervisory Analyst, Denver Institute for Psychoanalysis.

Yale Kramer, M.D.
Clinical Associate Professor, Department of Psychiatry, University of Medicine and Dentistry of New Jersey; Assistant Lecturer, New York Psychoanalytic Institute.

Steven T. Levy, M.D.
Professor and Chief of Psychiatry, Emory University School of Medicine at Grady Memorial Hospital; Clinical Professor of Psychiatry and Psychoanalysis, Morehouse School of Medicine; Faculty, Emory University Center for Psychoanalytic Training and Research.

Carol Lyle, M.D.
Resident in Psychiatry, Emory University School of Medicine at Grady Memorial Hospital.

Homer E. Olsen, M.D.
Associate Clinical Professor, University of Colorado Medical Center; Faculty, Denver Institute for Psychoanalysis.

Henri Parens, M.D.
Supervising and Training Analyst, Philadelphia Psychoanalytic Institute; Research Professor of Child Psychiatry and Director, Infant Psychiatry Section, Medical College of Pennsylvania.

Arnold D. Richards, M.D.
Assistant Clinical Professor of Psychiatry, New York University School of Medicine; Training and Supervising Analyst, New York Psychoanalytic Institute.

Roger L. Shapiro, M.D.
Clinical Professor of Psychiatry, George Washington University School of Medicine; Faculty, Washington Psychoanalytic Institute; Consultant on Family Treatment, Chestnut Lodge Hospital; Chief of Section on Personal Development, Adult Psychiatry Division, National Institute of Mental Health.

Samuel Wagonfeld, M.D.
Faculty, Denver Institute for Psychoanalysis; Assistant Clinical Professor of Psychiatry, University of Colorado Health Sciences Center.

Acknowledgments

We would like to acknowledge the editors and organizers of the various symposia from which papers for this volume were drawn, including Samuel Wagonfeld, M.D., Eugene Goldberg, M.D., Anita Weinreb Katz, Ph.D., and Waltraud Ireland, Ph.D. We would also like to thank the former Editorial Board of the International Journal of Psychoanalytic Psychotherapy, including Richard Atkins, M.D., E. James Anthony, M.D., Martin S. Bergmann, M.A., Stanley H. Cath, M.D., Bertram J. Cohler, Ph.D., Arnold M. Cooper, M.D., Peter Bruce Dunn, M.D., Steven J. Ellman, Ph.D., Eleanor Galenson, M.D., Peter L. Giovacchini, M.D., Alan Gurwitt, M.D., James M. Herzog, M.D., Richard A. Isay, M.D., Sudhir Kakar, Ph.D., Paulina F. Kernberg, M.D., Judith S. Kestenberg, M.D., Eva P. Lester, M.D., William W. Meissner, M.D., Helen C. Meyers, M.D., Gilbert J. Rose, M.D., Vamik Volkan, M.D., Judith S. Wallerstein, Ph.D., Emanuel Berman, Ph.D., Joyce McDougall, D. Ed., Peter Hartocollis, M.D., Ph.D., Prince Masud R. Khan, Roger L. Shapiro, M.D., and Contributing Editors, Professor Erik H. Erikson, Harold Blum, M.D., and Peter Blos, Sr., Ph.D.

Additionally, we would like to acknowledge and thank Keith W. Bradley for his administrative and organizational skills and care in helping to assemble this volume. We would also like to thank Katherine Ball Ross for her helpful and welcome editorial suggestions.

Finally, we would like to dedicate the book to the memory of former Editorial Board members, recently deceased, two distinguished psychoanalysts, Margaret S. Mahler and Nathaniel Ross.

Introduction

New Concepts in Psychoanalytic Psychotherapy is a volume intended to augment the knowledge of the psychoanalytically informed and interested clinician. Its aims are to extend the reach of psychoanalysis beyond the consulting room. In so doing, we hope to demonstrate the workaday applicability of psychoanalytic developmental and technical precepts to an array of treatment, training, and educational situations beyond the confines of the couch.

A diverse group of psychiatrists, social workers, and psychologists find themselves applying the precepts and techniques of classical psychoanalysis and, more broadly, dynamic psychotherapy to a wide variety of modalities and settings. Some of these include individual, group, and family outpatient treatment; inpatient therapy, management, and pharmacotherapy; teaching mental health professionals and educators; and consultation-liaison work. However, because the differences from the practice of psychoanalysis proper have not been systematically thought out, the uses of its concepts and procedures in these other arenas have been wanting in precision and, thus, in technical consistency and practical results. Even the seasoned psychoanalyst, expert in facilitating the psychoanalytic process, can find himself or herself at a loss outside the classical psychoanalytic situation—where, in fact, most clinical work is actually undertaken and where the "rules of the game" are yet to be established.

In many of the areas noted above, time-tested methods of practice and education, conducted according to "instinct" or "experience" alone, often seem but vaguely enunciated, if they can be found to exist at all. It is our hope that this volume will provide some guidelines for those clinicians seeking a flexible yet systematic methodology for the range of interventions used not only in the office but also in the psychiatric center, school health facilities, the classroom, the outreach center, and the general hospital. That is, our goal has been to begin providing technical anchorage for the practical clinician and the everyday needs of a varied practice.

New Concepts in Psychoanalytic Psychotherapy begins with a series of clinical papers (section 1) dealing with an area of profound psychopathology familiar to many therapists, more so perhaps than the symptom and character neuroses on which the more classic analytic formulations were based—developmental deficits. These contributions elucidate both the genesis of the ego and object relational defects themselves and the psychotherapeutic interventions geared to help understand and correct them. The specific subjects dealt with in this section include border-

line and narcissistic disorders of adolescence and adult life, the severe
masochistic character, early object loss and its sequelae, creative and
pathological adaptations to early traumata, and the uses of reality in
addition to transference in the relationship of therapist and patient. The
treatment modalities described here encompass classical psychoanalysis,
psychoanalytically oriented individual psychotherapy, and family therapy utilizing inpatient and outpatient settings simultaneously. In this
work, the authors' emphases are on exposing and filling old voids, reestablishing dialogues long ago derailed, and finding the best in the
worst—that is, on "ego building" rather than on the facilitation of a
transference neurosis and the dissection of the intrapsychic conflict typical of work with less primitive patients.

A second set of articles (section 2) oversees consultation and supervision in a variety of settings outside the realm of the therapist's office.
These focus on handling of masochistic character pathology (in patients
and staff) in a medical setting; the dynamics of school consultation;
analytic contributions to teaching parents about parenting; interracial
and transcultural factors in both the training situation and the primary
clinical encounter; and the complexities of the supervisory relationship.
In the past, such efforts have been attuned more to the content alone of
what is being dealt with or imparted. The authors of these pieces stress as
well the processes involved—the people and the modes of training, instruction, and emotional learning. Issues of technique and concomitant
self-reflection are seen to be as central as those in a classical analysis.

The third and final section in the volume details current controversies
concerning the theoretical understanding and therapeutic handling of
some of the important psychopathological entities seen commonly in
clinical practice. Several summaries and critiques of some of the major
theoreticians and strategists in these areas, such as Otto Kernberg, Heinz
Kohut, Anton Kris, and Merton Gill, are offered in the hope that they will
further a deeper understanding of the borderline, narcissistic and other
severe character pathology that these authors describe. Along with theoretical and diagnostic matters, these papers also confront basic diver-
gences with regard to the rationales underlying psychoanalytic and psychotherapeutic techniques. Indeed, they ask what it is that constitutes a
good or "good-enough" result, a relative cure in the clinical situation.

In conclusion, we wish to stress that despite the changing emphases in
the broad field of psychiatry in recent years, psychoanalytically oriented
psychotherapy has proven its durability and relevance over many decades. As several of the chapters aim to demonstrate, this mode of treatment can interdigitate with, enhance, and in turn benefit from many of
the new advances, biological and otherwise, hitherto often regarded as
outside its scope. Informed by such advances, the questions and concepts
tendered here, which are themselves aimed at sharpening the discipline

and extending its reach, can serve to enrich the knowledge, vitality, and skills of a wide variety of therapists and mental health consultants. In sum, we believe that the integrative focus exemplified here can help the dynamically minded clinician to find method and meaning in the expanding range of activities now benefiting from the psychoanalytic approach.

John Munder Ross, Ph.D.
Wayne A. Myers, M.D.

Developmental Deficits: Their Origin and Treatments

Edited by
Samuel Wagonfeld, M.D.

CHAPTER 1

Family Determinants of Borderline Conditions and Pathological Narcissism in Adolescents

Roger L. Shapiro, M.D.

Recent investigations into borderline and narcissistic disturbances in adolescents raise important questions about the relation of family experience to pathological development of the self. Building on the framework of ego psychology and object relations theory, the research of Erikson (1950, 1956, 1968), Jacobson (1964), Kernberg (1975), Kohut (1966, 1968, 1971, 1977), Mahler (1968, 1971, 1975), and Masterson (1972) is concerned with the development of the self and the nature of its structure and boundaries. This work conceptualizes disturbances in the development of the self in childhood, linking these disturbances to pathological manifestations in later life (Shapiro E, 1978). It is frequently during adolescence that such pathological manifestations are first clearly seen.

In the work of Kernberg, Kohut, and Masterson, psychoanalytic reconstructions relate borderline and narcissistic disturbances in adolescents and adults to important characteristics of parent–child relationships during the child's first three years of development. Members of my research group have reported a series of studies done at the National Institute of Mental Health of families of adolescents who manifest borderline or narcissistic pathology (Shapiro R, 1967, 1969, 1979; Shapiro R and Zinner 1971; Zinner and Shapiro R, 1972, 1974; Berkowitz et al. 1974a, 1974b; Shapiro E, et al. 1975, 1977).

There are significant differences between theories different investigators have advanced about the developmental experience and the nature of the structural deficit in borderline and narcissistic pathology (Kernberg 1975; Kohut 1971). These theories derive largely from the dyadic transference observations of the psychoanalytic situation. They reflect differences in assumptions and in frameworks of personality theory within which clinical observations and interventions are made. The differences are important, in that structural constructs of pathology and theories of developmental etiology dictate theory of therapy. In consequence there are important differences in therapeutic approaches to these disorders.

In our work with families we are able to explore the differences with reference to a new body of data. In addition to observations of the individual in a regressive transference situation in individual therapy, we observe him and his family in episodes of family regression in conjoint family therapy. We find striking similarities between conceptualizations of intrapsychic structure in borderline and narcissistic individuals and the characteristics of regressive group phenomena in their families. We believe that study of the family group is an important source of evidence about the links between constructs of intrapsychic structure and characteristics of primary object relationships, a source of evidence comparable to study of the transference.

Kernberg (1975) makes a clear distinction between normal and patho-

3

logical narcissism. He considers pathological narcissism to be similar to borderline personality with respect to the characteristics of the defensive organization—that is, in both conditions one sees a lower level defensive organization characterized by a predominance of splitting or primitive dissociation, reflected in mutually dissociated or split-off ego states. He conceives of the difference between narcissistic personality structure and borderline personality organization as resulting from the presence in the narcissistic personality of an integrated, highly pathological grandiose self. The integration of the pathological grandiose self compensates for the lack of integration of the normal self-concept, which is part of the underlying borderline personality.

Kernberg's formulations represent inferences from observations of dyadic transference manifestations in individual analytic therapy. I believe these formulations can be amplified through study of patients with borderline personality or pathological narcissism in the context of their families. Family observations suggest the inference that developmental experience in these patients contains repeated and characteristic episodes of regression within all family members; through internalization, such episodes are important determinants of borderline functioning and pathological narcissism in the developing individual. Furthermore, study of the family of the patient with pathological narcissism provides evidence of a narcissistic relationship between parent and child; I propose that such a relationship is an important determinant of the pathological grandiose self in the developing adolescent.

In this paper I shall consider evidence from family observations about the activation and characteristics of regression in the family where the adolescent manifests borderline pathology alone, and I shall contrast it with analogous evidence regarding borderline pathology manifested in pathological narcissism. It is my thesis that the similarity in characteristics of family regression in these two situations parallels the fundamental structural similarity in characteristics of regression described by Kernberg in individuals with borderline personality or pathological narcissism. The difference, deriving from the presence of a narcissistic relationship between parent and adolescent, determines the pathological narcissistic self-structure in the narcissistic adolescent. I propose that the finding of a narcissistic relationship between parent and adolescent in families where the adolescent manifests pathological narcissism is relevant to an understanding of the origin of the grandiose self and is in support of Kernberg's view that the grandiose self in narcissistic personalities is a pathological structure.

To elucidate this thesis, I shall discuss briefly the framework of family theory we use to organize our family observations, and then summarize our findings in families of adolescents manifesting severe borderline pathology or pathological narcissism. I shall then present clinical material from one of the families in our study to illustrate these findings.

AN ANALYTIC THEORY OF FAMILY FUNCTIONING: UNCONSCIOUS ASSUMPTIONS AND FAMILY REGRESSION

Direct observations of the family lead us to conclude that during the course of his development and depending upon his particular emotional meaning to his parents, the adolescent who is disturbed has not been adequately supported by his parents in his efforts to accomplish phase-appropriate life tasks. In contrast to parental behavior where there is good adolescent functioning, the parents of the seriously disturbed adolescent have responded to his development with anxiety and repudiation of change in their relationships with him. In the face of progressive individuation in the developing child and adolescent, characteristic defensive behaviors are mobilized in these parents, activated by their unconscious fantasies regarding the child. These fantasies distort the parents' perceptions of the child and adolescent and dominate their responses to him.

To explore the family contribution to pathologic outcome in these adolescents, it is necessary to move beyond dyadic observations. Observations of the family reveal that each family member participates in episodes of family regression that contribute to pathology. It is through the shared participation of all family members in these episodes that the level of family regression and primitive defensive organization achieves its stability and its power.

Our findings from family observations suggest links between the adolescent's character pathology and the characteristics of defenses, regression, and distortions in the family relationships, as the child and adolescent develops. To study these links we assess the level of regression and characteristics of defense in family transactions, and the nature of unconscious fantasies that are the motives for defense. From this evidence we define shared unconscious assumptions in the family and attempt to discern the participation, contribution, and collusion of each family member in the episodes of family regression that are dominated by unconscious assumptions, and which we consider to be decisive for the developmental disturbances we are discussing. We observe repetitive behaviors in families that appear to militate against change, development, and individuation of the adolescent, and we infer that shared unconscious assumptions in family members motivate and organize these behaviors. The assumptions appear to derive from the internalized developmental experience of both of the parents in their families of origin. An organization of motives and defenses evolves in the marriage; they are operative throughout the development of the child and adolescent.

The concepts of unconscious assumptions of the family group and of family regression are constructs that originate in clinical observation. They derive from the small group theory of Bion (1961), concerning both the conscious functions and tasks that define groups and the unconscious motives in group members that may dominate group behavior and give rise to group regression. Our study of family behavior has been facilitated by using a similar framework, that of conscious family functions and tasks in contrast to a variety of unconscious motives that may dominate family behavior and lead to family regression.

When the family is in a situation of anxiety mobilized by unconscious assumptions, we find conflicting motivations and behavior that appears to be determined more by fantasy than by reality. Confused, primary process thinking emerges; understanding and adequate communication fail; and the ability of the family to work cooperatively or creatively on a task, to maintain a meaningful, progressive discussion, or to respond realistically to the problems under discussion breaks down. In short, at such times, defensive behaviors activate disturbance in the family's reality functioning and contribute to family regression. In contrast, when unconscious assumptions are not mobilized, the family does not manifest anxiety and prominent defensive behavior. It remains clearly reality oriented, functions on a mature level, and functions well in relation to tasks that facilitate development of children and adolescents.

The concept of projective identification provides a highly useful means of conceptualizing one category of primitive defenses in episodes of family regression (Zinner and Shapiro R 1972). In these episodes there is a rapid reduction in usual ego discriminations. This results in impairment in self-object differentiation, with increased splitting and projection and increased confusion over the ownership of personal characteristics that are easily attributed to other family members. The projecting individual then attempts to control the projected characteristic in the other person. When an individual assumes a role compatible with the attributions of others in the family at the regressed level, he quickly becomes the recipient of projections that tend to fix him in that role. Family members project an aspect of their own personal characteristics into him and unconsciously identify with him. The power of these projections, with their accompanying unconscious identifications, may push the individual into more extreme role behavior and constrain other potentialities of development.

CHARACTERISTICS OF REGRESSION IN FAMILIES OF BORDERLINE AND NARCISSISTIC ADOLESCENTS

The borderline outcome is described by Kernberg (1975) as a failure in ego development characterized by nonspecific ego weakness with impairment in anxiety tolerance, impulse control, and sublimatory capacities, and shifts toward primary process thinking. In addition, one finds a level of regression to a specific structure of internalized object relationships in which there is an active splitting of all good (organized around pleasurable parent–child interactions) and all bad (derived from frustrating and aggressive interactions) self images, object images, and their affective links. This pathological fixation at a developmental level of splitting processes occurs after self-object differentiation but prior to object constancy. It is the consequence of a relative predominance of "bad" introjections in the child, which requires that they continue to be split off and projected outside in order to allow a consolidation and protection of good internalized self and object images. As development progresses, the continued defensive use of splitting results in limitations in the capacity to test reality, to tolerate anxiety and frustration, and to sustain a stable integrated object relationship. Although gross reality testing is intact in the borderline adolescent, he or she is unable to integrate positive (or good) and negative (or bad) aspects of the self and others into an integrated self-concept and an integrated and stable conception of whole objects in relation to the self.

Pathological narcissism is related to borderline pathology in that its manifestations are the consequence of failure of integration of parts of the self. In narcissistic adolescents, however, the pathology of the self is a failure to integrate real and ideal images of self and object into a self-concept with stable internal regulation of self-esteem. Pathological narcissism is characterized by extreme vacillations in self-regard, reflecting two contrasting and dissociated states of narcissistic equilibrium, with states of grandiosity and omnipotence on the one hand and states of inferiority and inadequacy on the other. Intimately connected to these alternate states of self-regard are an overdependence on the confirming approval of others and an extreme sensitivity to criticism.

Kohut (1971) describes a particular kind of relationship in narcissistic pathology in which the narcissistically disturbed individual relies on the behavior of an object to determine his subjective experience of self-esteem. Such a person uses others primarily to stabilize narcissistic equilibrium by substituting for his own lack of psychological structure, rather than appreciating others for their own qualities. The object is relied upon to regulate self-esteem for the subject and is experienced and treated as an extension of the subject rather than as a separate and independent person. Narcissistic objects (self-objects or "selfobjects," in Kohut's terminology) are objects that are emotionally experienced as part of the self, rather than being responded to as separate. For the narcissistic individual, a sense of control over an object experienced as part of the self is essential to the maintenance of self-esteem. Frustrations or disruptions in the relationship to the object give rise to vengeful rage and projections of devaluation in one who is narcissistically fixated.

When adolescents manifest borderline pathology or pathological narcissism, we consistently find evidence in members of their families of a powerful cluster of unconscious assumptions that equate separation–individuation with loss and abandonment. Family members' thoughts and actions that challenge these assumptions are then perceived and reacted to as destructive attacks (Shapiro R and Zinner 1971; Shapiro E, et al. 1975). There are similarities in the characteristics of regression in families of borderline adolescents and families of adolescents manifesting pathological narcissism. Regression is activated by behavior in family members signaling separation–individuation. During adolescent individuation there is clear evidence of anxiety in the family over a perceived threat of abandonment, with regression manifested in an organization of lower level defenses of denial, splitting, and projection. There is an active splitting of aspects of self and objects within family members and these split representations are then distributed among family members by projective identification. A situation of pathological mourning is evidenced in which the individuating and separating adolescent is no longer experienced and mourned as an integrated whole object. Instead, the primitive splitting in the parents, activated by the threat of loss, results in the projection of "badness" or "devaluation" into the developing adolescent.

However, the nature of the split in the self and object representations in the family where the adolescent manifests borderline pathology differs from the split in the family of the adolescent with narcissistic pathology, with consequent differences in the nature of projections. In the family of the borderline adolescent, a structure of internalized object relations is found in which there is splitting of all "good" and all "bad" self and object images (Shapiro E, et al. 1975). Family members split off the "bad" aspects of themselves that are associated with painful and aggressive experiences with objects in the past. In particular, past painful responses to autonomous strivings within individuals, or to individually expressed needs for nurture and support, give rise to shared unconscious assumptions in the family associating such behavior with destructiveness. When this behavior is enacted by the separating adolescent, other family members project the "bad" characteristics that are denied in themselves into him. Through identification, they repudiate him as they do the split-off qualities in themselves, rebuffing the adolescent in episodes of aggressive turmoil and withdrawal. The result in the adolescent is an identity formation dominated by negative self and object images, a continuation of splitting of positive and negative internalized relationships, and a clinical picture of identity diffusion.

In contrast, in the family where the adolescent manifests narcissistic disturbance, the unconscious assumptions focus around the specific meanings of a narcissistic relationship between parent and adolescent, felt to be required for the narcissistic equilibrium of the parent and, by extension, of the entire family (Berkowitz et al. 1974a, 1974b). If a parent projects valued aspects of himself or herself into a child or adolescent and utilizes him or her as a self-object, then the narcissistic equilibrium of the parent is disturbed during individuation when the child or adolescent moves into a position no longer complementary to the parent's narcissistic need. This disruption of a central narcissistic relationship in the family disturbs the self-regard of other family members, whose narcissistic equilibrium depends on the parent who is now suffering an abrupt disturbance in self-esteem.

In families where the adolescent manifests pathological narcissism, we find a structure of internalized object relationships in which there is an active splitting of grandiose and devalued self and object images. Real, in contrast to ideal, or devalued images of self and object are not integrated in family members into a self-concept that includes stable internal regulation of self-esteem differentiated from real, idealized, or devalued objects. Family members manifest instability in self-esteem, which reflects the split between grandiose and devalued self and object images. One can recognize an effort to stabilize self-esteem in the activation of a narcissistic relationship within the family, which is experienced internally by participating family members as a relationship between the grandiose self and an idealized object (a self-object or an idealized parental image). In these families a narcissistic relationship is found between a narcissistic parent (grandiose self) and the adolescent (idealized self-object). This external relationship helps maintain the split in both parent and adolescent between the internalized relationship of grandiose self to idealized self-object, which is dissociated from inferior and devalued self and object images. The child and adolescent who is utilized by the parent as a self-object also evolves a pathological narcissistic self structure. He requires the relationship to an omnipotent parental image in order to maintain narcissistic equilibrium. Separation–individuation produces narcissistic disequilibrium in both parent and adolescent, with episodes of narcissistic rage in each and projection of split-off and devalued self and object images into the other.

Family regression militates against further differentiation of the adolescent from the family. Instead, through projective identification, boundaries between family members become even more blurred, with parents and siblings projecting into the adolescent who is attempting to individuate those feelings of devaluation denied within themselves.

AN EXAMPLE OF REGRESSED FAMILY FUNCTIONING

The following are excerpts of interactions in a family in which one adolescent manifests only borderline pathology, while the other manifests borderline pathology in pathological narcissism.

The following case material illustrates characteristics of the regression we find in families of adolescents who manifest borderline personality functioning or pathological narcissism. The adolescents were hospitalized on an adolescent psychiatric unit in the Clinical Center of the National Institute of Mental Health or were seen as outpatients. The program of treatment included three individual psychotherapy sessions per week for the adolescents, one hour per week of conjoint family therapy, and one hour of marital therapy per week for the parents. Our focus in the analytic, group interpretive family therapy was on understanding episodes of family regression, a process of clarification and interpretation that led to formulations of unconscious assumptions of the family as a group.

The Grant Family

In this family, the older son manifests combined narcissistic and borderline pathology, while the younger son manifests only borderline pathology.

The Grant family consists of Mr. Grant, age 53; Mrs. Grant, age 48; son Michael, age 18; and son Paul, age 16. The father's work in the Foreign Service required frequent travel, and the family had lived overseas for several different periods. These tours of duty overseas had interfered with Mrs. Grant's work as a public service lawyer, and she resented them very much. Michael began to have major difficulties during the last period abroad, between ages 14 and 16. He refused to go to school, fought with his parents, and spent days wandering in the foreign city in which they lived. Several times he ran away from home, and delinquent activities got him into trouble with the local authorities.

During the same period, Paul became isolated and withdrawn. He had no friends and spent much time at home alone studying. He continued to do well in school.

Past history relevant to separation and loss includes the fact that each parent lost a mother during childhood—the father when he was 6 and the mother when she was 10. The father's father remarried after several years, but the new marriage was stormy and lasted only five years. The father described a difficult and distant relationship with his own father. The mother's father did not remarry, and she was cared for by her older sister.

Michael continued to have serious difficulties after the family's return to this country, when he was 16. He returned to school for several months but then was expelled for drinking and smoking marijuana. Fighting with his parents escalated, and he left home. He wandered around the country and worked sporadically for several months. Finally, he returned home, refused to work or go to school, and generally isolated himself from the family and from high school friends, except for his girlfriend, Katie. He became involved in Yoga and ate a vegetarian diet. He was frequently grandiose in his thinking, behaved contemptuously to his parents, and was hostile toward his brother Paul. At other times, he expressed anxiety and hopelessness about the future and complained of depression, lack of confidence in himself, and loss of interest in anything. After much fighting and persuasion, and with much hesitation, he finally saw a psychiatrist at his parents' insistence and was referred to NIMH and to our project.

Although Michael was the focus of his parents' concern, it was clear that Paul was also troubled. He continued to be quiet and withdrawn throughout this period, to have no friends, and to be extremely irritable toward his parents. However, his performance at school was good, and the parents did not seem particularly concerned about him. We later learned that his isolation was necessary, if he was not to experience paranoid anxiety over his own (projected) anger and sexual feelings.

Excerpt 1

The first excerpt of family therapy is from the assessment interview prior to Michael's admission to the adolescent unit. The interaction, which is early in the session, demonstrates an initial sharp difference in the parents' perceptions of Michael. The father expects him to be explicit about what his problems are. He clearly puts him into the role of being the family problem. The mother speaks for Michael and requires very little of him. Her perception of him as anxious prevents her from expecting anything of him in the interview, and she has difficulty distinguishing his anxiety from her own anxiety. She does not listen to him. We take this to be initial evidence of the mother's narcissistic relationship to Michael. She does not psychologically distinguish herself from him, treating him as a sensitive and fragile aspect of herself and as if he is having the same responses in the interview situation that she does. Michael's behavior early in the session is grandiose. He ignores his father's efforts to put him in the patient role and devalues the doctors. He attempts to dissociate himself from his mother's feelings of helplessness and sameness with him.

> Father: Isn't it true that some basic dissatisfaction with things as they are brings you here or forces you here in some sense?
>
> Michael: Yeah, but look—everybody, you know, has dissatisfactions— with things as they are, you know—I mean I just went to the shrink and the shrink said, "Why did you want to come see me?" and I said "Not particularly," and he says, "I think then, you know, you ought to do an inpatient thing," so that was the way he saw things. I mean there were a lot of things he could have said—he could have said, "Why don't you hitchhike to San Francisco?" or something like that. I don't know.
>
> Mother: Michael, I'm—you know, I have something going on in my gut—I'm sympathizing with you because I—could tell from what you were saying before that you were kind of—probably terrified by this thing—starting, and then you said something about your defenses and . . .
>
> Michael (interrupting): I'm not—I'm not terrified. It's like when I came in and talked with the doctor he said, "Well, why don't you talk to me, I'm a doctor?" You know, well I don't care if you're God, you know, that doesn't mean I should talk to you. Well—if you were God it might be different, you know, but I don't see *this* that way. But, just because you're a doctor doesn't mean I'm supposed to say, you know, it doesn't mean that it's all right that I should talk with him.
>
> Therapist (to mother): What were you starting to say? You were starting to say something about your response to Michael?
>
> Mother: Yeah—I think it's frightening—he's not used to coming into a room with a lot of people—and strangers, so I think it's natural for Michael to be—anxious right now and he doesn't know what to say— particularly—and so I feel like I understand that—what he's struggling with—ah, so when I say what's going on in my gut I am sympathizing and, ah, realizing that I have some anxieties too, and ah, ah, I think that probably we all have. You know, when we're searching and—we don't know the answers and we're here so, we're trusting you, you know, strangers to help us out.
>
> Michael: I haven't! I haven't tried trusting him—I'm not—I mean, you probably are, you've figured that one out. . . .

Excerpt 2

The next excerpt is from a family therapy session two months after Michael was admitted to the hospital. The parents are complaining about how abusive Michael has been to his mother over the weekend. Both adolescents complain about their parents' overprotection and over-concern. It is clear that the parents are hurt and angry when their wishes for closeness and control in relation to their sons are rebuffed. There is evidence in this excerpt for a shared assumption in the family that autonomous functioning of a family member is experienced as a loss and responded to as destructive behavior.

There is a clear difference in the mother's responses to her two sons. She is sad and bereft at separation from Michael and wants contact with him even though she is rebuffed. She projects her own feelings of being a deserted, angry, empty creature into him. She sees him as a scarecrow as he is leaving home to return to the hospital. When it is interpreted, she is able to see that much of the sadness really is her own response to the loss of a valued and exciting part of herself. Her response to Paul's with-drawal from her is far less intense. She acts oblivious of him and takes no account of what he says. She counters his separateness from her with repudiation of him.

The father is eager to effect a separation between his wife and Michael. He shares with his wife a tendency to overcontrol both sons. His willing-ness to acknowledge this is motivated by a hope that his wife will turn to him for the relationship she has for years sought in Michael.

Therapist: What abuse did Michael give you this weekend?

Mother: I don't know. It's just so routine—anything I ask him he just doesn't respond to—or he says leave me alone—or, if I knock on his door, it's locked and he won't come out, or he won't speak—or I'll ask if he wants any food, or, I mean, it's just such a multiple—most of the contexts are like this all the time—and you know—I don't feel *that's* Michael.

Therapist: Who is it?

Mother: I know it's a present expression of whatever he's like—but I mean—I can't feel this is anything but temporary—I feel—we've always been such good friends—we've always had such a good relationship—I find it very difficult to understand or explain—or anything—to have him behave this way.

Father: Well, you understand, his behavior of the moment is not of the stimulus–response type. I mean he's generalized something and he's just throwing it back at you no matter what you say—or what you offer him—or what you take away from him—you'll just get the same response. In this particular case, as I recall her telling me, he came into the kitchen wanting food and she offered him food—or something of this kind—and she got abuse for it—I think that was the situation.

Mother: Let me tell you something that happened last night. I'm aware that he has been angry at me for a long time—and last night before he went out I said, "Have a good week," and gave him a big hug as he went out the door—thereupon Paul fell to the floor—and he acted in exaggerated response to my saying that to Michael—he said, "My God," he was burlesquing and making fun in terms. . . .

Michael: I don't think so. . . .

Mother: What do you think?

Michael: Most of my responses are not so generalized—I think they're pretty specific—you know—I mean occasionally it just reaches a level—that's true—which is a bad thing—I mean—in general like say I'm sitting at the table, and you're saying, "Would you like some milk? Would you like some of this? Would you like some of that?"—you know, I mean, I think I'm perfectly capable of doing it myself, you know.

Father: What do you mean by doing it—do you mean getting it?

Michael: I mean pouring the milk in my glass—it's sitting right in front of me—you know—and it's pretty far out, I think, I mean this is the kind of thing I'm talking about.

Father: You think she's moved in on you—she's doing things for you that you want to do for yourself.

Michael: Well, she has been all my life, and it's really kind of a drag.

Mother: Michael, you don't respond like anybody else in the family—if you did, nobody would ask you these questions.

Michael: That's not true—you do it all the time—to everybody, anyway.

Paul: How do I respond to these things? I don't see any great difference between us.

Mother: If I ask you for something you say, "Yes, sure I'll have some," and I'll hand it to you or something.

Michael: Bull shit.

Mother: Or if you don't want any you say, "No," and if I'm. . . .

Michael: You're just doing the same thing. A little while ago you said how we've always been such great friends.

Paul: For the first ten times you ask me for something I give you an "Ugh"—then I get concerned about this—I think there's something wrong with me for not responding, and I try to make my position clear and sort of end the whole discussion right there by talking to you and saying, "No, thank you, will you please not bother me anymore."

Mother: Or I'll get it myself—or whatever you want.

Paul: And I expect you to be a little hurt by this—but also understand what my feelings are so that behavior like this on your part will not continue day after day—but. . . .

Therapist: Does it?

Paul: It does—it's not terminated by one lecture like this on my part.

Michael: Last night—right—so I said, "Goodbye, I'll see you tomorrow," and you just kept on talking, so I walked out the door—then I remembered I forgot my cigarettes—I didn't want to go back, but I went back anyway—and I got my cigarettes, and this time on my way out you grabbed me and hugged me—and I stood there, which was the only response that I could do—and that is what I think Paul got off on—was that I was just standing there and being. . . .

Father (laughing): A wooden Indian. . . .

Michael: Well, you think that it's amusing—I don't think that it's amusing at all—I mean, you know—it has an amusing side.

Mother (laughing): Well, we were—I was just responding to that aspect.

Michael: But just a little while ago you said we've always been friends and you can't understand how we're not friends anymore—which is another bunch of bull shit—I mean, nobody's ever always friends. We haven't always been friends—we haven't always gotten along well— and all that kind of jazz—and then you just tried to do the same thing again with Paul and say that Paul he always does it straight—Paul is more far out about it than I am—except you see that I get angry more than Paul does.

Father: Paul, you do the same thing to me if I hover over you too much. You let me have it too, and I think it's true that we don't learn in this respect—you know—we do too much for them—we're after them—we just overprotect them from A to Z—and with Michael—he's just got it up to here—he's smothered.

Michael: Yes.

Therapist: How was the fall on the floor a comment on that?

Father: Well, he falls apart laughing—it seems to me it's very clear.

Michael: He wasn't laughing.

Father: He must have been.

Mother: I think he was trying to get it through to me the incongruity of the act—and I think I saw this very clearly, and this was his attempt to convey it to me.

Therapist: What was incongruous?

Mother: Just what Michael said. You know, Michael stood there like this—and it was obvious that whatever I was doing was unwanted— completely rejected—and I was doing something very—from my point of view an entirely spontaneous simple act—and he, you know, this was terrible to him—and so it has its funny side.

Therapist: What was this spontaneous simple act from your point of view, Mrs. Grant?

Mother: Well, you know, as he went out of the door I said—I put my arms on him like this and said, "Have a good week"—or something like that—and obviously he didn't want this—now I rarely. . . .

Father: You put your arms around him I think is what we heard a minute ago.

Mother: I scarcely touch him in any way—because I feel that, you know, he doesn't want me to have anything to do with him—and he doesn't want to touch me or have me touch him or have me mother him or anything. So most of the time I try to be very careful about this—perhaps, I don't know, I had a surge of motherly something or other, and just as I would to anybody—my husband going out the door—or anybody—of my children—of my family. I don't touch people usually—I'm not demonstrative usually—I think that occasionally I feel badly about Michael, I guess, and so I react to this and. . . .

Father: But you see this is more of the same.

Michael: So you think if you hug me that's going to make everything really good?

Mother: No, I don't think any such thing.

Father: Michael is upset about it.

Therapist: I'm still wondering about the simplicity of the act. I don't think anyone in the family is all that simple.

Mother: Well, I think I was responding—I guess—to the sadness, you know, in Michael. He looks like a. . . .

Michael (interrupting): Obviously I didn't want you to hug me—why did you do it anyway?

Mother (interrupting): Scarecrow often—most of the time—pardon?

Michael: Obviously I didn't want you to hug me. Why did you do it anyway? Everytime when I leave and go out somewhere you always start talking, and, and, like it's really ridiculous—like I'm supposed to sit there and listen to whatever you have to say—you know, because I'm leaving, so you should put all this rap on me—I don't know—it's pretty far out—it's not very simple at all.

Therapist: It's even hard to locate the sadness, Mrs. Grant, because you say you see so much sadness in Michael, and he says he sees so much sadness in you. I think there's a great effort in the family to put the sadness someplace else instead of people thinking about their own. . . .

Mother: Well, I feel sad.

Therapist: I think you feel sad when he leaves and start seeing him like a scarecrow—but I think it may be your sadness at that moment.

Mother: Okay, it's my sadness, it was my impulsive need perhaps to get close to him or reassure myself—or something—I don't know. It was in that sense that I meant simple—it wasn't anything that one wouldn't do naturally with one's own family—it wasn't anything strange.

Excerpt 3

The next excerpt, taken from a family therapy session three months after Michael's admission to the hospital, provides a further view of Michael's relationship to his father. The father and son have been mutually antagonistic for years. The family has understood this as a consequence of the mother's special relationship to Michael. She felt Michael understood her better than her husband did.

The previous weekend the father found marijuana in Michael's room and flushed it down the toilet without talking to Michael about it at all. There was a fight later on, Michael saying he was furious at not being talked to. In the family session these events have been told. The father and son are both hurt by the distance between them. Each projects into the other split-off painful and disappointing experiences with a father, with the consequence of increasing alienation.

Father: Michael did say he's very angry—but then he got over it so he's plowed it under or something—you can't call it up now?

Michael: Call what up?

Father: Your angry feelings.

Michael: I'm angry all the time.

Father: What are you angry about—can you talk about it? As long as you can't talk about it, as long as you can't express it—particularly the part that relates to me—in some sense you are going to be tied to me—you're going to be hung up on it and you're never going to get rid of me.

Therapist: Maybe he thinks *you* want to get rid of *him*.

Father: Maybe he does. *Do* you?

Michael: I don't know—you seem to have gotten rid of yourself, you know.

Father: How did I get rid of myself?

Michael: Pardon me?

Father: How did I get rid of myself?

Michael: Well, you hid it away, I guess.

Father: You mean you don't see it.

Michael: No, I don't think I've ever seen it, actually.

Father: Okay, well maybe I turn you off, but unless you can get feelings against me which. . . .

Michael (interrupting): I have lots of feelings against you.

Father: . . . can be expressed, my thought is you're going to be tied to me—unless it's all hung up on your mother—but I don't know.

Michael: Well, you know—

Therapist: You said you had feelings against your father.

Michael: That's what I said.

Father: Name a few.

Michael: I'm not really up for it—you know.

Mother: Michael, I couldn't hear what you said, or I couldn't understand. You said he must have hid it away—what is it you felt he hid away?

Father: Myself.

Mother: Is that what you were saying?

Michael: Um hum, he [therapist] said he [father] wanted to get rid of me—I said he [father] already got rid of himself—so he is trying to get rid of me now.

Mother (to father): What do you think of this?

Father: Well, it bespeaks an alienation which is all too plain, but I feel his distance—I've felt it for some time—but I haven't known how to budge it. . . . I know that something at least comparable happened between my father and myself—I just crossed him off my list, so to speak. Maybe that's what Michael did to me. But it seems we ought to be able to talk about it in a way which would be wholesome.

Michael: Well. . . .

Father: I'm not asking you to like me—its not my right to—that's up to him.

Excerpt 4

The next excerpt is taken from a discussion in family therapy six months after Michael entered the hospital. The mother has just returned from a sudden visit to her older sister, who lives in another state and was hospitalized for a serious illness. The family is discussing some specific aspects of the way the mother left on this trip. Michael was at home with his girlfriend when the mother was called about her sister's illness and decided to go. The mother asked Michael to call his father and tell him, as she didn't want to "bother him" at work. Michael refused to do this, but did help his mother with arrangements for the trip. The mother didn't talk to Paul about the trip or say goodbye to him, although he was at home in his room. The mother was clearly upset at the serious illness of the sister, who had taken care of her after their mother died. She could relate to Michael as an idealized self-object, all giving and all loving to her during her time of need. She describes this in the excerpt despite Michael's protests. She did not want to talk to her husband or to Paul. The excerpt begins with her statement to her husband that she does not experience him as understanding or sharing and helpful (as she does Michael). The same is true of her experience of Paul. She does not idealize her husband or Paul as she does Michael (and her mother and her sister). She experiences Mr. Grant and Paul as she did her father—as remote, angry, depressed, and emotionally unavailable to her.

Mother (to father): Well, I think what bothers me some about it is that intellectually you say that you are willing to help and—you do—logistics; you do everything you can and you're very kind and very helpful, very supportive—but I think that the fact that you don't share your privacy with us—at all—ever, you know, you kind of cut up, and you cut off feeling so that there's not the feeling exchange. Do you understand what I mean?

Father: I'm thinking about it. Of course, I hear what you say and. . . .

Mother: There isn't the resonance—somehow.

Michael: Well, I mean, like when you went up to New York when you said you were going and you said: "Well, I'm going up to New York," I mean, I didn't get really upset. I just thought it was pretty far out, you know. And ah, I asked her [mother], you know, if she [mother's sister] was all right—if she was dying or something, and you said you didn't think she was dying and, ah. . . .

Mother: Well, Katie and Michael were together, and Michael came in and said, "You look very disturbed, Mother."

Michael: And then I said, "Well then, are you? Are you upset?" You know, 'cause I couldn't really tell because you were just acting kind of freaky I thought.

Mother: What's that word?

Michael: Kind of freaky.

Mother: Freaky, what does that mean?

Michael: I don't know.

Father: Upset.

Michael: Well, not upset, I couldn't tell. You said you weren't upset so I was. . . .

Mother: I said what?

Michael: That you weren't upset.

Mother: No. I said, "I don't know, Michael. I'm just going around doing the things I have to do as fast as I can do them." I just didn't have time to think whether I was upset or not.

Michael: Well, I mean I guess you were upset, but it wasn't really communicated to me, I mean, like I knew that you were.

Mother: Well, I wasn't crying. I was just seriously going about trying to, you know, the wheels were going around.

Michael: You were kind of—in a daze or something.

Mother: Michael, I thought you and I didn't have to talk! I didn't have to talk. I didn't have to explain anything or discuss it, or anything. You picked up just like that, and you went ahead and you did it. And you didn't argue about it. Ah, and this was great, you know, it was—just like a 100 percent support.

Therapist: I'm wondering, Paul was at home—what is the meaning? There didn't seem to be any calling you [Paul] to get you to do some of these things like call the airport, get a suitcase, or what not.

Michael: Well, I mean, any monkey can do things like that.

Mother: Well, whoever was around, you know, would have gotten corralled, and Paul was asleep and downstairs, and this all happened upstairs. So, he just wasn't, if he had been there and I asked him he would have gotten the suitcase immediately, too or even. . . .

Father: You didn't lack for hands, because both Michael and Katie were there.

Discussion of Excerpts

These excerpts contain examples of interaction of a family functioning at a regressed level that is dominated by unconscious assumptions equating individuation and separation with catastrophic loss. Family regression militates against any realistic experience of phase-appropriate separation and suffuses individuation with anxiety. This is true for the parents as well as the adolescents. Problems in the parents' individuation in their own adolescent development are reactivated at the time of separation–individuation of their adolescent offspring.

The excerpts contain evidence of a narcissistic relationship between Mrs. Grant and Michael, in which she has difficulty differentiating herself from him and projects idealized aspects of herself into him. The qualities of sensitivity, gentleness, empathy, and helpfulness that are projected into Michael originate in the internalized idealized relationship to her own mother, which is vital to her self-esteem. The relationship with an idealized mother is split off from the traumatic relationship to a mother of separation ending in death. The idealized relationship is stabilized by enlisting Michael as a self-object into whom she projects the characteristics of the idealized parental image. She responds to Michael's separation and individuation from her as narcissistic injury, as she did to her mother's death. In her narcissistic rage and depression, she projects into Michael split-off helpless and devalued aspects of herself in relation to a dying mother who left her.

Mrs. Grant is unable to invest her husband or Paul with the idealized qualities she projects into Michael. Both Mr. Grant and Paul are perceived by her as unempathic, remote, and critical. She relates to them as she did to her distant and critical father, and ignores and repudiates them as she felt he ignored and repudiated her.

Mr. Grant is an isolated, depressed, highly controlled, and intellectualizing man, who is pessimistic about the possibility of a good relationship with either of his sons. He responds to their rejection of him with intellectualizations and split-off hopelessness and angry repudiation, projecting into them his own angry behavior with his own father. His rivalry with Michael for Mrs. Grant's interest is intense and overt. Mr. Grant's relationship with his wife is built upon his internal relationship with his own mother. His mother's death when he was 6 was experienced by him as a traumatic desertion, and he projects his split-off bad experience with a dying mother into his wife when she withdraws from him, with ensuing rage and repudiation of her.

Michael manifests predominantly narcissistic pathology. He participates with his mother in a relationship in which his narcissistic equilibrium depends upon his involvement with her as a self-object. With separation–individuation, loss of this relationship with his mother has resulted in his grandiose feelings giving way to feelings of inferiority and worthlessness, with rage and efforts to project devaluation into his mother. He attempts to regain narcissistic equilibrium through a relationship with Katie, which is sexual and highly dependent, and modeled on the narcissism of his relationship with his mother. However, his fragile self-esteem cannot withstand the real challenges of school or work. He is very threatened by competition with men or peers, and fears of their malevolence have their origin in his relationship with his father.

Paul manifests overt borderline pathology. He is greatly impaired in personal relationships, experiencing paranoid anxiety with projection of destructiveness into any relationship with another person in which he attempts to initiate satisfying activity and exert independent control. He does not feel safe either in the expression of autonomous behavior or in the expression of emotional needs for nurture and satisfaction. He experiences himself as controlled by the other person, then feels enraged and projects that rage into the other person, who, he feels, hates him. His long-standing repudiation of his mother has gained him her disinterest. She usually behaves as if she were oblivious of him. His father reacts to Paul's anger with distancing, and controlled rage. Paul has retained his competence in school, a predictable arena in which he can easily fulfill expectations. However, his personal relationships are painful and frightening and dominated by projections of internalized bad self and object relationships. His limited capacity to maintain a relationship to the good internalized object requires that he experience himself as conforming and controlled. He becomes anxious in any situation of need satisfaction and has no internal permission for any sort of sexual expression.

The family has the characteristics we have described in families of borderline and narcissistic adolescents—vulnerability to separation–individuation, and regression to an organization of splitting of positive and negative self and object representations in family members, with defensive projective identification.

Projections into Paul from both parents are of negative self and object representations organized around pain and aggression. Both parents have denied and dissociated their own needs for support and nurture during individuation, which have been linked to painful experiences with objects in the past. When these demands are enacted by Paul, the parents, through identification, repudiate him as they do these split-off qualities in themselves.

The situation is different for Michael, whose development has been decisively influenced by an enduring narcissistic relationship with his mother. She has utilized him as a self-object and has projected valued and idealized aspects of herself into him. His efforts to separate give rise to withdrawal in him and narcissistic rage and depression in his mother, affecting the narcissistic equilibrium of the entire family.

DISCUSSION: FAMILY DETERMINANTS OF BORDERLINE CONDITIONS AND PATHOLOGICAL NARCISSISM IN ADOLESCENTS

The findings that I have discussed about characteristics of family regression reveal both similarities and differences in families of borderline adolescents and families of narcissistic adolescents. I believe these are related to structural similarities and differences in individuals manifesting borderline personality and pathological narcissism. Our findings in families have a close relationship to Kernberg's discussion of structural similarities and differences between individuals with borderline personality organization and pathological narcissism. Kernberg states that the similarities are reflected in the predominance of mechanisms of splitting in both conditions, reflected in the presence of mutually dissociated or split-off ego states. Thus, for example, in pathological narcissism haughty grandiosity and feelings of inferiority may co-exist without affecting each other. These splitting operations are maintained and reinforced by primitive forms of projections, particularly projective identification, omnipotent control, narcissistic withdrawal, and devaluation. In addition, narcissistic personalities and borderline personality organization are characterized, from a dynamic point of view, by similar pathological condensation of genital and pregenital needs under the overriding influence of pregenital aggression.

Kernberg discusses the differences between narcissistic personality structure and borderline personality organization through use of the construct (in the narcissistic personality) of an integrated although highly pathological grandiose self. He defines the grandiose self as a pathological condensation of some aspect of the real self (the "specialness" of the child reinforced by early experience), the ideal self (the fantasies and self images of power, wealth, omniscience, and beauty that compensated the small child for experiences of severe oral frustrations, rage, and envy), and the ideal object (the fantasy of an ever-giving, ever-loving, and accepting parent in contrast to the child's experience in reality; a replacement of the devalued real parental object).

Kernberg goes on to say that the integration of the pathological grandiose self in narcissistic personality compensates for the lack of a normal integrated concept of self, which is a consequence of their underlying borderline personality organization. In this way he explains the paradox in narcissistic personality of relatively good ego functioning and surface adaptation in the presence of a predominance of splitting mechanisms, a related constellation of primitive defenses, and the lack of integration of object relations.

Kernberg notes that his description of the general characteristics of the pathological grandiose self coincides with clinical descriptions of this condition by many authors. However, he points to a basic disagreement with Kohut regarding the origin of the grandiose self. In Kohut's view, the grandiose self represents the fixation of an archaic "normal" primitive self. In Kernberg's view, it reflects a pathological structure clearly different from normal infantile narcissism.

I believe that the consistent findings of a narcissistic relationship between parent and adolescent in families where the adolescent manifests pathological narcissism is relevant to an understanding of the origin of the grandiose self and is in support of Kernberg's view that the grandiose self in narcissistic personalities is a pathological structure.

Our evidence indicates that both in families of borderline adolescents and in families of narcissistic adolescents, early experience in the family as well as current experience is deficient in empathy, is highly frustrating, and is lacking in age-appropriate idealization by parents. However, the pathological narcissistic structure of the grandiose self does not develop in the borderline adolescent, as would be expected if it resulted, as Kohut postulates, from the fixation of an archaic normal primitive self brought about by early frustration, lack of empathy, and lack of age-appropriate idealization by parents. This calls into question the view advanced by Kohut. We find evidence of pathological narcissism only in adolescents from families where a narcissistic relationship between parent and adolescent is found, in which a narcissistic parent utilizes the child and adolescent as a self-object. This suggests that the pathological structure of the grandiose self is determined by the child and adolescent's experience during development in an actual relationship with a narcissistic parent who is impaired in his or her capacity to differentiate from the child. Kernberg states that the pathological condensation of the grandiose self in the adolescent contains a component of the real self that reflects certain early experiences in addition to the usual specialness of the child.

I would suggest it is the child's experiences as the self-object of a parent, vital to that parent's self-esteem, which are crucial internalizations of the real self in pathological narcissism.

In the narcissistic relationship to a child, the parent is frequently attempting to revive a special relationship from his or her family of origin, which has been important to the maintenance of narcissistic equilibrium in the parent. The parent projects idealized qualities of the lost object into the child and adolescent and suffers an acute disturbance of self-esteem when the child and adolescent differentiates himself from the limitations of parental projections. These parental projections are extremely coercive in that they are required by the parent in order to maintain his or her narcissistic equilibrium, and by extension the narcissistic equilibrium of the entire family. This gives the child and adolescent unusual power, an aspect of the real self that is frequently reflected in the grandiose self of the narcissistic adolescent.

The pathological grandiose self postulated by Kernberg also contains the ideal self, which has developed to defend against parental devaluation in episodes of narcissistic rage. It also helps the child and adolescent to withstand his own rage and envy when the narcissistic parent becomes occupied with other family members or other interests, which the adolescent experiences as a loss.

Finally, the pathological condensation of the grandiose self contains a component that is the ideal object, which also reflects the child and adolescent's experience in a narcissistic relationship with a parent. Here, the fantasy of an ever-giving, ever-loving, and accepting parent is not entirely a contrast to the child's experience in reality. Kernberg states (1975, p. 265) that the ideal object does not accord with the child's experience with the object in reality. In my view, the fantasy of the ideal object does reflect the child's experience in reality when the narcissistic relationship with the parent is in equilibrium and he or she is the recipient of inappropriate idealizations from an "ideal" parent. When through separation–individuation, the child and adolescent disturbs this equilibrium, the parent's narcissistic rage and devaluation is defended against through reciprocal devaluation of the parent and defensive reinforcement of the internal "ideal" parental image, which is condensed into the pathological grandiose self.

The split, bad, devalued self in the child and adolescent contains internalizations of negative self and object images that reflect experiences with the narcissistic parent, where attempts at separation–individuation result in narcissistic rage and projections of badness and devaluation into the child and adolescent.

Work with these families in family therapy provides us with detailed historical material, as well as current observations of the narcissistic relationship. From this we can reconstruct evidence about the early narcissistic relationship between parent and child, which has relative stability over time and becomes crucial to the narcissistic equilibrium of the entire family. The consistent finding of such a relationship in a family where the adolescent manifests a narcissistic structure leads me to conclude that the grandiose self in narcissistic patients is a pathological structure, whose characteristics are determined by a narcissistic relationship to a parent. I agree with Kernberg that it is a pathological structure clearly different from normal infantile narcissism, and I disagree with Kohut that the grandiose self in the narcissistic patient simply reflects the fixation of an archaic normal primitive self. Neither Kernberg nor Kohut adequately conceptualizes structural consequences of a narcissistic relationship with a parent in the formation of the grandiose self, although both frequently provide clinical evidence of such a narcissistic relationship in their reconstructions of childhood experiences of narcissistic patients.

REFERENCES

Berkowitz D, Shapiro R, Zinner J, et al: Concurrent family treatment in narcissistic disorders in adolescence. Int J Psychoanal Psychother 1974a; 3:370-396

Berkowitz D, Shapiro R, Zinner J, et al: Family contributions to narcissistic disturbances in adolescence. International Review of Psychoanalysis 1974b; 1:353-362

Bion W: Experiences in Groups. London, Tavistock, 1961

Erikson E: Childhood and Society. New York, Norton, 1950

Erikson E: The problem of ego identity. J Am Psychoanal Assoc 1956; 4:56-121

Erikson E: Identity: Youth and Crisis. New York, Norton, 1968

Jacobson E: The Self and The Object World. New York, International Universities Press, 1964

Kernberg O: Borderline Conditions and Pathological Narcissism. New York, Aronson, 1975

Kohut H: Forms and transformations of narcissism. J Am Psychoanal Assoc 1966; 14:243-272

Kohut H: The psychoanalytic treatment of narcissistic personality disorders. Psychoanal Study Child 1968; 23:86-113

Kohut H: The Analysis of the Self. New York, International Universities Press, 1971

Kohut H: The Restoration of the Self. New York, International Universities Press, 1977

Mahler M: On Human Symbiosis and the Vicissitudes of Individuation,

Vol. I: Infantile Psychosis. New York, International Universities Press, 1968

Mahler M: A study of the separation–individuation process and its possible application to borderline phenomena in the psychoanalytic situation. Psychoanal Study Child 1971; 26:403-424

Mahler M: The Psychological Birth of the Human Infant. New York, Basic Books, 1975

Masterson J: Treatment of the Borderline Adolescent: A Developmental Approach. New York, Wiley, 1972

Shapiro E: The psychodynamics and developmental psychology of the borderline patient: a review of the literature. Am J Psychiatry 1978; 134:1305-1315

Shapiro E, Zinner J, Shapiro R, et al: The influence of family experience on borderline personality development. International Review of Psychoanalysis 1975; 2:399-411

Shapiro E, Shapiro R, Zinner J, et al: The borderline ego and the working alliance: indications for family and individual treatment in adolescence. Int J Psychoanal 1977; 58:77-89

Shapiro R: The origin of adolescent disturbances in the family: some considerations in theory and implications for therapy, in Family Therapy and Disturbed Families. Edited by Zuk G, Boszormeny I. Palo Alto, CA, Science and Behavior Books, 1967

Shapiro R: Adolescent ego autonomy and the family, in Adolescence: Psychosocial Perspectives. Edited by Caplan G, Lebovici S. New York, Basic Books, 1969

Shapiro R: Family dynamics and object-relations theory. Adolesc Psychiatry 1979; 7:118-135

Shapiro R, Zinner J: Family organization and adolescent development (1971), in Task and Organization. Edited by Miller E. London, Wiley, 1976

Zinner J, Shapiro R: Projective identification as a mode of perception and behavior in families of adolescents. International Journal of Psychoanalysis 1972; 52:523-530

Zinner J, Shapiro R: The family group as a single psychic entity: implications for acting out in adolescence. International Review of Psychoanalysis 1974; 1:179-186

CHAPTER 2

From Transitional Object and Imaginary Companion in Childhood to Agoraphobic Companion in Adult Life: A Creative–Pathological Continuum

Wayne A. Myers, M.D.

In this chapter, clinical material will be presented from the analysis of a woman who suffered from agoraphobia with panic attacks in adult life. What is unusual about her case is that the data from the treatment brought to light a continuum in her life, which oscillated between the creative and the pathological. An early transitional object, which was later also used as an infantile fetish object, served in part as the basis for imaginary companion fantasies during her latency years. These, in turn, became incorporated into her adolescent masturbatory sagas, as well as into her childhood and adult creative writing. Finally, all of the preceding objects could be seen to play a significant role in the determination of her choice of her husband as her adult agoraphobic companion.

I do not wish to imply here that there is an absolutely predictable relationship between the specific childhood phenomena delineated above and the specific adult neurotic symptom, agoraphobia, and the presence of an agoraphobic companion, though I believe that this may be true in other instances than the one case described here. Any such far-reaching generalizations would be beyond the scope of the data that I thus far possess and would also tend to give short shrift to the significant body of evidence accumulated in the general psychiatric literature concerning the possible biological substratum of agoraphobic panic attacks. What I most wish to call attention to here is that these phenomena sequentially, and I believe interrelatedly, existed in this patient, thus raising the old issue of the genetic determinants of the choice of the adult neurosis in at least some patients suffering from agoraphobia. It is my hope that other investigators will come forth with subsequent case reports that may help to further elucidate the psychodynamic and developmental interrelationships that I have touched upon in this chapter.

In addition to the above, I will present a review of the psychoanalytic literature on agoraphobia, giving especial emphasis to the subject of the agoraphobic companion. In addition, I will more briefly review the literature on imaginary companions. I do this in the hope of putting the clinical data from the case into historical perspective with respect to the findings of other investigators working in these fascinating areas.

CLINICAL MATERIAL

Mrs. A, a successful free-lance writer, entered analysis shortly after her 30th birthday. She had one sibling, a brother, who was six years her junior. Her presenting complaint was anxiety attacks when she was by herself in crowds. These attacks had increasingly resulted in her being confined to her apartment, unless she went out with her husband.

She had first experienced anxiety attacks some eight years earlier, when after graduating college, she moved out of her parents' home into

29

an apartment of her own. Her mother criticized her at the time for being a "loose woman," though she dated infrequently and did not engage in sexual intercourse until she married at the age of 25. Her attacks at that time were controlled with Valium, and she did not require the presence of a companion figure in order to travel about. The attacks did not entirely disappear, however, until she moved back into her parents' home, where she remained until the marriage.

When Mrs. A met her husband, she became enamored of a number of qualities that he possessed. In particular, she admired his athletic abilities, especially his considerable prowess as an equestrian, and the fact that he was something of a rugged individualist and a loner, who was not especially close to his parents. The patient perceived the latter trait in her husband as one that would aid her in her desire to separate from her own parents.

Shortly after their marriage, the couple moved to New York City, where Mrs. A's anxiety attacks returned once more. The attacks became more frequent as the subject of their having children arose, and the fears became quite paralyzing in intensity. She finally became incapable of moving about the city on her own, and her husband became her agoraphobic companion in her travels. Without him, she feared that she would "lose control of" herself or would "go crazy," by which she meant that she would either wet or soil herself, lose her identity, do something "reprehensible sexually," or die. These frightening possibilities left her, in her fantasies, completely dependent on the vagaries of strangers— hence the need for the husband as a companion.

In her past history, the patient and her mother had been nearly inseparable during the first few years of Mrs. A's life, to the extent that the patient even spent her first four years in the parental bedroom. The sleeping arrangement and the closeness to the mother changed considerably when the maternal grandmother, who suffered from hypertension, moved into the family household when the patient was aged 4. At this time, the patient was moved into a bedroom of her own, and the grandmother was placed in a room adjacent to that of the parents. The older woman remained in the patient's household until she died when Mrs. A was 12. During this time, she suffered from several cerebrovascular accidents, which led to a loss of bowel and bladder control. Because of such difficulties, the patient's mother devoted a good deal of her physical and emotional energies to the grandmother.

Mrs. A thus felt neglected and abandoned by her mother and attempted to turn to her father for succor. He, however, was unavailable emotionally and always seemed critical and unaccepting of her. In addition, he frequently verbalized his longings for a male child and heir. When her brother was born when she was aged 6, the father became even less available to the patient, as did the mother, who now had to divide her attentions between her sick mother and the new baby.

Going off to school also intensified the sense of separation and loss from the parents. When the grandmother died, however, the mother once more turned the full force of her attentions upon the 12-year-old patient. In so doing, she even attempted to encroach upon the patient's autonomy during her adolescence and was particularly critical of any attempts by the patient to establish herself both as an independent person and as a sexual being, such as by staying overnight with her girlfriends or by dating male classmates.

Mrs. A felt resentful of her mother's hovering over her, but she also felt guilty when she thought of moving away from and thus hurting her mother, whom she saw as needy. She desperately longed for a life of her own, though, away from the ups and downs of her mother's moods and needs. When she attempted to establish a separate existence after graduating from college, by moving into an apartment of her own, she experienced the onset of her anxiety symptoms. Because of these, ultimately she had to move back in with her parents. In this setting, the idea of a husband and marriage seemed to her like the only way out of her conflict.

In Mrs. A's fantasies, her husband was to be the man who would make up for all the deprivation and rejection she had experienced at the hands of the father. His masculinity would enable her to perceive of herself as a "sexual woman" in a setting that her mother could not make her feel guilty about. When she did marry, however, she was unable to experience orgasms during intercourse and could achieve them only in solitary masturbation. She began to withdraw from her husband and to resort to "faking" sexual pleasure, so as not to risk his rejecting her as well, for being "defective" and "lacking as a woman." Yet when the possibility of having children arose, and of "becoming a woman" in another sense of the word, the patient began to experience a recrudescence of her anxiety attacks, which precipitated her entry into treatment.

After several months of treatment, Mrs. A was able to give up the use of her husband as the agoraphobic companion and to come to sessions and get about town on her own. She soon began to verbalize her anger toward her father for his rejection of her and his preference of her brother because he was a boy. As she additionally began to experience anger toward her mother, and to recognize her feelings of guilt over having achieved some modicum of autonomy from both her mother and her husband, she had periodic upsurges of anxieties and occasionally had to use her husband as agoraphobic companion. These feelings largely disappeared, though, by the end of the first year of the treatment, as she was able to verbalize that I now provided the safety zone that her husband had previously afforded.

At that time, the strongest affect manifest in the sessions was the patient's intense sexual feelings toward me in the transference. With great difficulty, she began to reveal her masturbatory fantasies involving me and to discuss her lifelong conflict about her masturbation. She was able to reach orgasms only with clitoral manipulation, accompanied by masochistic fantasies of being subjugated by strong men or of being dragged naked and having her legs spread apart by wild, white horses. She would imagine that the animals belonged to some desert chieftain or to an outlaw band. The chieftain (often seen as looking or acting like me in the fantasies) and his tribesmen or the band of brigands would look on at the exciting sight, become aroused, and then have intercourse with her. Following occasions of disappointing sexual intercourse with her husband in reality, she would generally masturbate, along with fantasies of me as a Turkish Bey and her husband as the court eunuch, a clear-cut indication of her feelings of castrating rage toward him for disappointing her and not "making her into a woman."

When I questioned her about the content of the fantasies and about her use of the words "horsing around" as a code phrase for actual sexual activity with her husband or for fantasied activity with me, she revealed that she had a long-standing and deep attachment to horses. She had even carried her childhood transitional object, a toy white horse, about with her as a magical talisman during her early anxiety attacks. "That white horse has always meant a great deal to me," she said; "I've had it since I was born. It's a little ratty now, but I don't really want to give it up. The first story I ever wrote, when I was about 7 years old, was about the horse. It involved a brave boy taming a wild, white horse. I used to love to ride horses then, something about the sense of control over them. All that power between my legs. Yet once you tame them, they're loyal to you forever and never leave you."

In her associations over the next few months to the underlying issues subsumed in these comments, Mrs. A spoke of the horse as a kind of companion that kept her from feeling left alone. Her profound anxiety at being left by me during the analysis was often manifested during weekend and vacation separations. She became quite angry at me for these separations, but feared expressing her rage too strongly, lest I also reject her, as the father had. Similarly, she feared that I would reject her for the masturbation, as her mother had.

In speaking of the phallic connotations of the horse, in terms of her statement about the feeling of power between her legs, she revealed her lifelong conscious desire to be the boy whom her father had wished for prior to the brother's birth. In that way, she would displace the hated usurper brother and gain ascendancy in her father's affections. In this context, she remembered how angry she had felt at her mother when she had first gotten her menstrual periods at the age of 12, because this signaled to her both the concrete reality of being a woman and the ultimate denouement of her fantasy of becoming the father's favored son.

Similarly, the idea of having children of her own led to a return of these feelings, with an attendant sense of despair and rage—hence the upsurge of anxiety attacks that had brought her into the analysis. Her husband's prowess as an equestrian was an important determinant in her initial choice of him as a lifemate and in her later choice of him as the agoraphobic companion. She saw him as the latter-day prototype of the "brave boy" of her early stories, whose phallic strength would osmotically pass over to her and would imbue her with an aura of acceptability in the eyes of her father. When this failed to work, however, she grew disappointed in him and turned to me in the transference. When I, too, failed to gratify the fantasy of magically turning her into either a man or a woman endowed with phallic qualities, she became angry and disenchanted with me as well, and suffered a brief resurgence of her anxiety symptoms. The rage toward me was largely turned against herself, though, in her masochistic masturbatory fantasies, as she had earlier turned the rage toward both of her parents against herself, in order to maintain the early and fragile object ties.

In further associations to the white horse fantasy, late in the second year of the analysis, Mrs. A began to recall a multitude of other childhood fantasies that she had created. These were related to the escapades of a group of imaginary companions whom she had invented. The earliest of these companions were girls, imaginary sisters whom she had created when she herself was about 4 or 5 years old, apparently as a response to the grandmother's usurping the attention of the mother and the concomitant expulsion of the little girl from the parental bedroom.

In the tales about these girls, their mother would let them stray long distances away from her and would allow them to play at having imaginary teas, where they would practice their "grown up, ladylike manners." Then they would go back home, where their mother (a more idealized, less depressed version of her own mother) would serve them cookies that she had baked for them. The patient revealed these stories to her mother and would set the table for the girls and insist on waiting for them when crossing streets, much to the consternation of the mother. What seemed most apparent to us from these early stories, though, was that the grandmother was conspicuously absent from them, and the patient still appeared content to be a girl in them, despite the anxiety she felt in the absence of the mother. To put it another way, the early stories focused in large measure on her creative way of dealing with the conflicting wishes and passions aroused in the process of her being abruptly separated from her mother after the grandmother "invaded" the familial household.

After the birth of the brother when she was 6, the stories changed to a considerable degree. The imaginary companions, now boys or tomboys, were no longer freely spoken of with her mother, as the patient felt embarrassed at revealing her desire to replace the favored brother in the competition for the father's love. These boys or tomboys were envisioned as engaged in "boyish" ball games, or riding wild, white horses, or at play as desert warriors or outlaws. In these tales, the boys or tomboys shared a quality of being "outsiders," not bound by the usual laws of society. These fantasies clearly served as the anlage for the later masturbation sagas.

Mrs. A had a number of dreams that involved her watching scenes of other people making love. From her associations to these dreams, it became clear to us that the fusion of separation and castration material in her fantasies could best be related to her having experienced chronic primal scene exposure when she shared the bedroom with the parents for the first four years of her life (before the brother's birth). We also learned that there were brief periods after the grandmother's move into the household and even after the brother's birth, when her night terrors and her crying "forced" the mother to bring her into the parental bedroom once again. We could only speculate about whether or not she was reexposed to the primal scene on these occasions, but certainly the brief later forays into the parental bedroom caused a revival of her memories about earlier experiences of this kind. All of this and a number of other interesting aspects of the patient are illustrated in the following dream and associations, which she presented late in the third year of the analysis. This dream occurred the night after a session in which Mrs. A felt "thrown out" of my office, at the height of her erotized transference, in order to make way for the next patient, a man.

> I was lying in a small bed or crib, here in your office. I was a child, I guess, or a baby. I think the moon was shining in through the window, because the room was pretty well lit up. I had my white horse in my hands and I was cradling it, as if I wanted to give it comfort or to derive some from it. Then I saw you, or someone who looked just like you, making love to a woman whom I assumed to be your wife on the couch or a bed. I tried to cry out to tell you to stop it, that it was hurting me, only no words came out. I suppose I wasn't old enough to speak yet.
>
> The moon lit up the genitals of both persons in the dream, making them look a sort of unearthly white. It was hard to distinguish just who had what. Then she or you began to moan. Again, I couldn't tell who it was. Then one of you said "Ride me, Honey, please ride me hard." And I woke up.
>
> I felt very sad and lonely then, bereft I suppose. It was the way that I felt when you made me leave the office yesterday. I took the white horse to bed with me last night to comfort me. Only it

wasn't in my arms, as it was in the dream, but the way I used to
hold it as a kid, between my legs. It was as if I were the one trying
to ride it, trying to be part of the sexual scene within the dream.

In her associations to the dream, the patient recalled that she had
begun her childhood masturbation by placing the white horse between
her legs and rubbing it against her clitoris in an arousing way. At other
times, she would simply hold the horse between her legs in an identification with her father's penis, and later her brother's. It was at a moment
such as the former, that her mother caught her as a child and severely
chastized her for the "dirty practice." From her thoughts at this time, it
seemed clear to us that the behavior with the horse had been a method of
dealing both with the separation anxiety aroused by the realities of being
excluded from the sexual act and the bedroom by the parents (and from
my office by me) and with the sense of being castrated, derived from the
observation of first the father's penis and later the brother's.

The confusion between the sexes engendered by the observations was
clear, which intensified the wish to be a boy. This confusion meant to her
that she could obtain the genitals of either sex during intercourse and was
one of the later reasons for her disappointment in intercourse with her
husband. The confusion is also apparent in the idea of "just who" was
involved in riding whom in the sexual act in the dream. She saw the latter
idea as being one of the important linkages between the early use of the
horse as a transitional and fetish object (see Myers 1980), the later use of
it in the imaginary companion stories about the brave boys and tomboys,
and the still later masturbatory sagas and creative writing. She recognized that it was also instrumental in her choice of her husband, the
equestrian, as the adult agoraphobic companion.

These linkages between the latency imaginary companion fantasies,
the adolescent masturbatory sagas, and the adult creative writing are in
keeping with my experience with other patients who had imaginary
companions as children and became involved in creative pursuits as
adults (Myers 1979b). Let me also underscore some thoughts about the
above themes and their linkage to the choice of the husband as the adult
agoraphobic companion. He most clearly was chosen because of his ability as an equestrian (the rider of the wild, white horses) and because of
his qualities of independence and separation from his parents. I was
viewed as having similar qualities in the transference, particularly because of a lithograph of a wild horse on my office wall. In fantasy, then,
by being in apposition with a man such as the husband or me, the patient
could share in our assumed independence and our phallic powers and
thus need feel no separation or castration anxiety.

A few final thoughts about Mrs. A seem in order now. During the fourth year of the analysis, she became pregnant and gave birth to a baby girl. When I asked her about the unequivocally feminine name she had chosen for her daughter, as compared with her own ambisexual name, she replied that she did not want her daughter to be confused in the way that she had been. When the time came to select an object that her daughter might become close to—an object analogous to her own white horse—she chose a Raggedy Ann doll, in keeping with the tenor of her remarks about the name. Even her adult writing began to reflect a clear-cut movement away from the ubiquitous horse and brave boy themes of former days.

REVIEW OF THE LITERATURE

I wish to turn now to a review of the psychoanalytic literature on agoraphobia. Among the early authors discussing the subject, Abraham (1913) spoke of the concept of libidinization of locomotion in such patients. He related the outbreaks of agoraphobic anxiety to a threatened disruption of the erotic attachment to the oedipal mother. He saw the incestuous tie to the mother as the basis for the choice of her as the agoraphobic companion.

In her classic paper on the subject, Deutsch (1928) saw the "identification with the [maternal] object of the hostile tendencies to be the characteristic element in agoraphobia" (p. 114). She noted that "As a result of this identification the aggressive impulses . . . which are directed against this identified object, are turned against the ego" (p. 114). She further stated that "the tensions between the ego and the . . . superego will be released only when the presence of the protecting object confirms the fact that the object is not in danger and has not deserted the ego" (p. 114). Thus she saw the companion as the "protected protector" (p. 102), an auxiliary superego representation, which helps guard the patient from feelings of guilt by controlling the underlying hostile impulses. Deutsch's formulations are clearly in keeping with Mrs. A's needs to ward off her hostility toward both her mother and her husband.

Bergler (1935), Fenichel (1944), and Katan (1951), while accepting Deutsch's findings about the underlying hostility to the companion, primarily conceptualize the anxiety attacks in libidinal terms, regarding them as failures of defense against derivatives of oedipal sexual wishes, such as fantasies of prostitution in women. Their specific discussions about the companion add little to Deutsch's conceptualizations, as is also true of Tausend (1956). All of these formulations are of value in understanding the patient's fears of doing something "reprehensible sexually" during her anxiety attacks. They should be supplemented, however, with the more recent psychiatric data about the biological substratum of the anxiety attacks.

Miller (1953) relates the agoraphobic patient's conflicts over unconscious exhibitionistic wishes to early primal scene exposure and sees the anxiety attacks in the street as being derived from fears of impregnation by representations of the oedipal father. He, too, emphasizes defective superego development in such individuals and consequently views the companion as an auxiliary superego to help guard the patient from giving vent to guilt-provoking, oedipal, drive-derivative wishes. Mrs. A's primal scene exposures are consistent with this formulation as well.

A shift of emphasis is noted in Ruddick's (1961) paper on this subject, as he stresses early oral traumata in the genesis of agoraphobia. While he also mentions the superego defect in such patients, he clearly underlines the symbiotic ties to the companion, a theme also described in the works of Garbarino (1965) and Chatterji (1967). Rhead (1969) sees a failure in separation–individuation as being at the core of the anxiety state in agoraphobia and links the need for the companion with the unresolved symbiotic bond to the preoedipal mother. Bowlby (1973), too, conceptualizes agoraphobia as arising from a disturbed familial interaction in which an anxious symbiotic attachment to the mother, later reduplicated with the companion, predominates. One problem with such conceptualizations of agoraphobia, and of the function ascribed to the agoraphobic companion in these articles, is the lack of specificity concerning why such early disruptions in the separation–individuation process should necessarily predispose an individual to agoraphobic attacks and not, for example, to anorexia nervosa or some other disorder.

While Mrs. A clearly had a profound disturbance in separation–individuation when she was removed from the early and intense closeness in the parental bedroom at the time of the grandmother's entrance into the family household, there is no obvious reason why that event should have led her to develop agoraphobia as an adult. Even assuming the presence of a biological substrate predisposing the patient to panic attacks, it seems more logical to implicate the creative–pathological continuum in her life as being of greater causal significance in terms of increasing her vulnerability to the later development of agoraphobia.

Stamm (1972) attempts to address the problem of why agoraphobia develops in later life, relating his female patient's lifelong narcissistic vulnerability to early traumatic exposures to familial nudity. He sees these early exposures as engendering an intense sense of castration in his patient, which can only be mitigated by external approval of her beauty from a host of male admirers. He specifically mentions the mercilessly unrealistic quality of her ego ideal, which was patterned on a phallic model. In this sense, his findings show similarities to mine in the case of Mrs. A, though nudity per se, as in the primal scene exposures, may have multiple sequelae (see my earlier article, Myers 1979a). Stamm further infers from his data that the companion serves as an idealized phallic self-representation and as an external embodiment of the ego ideal. By receiving the admiring glances of the desired men—that is, of the companions—further narcissistic mortifications are aborted and prior ones are ameliorated. In this regard, he comes close to what I (Myers 1976, 1979b) and others (see below) have described as one of the important functions of the imaginary companion. This gives credence to the idea that the creative–pathological continuum is of significance in predisposing Mrs. A to her unconscious choice of agoraphobia and a related agoraphobic companion as the basis of her adult symptom neurosis.

Before turning to a paper that I see as most germane to the theses being expounded here, let me briefly note that the nonpsychoanalytic literature on agoraphobia sheds little light on our understanding of the genesis of the agoraphobic companion, with most of the current articles dealing with the biological substratum. Those that deal with other factors, such as one by Marks and Herst (1970) that describes a survey of 1200 adult agoraphobics in Britain, limit their discussions to social and occupational phenomena and not to genetic or psychodynamic ones. The issue of the companion is not even mentioned in this survey. In two other British articles of this kind, by Hafner (1977a,b), a study of 33 agoraphobic women and their husbands is presented. The author notes that the husbands were chosen by a process of assortive mating, the implication being that unconscious motivational factors were at work. He describes how improvements in the patients often led to deterioration in the husbands. It is difficult, however, to infer from the behaviorally oriented material presented in the papers at what developmental level(s) the pathological interaction(s) between patient and companion might be occurring.

Turning back to the analytic literature, I want to emphasize the article that I see as being most relevant to the patient described here—a 1975 paper—by Frances and Dunn. They approach the subject of agoraphobia from the point of view of object relations theory and note that for the child, "A given territory becomes safe because it becomes equated with and or symbolizes mother and protection. The outside is feared for its inherent uncertainty but especially because entering it implies leaving the safety of mother, i.e., separation" (p. 436). They go on to relate these ideas to the study of the adult agoraphobic and suggest that the phobic partners "are the people most closely involved with him, often with blurring of psychic differentiation. The agoraphobic patient, with his symptoms, binds the phobic partner within the safe territory and ultimately to himself. He finds it necessary to elaborate symptoms in order to ensure his dependency sources" (p. 436). They observed three levels of agoraphobic self–partner connectedness, defining them as: the psychotic symbiotic, where self and object differentiation is lacking; the narcissistic, where the presence of the phobic partner, who is experienced as a self-object, enables the patient to maintain a stable level of self-constancy; and the differentiated dependent, where there is an over-close dependency between the phobic partners but self and object constancy have been achieved. Mrs. A fits most closely into their differentiated dependent category. Her self-constancy was never in any real jeopardy, despite her frequently voiced fears of loss of her identity in her panic attacks.

What is of especially great interest here, however, is Frances and Dunn's suggestion that "The concept of the phobic partner can also be extended further to include intrapsychic events which are experienced at the border of the self and object worlds. Repetitive fantasies, ruminations, imaginary friends, and hallucinations occurring in agoraphobic patients are often incompletely internalized representations of a safety-providing object relation" (p. 430). Mrs. A's imaginary friends, and her ability to give up her husband's function as agoraphobic companion when she felt in a "safety zone" with me, are similar to the phenomena described by France and Dunn.

Let me turn now to a brief review of some of the prior psychoanalytic and psychiatric contributions on the subject of the imaginary companion. Green (1922), Hurlock and Burstein (1932), and Svendsen (1934) observed that most of the children with such companions were either only children or very lonely ones, which is certainly in keeping with Mrs. A's history. Jersild et al. (1933) noted that a number of children with such companions shared them with their friends, which my patient did as well.

Anna Freud (1937), in writing of imaginary animal companions, conceptualized such creations as helping the patient to avoid painful realities by a mechanism of denial in fantasy. Mrs. A's early childhood companions, her later stories, and her adult agoraphobic companion clearly performed the same function for her.

Bender and Vogel (1941) described the phenomenon as one used by the child to supplement deficient environmental experiences and unsatisfactory parent–child relationships—a formulation that is also consistent with the findings regarding my patient. Sperling (1954), in his description of a late anal stage male child with an imaginary playmate, noted that the companion was perceived of as possessing the "superman-like" virtues of the child's father, thus serving as a prototype for early ego-ideal formation; here, too, the example is consistent with what I observed in Mrs. A's case. Nagera (1969) also conceptualized the companion as a representation of the ego ideal, particularly in children who were rejected by their parents. By endowing the fantasied companion with all of the attributes that the children felt they were lacking in reality, they could undo in fantasy the feelings of deprivation. Similarly, my patient attempted, via the medium of the outsider boy stories, to undo the rejection by her father after the birth of her brother.

Bach (1971) also described the imaginary companion as a primitive ego-ideal precursor, as did Benson and Pryor (1973), who conceptualized such companions as narcissistic guardians who helped the individual maintain his "inner sense of perfection and worth" (p. 469). Schwartz (1974), in a paper discussing the adult analysis of a male with a narcissistic personality disorder, described a companion who was seen by the patient as a representation of both the paternal phallus and the phallic mother—in other words, as an idealized phallic self-representation, much in the manner of Mrs. A's outsider boy companions. My own findings in earlier articles on this subject (Myers 1976, 1979b) concur with this viewpoint.

DISCUSSION

In what follows, I would like to synthesize briefly some of the thoughts that have been presented in the clinical material and in the review of the literature. Of major importance, the patient's overly close relationship with the mother had been acutely interrupted, initially by the introduction of the grandmother into the household and then by the birth of the brother. Prior to these events, the exposure to the primal scene had introduced a strong element of genital confusion, and this, along with the rejection by the father, intensified the patient's sense of herself as castrated. The indifference shown to the patient's individuality by exposing her to chronic primal scene experiences also contributed to the confluence of separation and castration anxiety seen in this case.

Given these events, the patient attempted to deal creatively with anxieties and narcissistic mortifications—first, by adopting her toy white horse as transitional object. Sometime during the primal scene exposures, this creatively enhanced object was transposed into an infantile fetish object as well (Roiphe and Galenson 1973), or what Bak (1974) calls a prosthetic object. Subsequently, the imaginary companion stories evolved. Initially, they focused on a feminine girl in an identification with the mother, and later they progressed to a phallic identification with the favored brother and the idealized father. Thus, through these creative acts and fantasies, Mrs. A can be seen as struggling with the felt discrepancies in her perceptions of her real and of her idealized selves (her narcissistic wounds), and with her separation and castration anxieties as well. The later written stories and masturbatory sagas seemed to have similar functions. Finally, the utilization of the husband and later the analyst as embodiments of the brave boy–horsemen of her early tales helped her to manage the separation and castration traumata inherent in moving away from the parents and competing with the mother—especially when contemplating becoming a mother herself. Thus, we can see the continuum of creative–pathological acts from childhood to adult life that profoundly affected Mrs. A's behavior.

The change from the initial utilization of the mother to ward off the panic attacks to the later utilization of the husband and the analyst in a similar role paralleled the modifications within the use of the transitional object and the progression within the imaginary companion stories. Since the ego-ideal formation had crystallized at the end of the oedipal phase (concomitant with the birth of the favored brother) around the idealized phallic self-representations (as exemplified in the outsider boy stories), the choice of the husband as an idealized alter ego to help ward off her sense of shame, narcissistic mortification, and loss of self-esteem can be traced to the patient's perceptions of the husband as the personification of the idealized brother–father imago of her fantasies. With her disappointment in him sexually, she turned to me and formed an idealization of me in the transference. Through the analysis of this idealization, we were able to follow clearly the evolution in the patient of the continuum described above.

While it is not my intention to proclaim that an absolute, psychodynamically isomorphic congruence should be drawn between the patient's childhood and adolescent creations and the choice of her adult agoraphobia and agoraphobic companion, the data are highly suggestive of such a relationship and need further investigation. I hope that the material delineated here will stimulate other investigators to come forth with similar case reports about other adult patients that might further elucidate some of the thorny points involved in understanding the specificity of this symptom choice—agoraphobia and the use of an agoraphobic companion.

REFERENCES

Abraham K: On the psychogenesis of agoraphobia in childhood (1913), in Clinical Papers and Essays on Psychoanalysis. New York, Basic Books, 1955

Bach S: Notes on some imaginary companions. Psychoanal Study Child 1971; 26:159-171

Bak R: Distortions of the concept of fetishism. Psychoanal Study Child 1974; 29:191-215

Bender L, Vogel F: Imaginary companions of children. Am J Orthopsychiatry 1941; 11:56-66

Benson RM, Pryor DB: "When friends fall out": developmental interference with the function of some imaginary companions. J Am Psychoanal Assoc 1973; 21:457-473

Bergler E: Psychoanalysis of a case of agoraphobia. Psychoanal Rev 1935; 22:392-408

Bowlby J: Separation. New York, Basic Books, 1973

Chatterji N: The agoraphobic companion. Samiksa 1967; 21:81-92

Deutsch H: Agoraphobia (1928) in Neuroses and Character Types: Clinical Psychoanalytic Studies. New York, International Universities Press, 1965

Fenichel O: Remarks on the common phobias. Psychoanal Q 1944; 13:313-326

Frances A, Dunn P: The attachment–autonomy conflict in agoraphobia. Int J Psychoanal 1975; 56:435-439

Freud A: The Ego and the Mechanisms of Defense. New York, International Universities Press, 1946

Garbarino H: Theoretical and technical aspects of agoraphobia: its implications derived from the 'umbilical stage'. Psychoanal Q 1965; 34:627 (abstract)

Green GH: Psychoanalysis in the Classroom. London, Putnam, 1922

Hafner RJ: The husbands of agoraphobic women: assortive mating or pathogenic interaction? Br J Psychiatry 1977a; 130:233-239

Hafner RJ: The husbands of agoraphobic women and their influence on treatment outcome. Br J Psychiatry 1977b; 131:289-294

Hurlock EB, Burstein W: The imaginary playmate. J Genet Psychol 1932; 41:380-392

Jersild AT, Markey FV, Jersild CL: Fears, Dreams, Wishes, Daydreams, Likes, Dislikes, Pleasant and Unpleasant Memories: A Study by the Interview Method of 400 Children Aged 5 to 12. New York, Teachers College, Columbia University, 1933

Katan A: The role of 'displacement' in agoraphobia. Int J Psychoanal 1951; 32:41-50

Marks IM, Herst ER: A survey of 1200 agoraphobics in Britain: features associated with treatment and ability to work. Social Psychology, 1970-1971; 5–6:16-24

Miller ML: On street fear. Int J Psychoanal 1953; 34:232-240

Myers WA: Imaginary companions, fantasy twins, mirror dreams and depersonalization. Psychonal Q 1976; 45:503-524

Myers WA: Clinical consequences of chronic primal scene exposure. Psychoanal Q 1979a; 48:1-26

Myers WA: Imaginary companions in childhood and adult creativity. Psychoanal Q 1979b; 48:292-307

Myers WA: The psychodynamics of a beating fantasy. Int J Psychoanal Psychother 1980; 8:623-648

Nagera H: The imaginary companion: its significance for ego development and conflict solution. Psychoanal Study Child 1969; 24:165-196

Rhead C: The role of pregenital fixations in agoraphobia. J Am Psychoanal Assoc 1969; 17:848-861

Roiphe H, Galenson E: The infantile fetish. Psychoanal Study Child 1973; 28:147-169.

Ruddick B: Agoraphobia. Int J Psychoanal 1961; 42:537-543

Schwartz L: Narcissistic personality disorders—a clinical discussion. Psychoanal Q 1974; 22:292-306

Sperling OE: An imaginary companion representing a pre-stage of the superego. Psychoanal Study Child 1954; 9:252-258

Stamm JL: Infantile trauma, narcissistic injury and agoraphobia. Psychiatr Q 1972; 46:1-19

Svendsen M: Children's imaginary companions. Archives of Neurology and Psychiatry 1934; 2:985-999

Tausend H: Psychoanalysis of a case of agoraphobia. Samiksa 1956; 10:175-200

CHAPTER 3

The Real Relationship in Psychoanalytic Psychotherapy

John F. Kelly, M.D.
Homer E. Olsen, M.D.

The role of the real relationship in psychoanalysis and psychoanalytic psychotherapy has long been the subject of debate. We find that an understanding of this role is valuable and sometimes essential in working with our patients. We will attempt to illustrate this in the clinical examples that follow.

Example 1

A 32-year-old professional woman had been in twice-weekly psychotherapy for five months, and her progress had taken an increasingly downhill course. She viewed the therapist as critical but second only to her own self-criticism. It became clear that she was using the "therapeutic" relationship increasingly to attack herself and the therapist. He had attempted to interpret the hostility that was being expressed in the transference, as well as her identifying and merging with negative figures of her past. She seemed superficially interested in these interventions, but nothing therapeutic took place as she adamantly continued to destroy the therapy, herself, and the therapist. She paid no serious attention to our lack of progress with her depression. The therapist felt angry, stymied, and helpless to change anything, and yet he felt an urgent need to do more, to do better. The therapist felt he was somehow doing something wrong. Though she had some worrisome suicidal thoughts, her ability to function, while limited, did not point toward hospitalization.

After some inner struggle and introspection, the therapist decided to change his focus from what was being repeated to the current reality. He told her that they were on a destructive downhill course and that despite his efforts, he was not helping her, and he was unwilling to continue this process. At first she did not believe that the therapist would be willing to stop the therapy. When he made it quite clear that he would not participate in such a destructive process, after a short period of angry protest she collapsed in relief and said tearfully, "I could never say no."

In our view this vignette illustrates a key to therapeutic leverage: in order to work in therapy using interpretation of transference, the patient must have two parallel experiences, one of the real relationship in the present, and the other a reliving in transference of the past. Just as the real relationship may be used to avoid the transference, the transference may be used to avoid the real relationship. Both patient and therapist may experience resistance to the real relationship, just as both might have resistance to the transference relationship.

The vignette also illustrates our expectation that the therapist will be emotionally involved in the therapy relationship, at times beyond a signal level. Since there is no real relationship free of transference, either in the patient or the therapist, our use of the terms refers to the predominant aspect that is operative at a given time in the therapy.

Although interpretation of the transference relationship is of major importance, in this clinical example recognition of the reality of the therapeutic situation and the reality relationship became the overriding issue. The patient was having one predominant experience, in which she relived the past. Transference interpretations were ineffective in the face of the patient's inability to test reality and the increasingly destructive course of the therapy. She could not contain an aggressive current in herself. The reality confrontation—that the therapist refused to participate in what he believed had become a verbally uninterpretable reenactment of a sadomasochistic scenario of the past—clarified the relationship in the present. Without this clarification the patient could not find a new perspective on the past but could only repeat it behind a veneer of living in the present.

The patient was an intelligent, talented woman who had gone far beyond her limited socioeconomic background. Though there was no overt physical abuse in her history, both parents were quite unresponsive figures who reacted indifferently or with anger to her needs. For example, she had been forced to wear clothes discarded by relatives during her childhood, even though her parents could well afford new ones. When she finally protested, she was slapped by her father. She was not allowed to say no, and she repeated her experience (and told the therapist about it in action language) by coercing the therapist until he said no. Words did not suffice; he had to meet her action with action in the present (the willingness to stop the therapy) and do what she had never been able to do. The refusal to participate in her abuse and self-abuse communicated a different order of integration of aggression from that available to her in her projected dilemma. This interaction was in keeping with Loewald's (1960) view that the therapist is a new object who "functions as a representative of a higher stage of organization and mediates this to the patient" (p. 24).

The process described in the vignette can also be conceptualized as projective identification (Ogden 1979), in which the patient's inner dilemma is induced in the therapist, who must then come to terms with it in himself before conveying it back to the patient. In this instance something is required of the therapist that is beyond the usual therapeutic interaction: the patient draws the therapist into experiencing her struggle in a compelling way, and the interpretive activity is conveyed in terms of the real relationship. The projective identification transaction in Example 1 implies some instability of self organization. The patient's "identification with the aggressor" involving the therapist was not an identification of a truly separate self with a separate object but a less differentiated imitation, since she concomitantly directed this aggression toward herself.

Following the session in which the therapist confronted her with a refusal to continue in the destructive process, the patient slowly began to use him and the therapy in a new way. She tentatively began to explore her past and present circumstances, questioning and trying to understand the punitive, self-critical view of herself. Her depression lifted, and her life situation improved considerably. She was able to allow her talents as a musician to develop much more fully. The discord in her marriage diminished, and some months later she gave birth to a child. In the confrontation, the therapist had used himself as a "real" person to convey what was pathological in the interaction, which interrupted a malignant, regressive experience. She was then able to make more positive use of transference interpretations and her relationship with the therapist.

At times the real relationship is the major vehicle for structural change, as in Example 2, in which the structural change begins with consolidation of self and object constancies.

Example 2

A young woman presented with complaints of long-standing unhappiness and depression. She was bright and charming, she had done well academically through graduate school, she had many friends, but life felt empty and painful. Her image of herself was the opposite of bright and charming. She was wary of any attachment to her therapist.

She had been thoroughly neglected by her professional parents, but as obvious as that was, she worried that she was "making it up," since she had been given material things and a substantial trust fund. The therapist repeatedly stated that she had in fact been neglected and reviewed the evidence with the patient. She had been saved by a loving nanny, who looked after her as an infant and intermittently after that until she was 10 years old, when the nanny died. Her relationship with her nanny, maintained in fantasy, was her most important attachment when she began therapy. She hinted that the therapist was like her nanny; only years later did she say that she had a conscious belief during this time that he was actually her nanny, returned to help her, just as she had fantasized.

After several months, the therapist went away for three weeks. Her menstrual period, which had begun two days before the separation, stopped on the day he left and resumed on the day of his return. She felt empty, hopeless, and despairing and lost 15 pounds during the separation. After this he was careful to maintain the patient's connection with him over separations, using telephone calls and a picture of him that the patient carried (see Adler and Buie's 1979 discussion of treatment of the problem of aloneness).

The patient was gradually able to call the therapist's voice to mind, which helped to contain her distress. After two years she came to a crisis that proved to be a watershed in her therapy. She began to be able to call to mind a visual image of him, whereupon she became seriously suicidal. She was emotionally distinguishing him from her nanny, which caused her to feel an almost unbearable sense of loss. She said she felt she had to choose whether to die and thereby rejoin her nanny, or remain in her present life. Ultimately she chose not to die because it would mean losing contact with her therapist, and their relationship had become too important to lose.

Up to this time she had lived her life in fantasy, going through the motions of life, putting up a façade that protected her emotional life from the threat of another overwhelming loss. Now she began to move into living her life in the present, buying clothes and pictures for her office, and developing a relationship with a boyfriend in which she revealed what she felt, all for the first time. She experienced this as a radical improvement in her life.

The crisis in her therapy came at the point when her relationship with her therapist became emotionally real to her in the present. Up to this time she had lived her life in fantasy, and he was experienced as her nanny. The "nanny transference" took up the whole relationship. Rather than resisting the transference, she resisted the real relationship.

Gradually a real relationship was built up that provided a feeling of security. Her image of the therapist was slowly internalized—first only the memory of his voice, then a memory of his voice that felt soothing and reassuring: a new level of object constancy. When she felt secure enough, she proceeded to the next step of calling his visual image to mind, which led to emotionally distinguishing him from her nanny and recalling the intense pain of losing her nanny. She now could bear this pain because of stronger inner structure, supplemented by the continuing relationship with him.

When the therapist became emotionally real, she was flooded with the pain of loss that she had avoided at all costs since she was 10. The degree of this avoidance suggested unstable self and object constancies, with a threat of loss of the object and annihilation, rather than the dangers associated with higher levels of organization. When she was 10 years old, her psychological survival was at stake; now it felt the same when the transference relationship yielded to an emotionally real relationship with him in the present. The strongest resistance was not against a transference regression, but against experiencing the real relationship in the present.

If a patient has not had a "good enough mother" (Winnicott 1953), the resulting impairment will likely be not only in regulatory structure but also in reality testing. The therapist will need to respond to distortions or omissions of reality in the patient's representational world, including what did and did not happen to him as a child, what he needed, what was and was not supplied by the parenting figures, what the patient contributed to his difficulties and successes, and his current image of himself, as well as what was internalized and is reproduced in transference. As these elements present themselves in the process of the therapy, the therapist helps the patient to assemble and integrate a more objective view of himself and his world, past and present, both by interpreting transference and by constructing past and present reality.

Example 3

A 30-year-old lawyer called, indicating during the phone contact that he was interested in once-a-week psychotherapy. In the first interview he revealed he had been in five years of intensive therapy, and the experience had left him angry, embittered, and unrelieved of the symptoms of anxiety and depression that had worsened during law school. Though he spoke negatively about this psychotherapeutic experience, he did believe he had become more sensitive to his inner life and past. There seemed to have been an achievement of insight with little or no change in his symptoms during this therapy. In an early session the patient, who tended to present himself in a depreciated light, made a witty remark at which the therapist spontaneously laughed. Though he initially joined the therapist in laughter, he then teared and related how important it was to him that the therapist had laughed. He went on to describe how his previous therapist had never laughed at any of his witty remarks, which were always interpreted as seductive, hostile, manipulative, and so forth, depending on the process of therapy at the moment. The patient then said in a self-deprecating way that he knew he used humor defensively at times. He realized that the therapist was not laughing at him and did not react to him in the disdainful manner that he felt his previous therapist had adopted in his zeal to reach unconscious meanings of the patient's productions. Through his interpretations, that therapist seemed to have participated in the same negative view that the patient had of himself.

After the patient had noted the therapist's appreciative response to him, he brought up an early sexual memory in which he felt he had taken advantage of another person, even though he was a child and the other person was an adult. When the therapist commented on the adult's highly pleasurable participation in the activity, the patient said, "You're not really against me!" The patient continually was surprised at the therapist's "accepting manner" with him, and when he felt relieved of a chronic sense of depression, he then realized he was anxious about "getting better."

The patient had been physically abused by his father and his mother, who were quite narcissistic and were inconsistently available to him in his early years. As therapy continued, the patient became more aware that though he felt increasingly more able to assert himself in his professional activities and enjoy his wife and children, he felt a "dread of moving out of the dark cloud I've walked under all my life." He saw the therapist's more accepting attitude toward him as a new way for him to think about himself, but it frightened him to give up these more negative views. When the therapist suggested that the negative orientation kept him from feeling painful feelings, he teared and said he sensed there was a "deep well of sadness" in himself that he had always fended off.

In this example, the therapist's laughter in response to the patient's joke was a moment in the interpretive process when an acknowledgment of a healthy part of the patient clarified the real relationship between patient and therapist and facilitated the patient's understanding of something real and valid in himself. His sense of humor, which at times he used defensively, also had a healthy aspect, which the patient could see only dimly. In our view, this aspect of the interpretation is an integral part of the therapeutic work: to convey to the patient his real characteristics, including talents, strengths, and potential, rather than only interpreting his conflicts and expressions of psychopathology. Acknowledgment and acceptance of aspects of the patient's healthy ego and realistic responses increase the patient's capacity to utilize new interpretations and insights into his unconscious.

Though this patient had many neurotic features, with problems around success, his self-representation was organized partly around negative introjects that were also reflected in early superego structuring. When the therapist did not participate in the patient's projections of his harsh superego and attacking introjects, which his previous therapist had unwittingly done, there was a threat to the negative organization by his internalizing a more current real relationship. The threat came from loosening a structural organization consisting of internalized aggressive, punitive objects that had prevented the experience of rage and despair.

> At a later point in therapy, the patient mentioned that he had an important business meeting in the early evening and needed a ride to a repair shop where he had left his car for the afternoon. He had taken a taxi to get to the late afternoon appointment. He "jokingly" asked if the therapist might give him a ride to the shop. When the therapist asked what his thoughts were about that, he replied, "I know I'm setting myself up to be hurt, because of course you'll say no." The therapist said, "But what if I don't?" He became anxious and said, "Well, you'd have to." The therapist said, "Oh?" He immediately changed the subject. A bit later the therapist pointed out that he had moved away from the subject of the ride. He responded with "I couldn't stand it if you did, but I don't know why except it would be too nice." The therapist responded that for him to be "too nice" and responsive to the patient was not only not what he was used to but also made him anxious. He stated, "It wouldn't feel like me to be treated in a nice way by you or me."

Another interpretive task having to do with reconstruction is to formulate with the patient what the facts were in his childhood, both from his perspective as a child and from a more objective adult perspective. In this example, it was helpful to point out the adult's role in the sexual event in his childhood in addition to his own participation as a child. Although this type of intervention can be seen as "teaching" the patient, it can also be seen as clarifying a part of past reality that has been distorted by the child's needs and the parents' needs in the past. Abused children are often all too willing to take responsibility for pain in their lives. An identification with the aggressor is used by the child, which supports an omnipotent view of the self and protects against overwhelming feelings of helplessness, aloneness, or disorganization. Thus, for defensive reasons patients resist seeing the role adults actually played in pathogenic events in their childhood. Clarifying and interpreting both the current real relationship and the related reconstruction of the abusive reality of the past often uncover painful affects. These affects derive not necessarily from conflict over forbidden impulses of childhood but from remembering overwhelming past external realities.

Something similar may happen in the course of clarifying those legitimate needs, desires, and affects that were treated in childhood as being in some way bad, shameful, or otherwise objectionable. When they surface in the therapy relationship, they are likely to be harshly treated by the patient for defensive reasons, in a way similar to how he was treated as a child. Fixed self and object constellations are needed to maintain what Fairbairn (1959) described as a "closed system" of repetitive experience, partly to ward off threatening affects and impulses (Fraiberg 1982). The therapist needs to intervene on behalf of the patient's true self (Winnicott 1965a) as a child, to clarify what he needed but did not get but also to understand the patient's defensive need to ward off (by using a false self) intense pain by clinging to his identification with his parents' harsh judgment of himself. The "abusing" parents may have been those who were indifferent or oblivious to the child's needs—that is, warmth, attention, and appropriate validation. The frustration and rage that result from such omissions are invested in the parental object representations that become internalized by the child. The child of inadequate, indifferent parents now lives with intensely demanding and rageful internalized images (introjects) that strongly influence his perception of his self, his needs, and his parents. These distorted perceptions have major influences on later periods of development—for example, the oedipal period.

It is frequently pointed out that countertransference gratifications or inappropriate object needs of the therapist may get into the therapy (Langs 1985). In our view, such experiences in the therapist cannot be entirely eliminated, and in fact belong to the therapy experience. Discovering such experiences and using them interpretively is a central part of the therapeutic action (Hoffman 1983). Similarly, concern over inappropriate transference gratifications in the patient can contribute to avoiding the recognition and acknowledgment of real aspects of the patient in the present and the past. Such acknowledgment can at times have a powerful therapeutic effect.

Example 4

In their paper "Preverbal Experience and Loss: Mourning the Death of a Parent" (1985, unpublished), Samuel Wagonfeld and Lupe Samaniego give a vivid account of treatment of a 27-year-old woman, who resolved both the loss of her father, who had died when she was 6, and a preoedipal developmental arrest, during 6½ years of psychotherapy. The patient, Amy, initially complained of uncontrollable crying following the loss of a boyfriend. She sobbed vehemently in the first session, and she conveyed to the therapist in a powerful way an overwhelming sense of loss and pain. The desperate, hopeless quality of her ego state, the rocking back and forth while holding her hand to her mouth as if sucking her thumb, called to the therapist's mind Spitz's films of anaclitic depression in infancy. Subsequent history from the patient's mother confirmed that the mother had experienced a major depression when the patient was about 10 months old.

As the therapy unfolded and the patient's preverbal depletion and hopelessness became clearer, she continued to sob desperately and attempted to comfort herself by holding herself. The therapist put the experience into words speaking "very softly, as though talking to a very small and scared child, 'Amy, you need and want a mom so much—a mom who can hold you and hug you.'" Later, when the therapist inquired about the patient's practice of bringing her own Kleenex to the sessions, the patient told of her fears that her intense neediness would deplete the therapist and leave her [the therapist] with nothing. The therapist responded, "I have lots of Kleenex boxes. I also have lots of energy. You look so scared—as if you're wondering if I can tolerate your needs. I'm a pretty strong lady, you know." The patient smiled, and said, "Yes, I know . . . my mom seemed to be depleted . . . (cries)." As the patient felt more confidence in the therapeutic process, she said "I'm beginning to feel like I'm talking to a new parent." The therapist's view of this phase of treatment was that "Tones and sound were rather crucial. Words were less important. What she noticed was the cooing— the 'softness' and later the 'laughter'—the 'aliveness' as she came to call it. The unfolding expressions of her needs and of her 'self' were interrupted when words were used prematurely in impatient attempts to help her reach a higher level of self-integration."

As the patient improved, she went through a phase of playfulness and games, for example, peek-a-boo, and showing off the new skill she had learned at belly-dancing lessons. During this time she insisted that no words be used in the therapy; later, these experiences also were conceptualized in words and integrated. As the therapy proceeded, it gradually moved beyond preverbal and nonverbal modes, and took the more familiar form of a process of mourning. The patient went on to resolve her grief and to marry, and terminated the therapy successfully.

In this therapy the real relationship played an unusual and essential role. The therapist was guided by her countertransference—that is, her response to the patient's intense transference longings—into supplying what the patient needed to resume her development. In specific and limited ways, a maternal soothing, a "holding environment," was necessary as well as the usual verbal interpretation and reconstruction that organized the patient's experience. Timing verbal interventions was important, since impatient, premature interpretations interrupted the patient's unfolding expressions of her needs. During the playful phase, the therapist had to allow "[being] used as an object who could tolerate [the patient's] developmental needs," who could be involved and attentive and patient in the present. "In essence, one had to allow her to be the initiator of the transition of her need 'not to verbalize' to a capacity to 'talk' about her actions."

The therapist realized that interpretation of conflict alone would not suffice, that a new experience was necessary, and that in specific ways the therapist needed to allow herself to follow the pull of her countertransference in action rather than to use it only to guide verbal interpretation. Sometimes the therapeutic process was best facilitated by allowing the patient to have an experience, or to "play," without immediately supplying an interpretation. At other times, for example in the Kleenex instance, the therapist added explicit verbal clarification of who she was in the present, in order to help the patient distinguish the real relationship from the transference relationship.

THEORETICAL CONSIDERATIONS

There is considerable literature regarding the technique of interpretations along drive/defense lines (Bird 1972; Brenner 1969; Gray 1973; Kanzer 1952; Lowenstein 1954), which generally assumes that the patient suffers from structural conflict arising in the oedipal phase of development. More recently, a growing body of writing considers techniques of therapy with patients with problems around ego deficits, developmental arrests, and varying degrees of pathology in self and object relationships (Mahler 1971; Greenacre 1954, 1959; Kramer 1979; Winnicott 1965a, b; Little 1966; Kohut 1971; Sandler 1976; Adler and Buie 1979; Lachman and Stolorow 1976; Miller 1979; Kernberg 1976; Searles 1965). There has been only limited focus on the technical use of the real relationship in psychoanalytic psychotherapy, and that has been directed mostly to patients with more severe pathology.

For the sake of emphasis, we stress the real relationship in contrast to the transference relationship, though this contrast is an oversimplification. These two "relationships" are relative and overlapping. In every transference relationship there is always some grain of "reality," and there is some degree of transference in "real" interactions. In certain patients and at particular times in a therapeutic process, one of the two relationships may be more prominent than the other. Many authors have commented on the importance of the real, or nontransference, relationship in the therapeutic process.

Anna Freud, in her 1954 discussion of Leo Stone's (1954) paper "The Widening Scope of Indications for Psychoanalysis," said,

Further, I refer briefly to Dr. Stone's remarks concerning the "real personal relationship" between analyst and patient versus the "true transference reactions." . . . [Even in the middle of a transference neurosis] so far as the patient has a healthy part of his personality, his real relationship to the analyst is never wholly submerged. With due respect for the necessary strictest handling and interpretation of the transference, I feel still that we should leave room somewhere for the realization that analyst and patient are also two real people, of equal adult status, in a real personal relationship to each other. I wonder whether our—at times complete—neglect of this side of the matter is not responsible for some of the hostile reactions which we get from our patients and which we are apt to ascribe to "true transference only."

Greenson and Wexler pursue this aspect of the treatment further in "The Non-transference Relationship in the Psychoanalytic Situation" (1969): "To facilitate the full flowering and ultimate resolution of the patient's transference reactions, it is essential in all cases to recognize, acknowledge, clarify, differentiate, and even nurture the non-transference or relatively transference-free reactions between patient and analyst" (p. 27).

Loewald, in his 1960 paper, "On the Therapeutic Action of Psychoanalysis," puts the real relationship into a developmental perspective, stating that ego-development is resumed in the therapeutic process.

And this resumption of ego-development is contingent on the relationship with a new object . . . this not primarily in the sense of an object not previously met, but the newness consists in the patient's rediscovery of the early paths of the development of object-relations leading to a new way of relating to objects and of being oneself. . . . The parent-child relationship can serve as a model here. The parent ideally is in an empathic relationship of understanding the child's particular stage in development, yet ahead in his vision of the child's future and mediating this vision to the child in his dealing with him. . . . [In contrast to the analysis of the classical psychoneuroses,] in cases with obvious ego defects . . . especially in borderline cases and psychoses, processes such as I tried to sketch in the child-parent relationship take place in the therapeutic situations on levels relatively close and similar to those of the early child-parent relationship. The further we move away from gross ego defect cases, the more do the integrative processes take place on higher levels of sublimation and by modes of communication which show much more complex stages of organization. (pp. 16–21)

Lipton (1977) notes that "without the actuality of the nontechnical personal relationship, irrational elements of the transference remain imaginary or intellectual" (p. 271). He explained that it is through the vehicle of the real relationship that transference elements may find an expression and elaboration. Without the opportunity of establishing an object relationship with the therapist as a person, there is a danger of establishing an iatrogenic narcissistic disorder in the patient, or aggravating such a disorder if it already exists. Gill (1982) makes a related point about technique in regard to realistic relationship between patient and analyst: "Much of the criticism of Freud's technique stems from his unabashed personal relationship with his patients. Important though the recognition of the distinction between the technical and personal role of the analyst is, I believe the current tendency to dissolve this distinction completely is a sign of a more basic problem—the failure to recognize the importance of the analyst's real behavior and the patient's realistic attitudes and how they must be taken into account in technique" (p. 106). The thrust of his thesis regarding technical issues is mainly in the direction of dealing with the patient's resistances to transference through examining the reality relationship, in order to discover those elements "not to be accounted for by the actual situation (Freud 1925)" (Gill, p. 15). We would agree with this point but believe there are also further technical uses of the real relationship.

Carrying Gill's argument further, Hoffman (1983) questions whether there is such a thing as a real relationship that can be separated from the transference relationship. He quotes Racker (1968), who said, "The analyst's relation to his patient is a libidinal one and is a constant emotional experience" (p. 31). And Heimann (1959): "The analyst's countertransference is not only part and parcel of the analytic relationship, but it is the patient's creation, it is part of the patient's personality" (p. 83). Although we agree that the therapist's emotional response may be the best key the therapist has to understanding the patient's experience, we do not see it as dominating the therapist's experience (except very occasionally), and we still find it useful to conceptualize a process involving a real relationship.

Greenson and Wexler (1969) defined the "real," nontransference relationship as differing from the transference relationship in the degree of relevance, appropriateness, accuracy, and immediacy of what is expressed and in being adaptive. Gill (1982) stressed the cognitive and less affectual attributes of the reality relationship. Gill, following Freud (1973), made clear the distinction between the real relationship, which is a current phenomenon, and the positive transference, which is a product of the past.

To distinguish between these two relationships is not always easy in view of their overlapping natures. Nontransference elements can be influenced by the personality and theoretical orientation of the therapist. Greenson and Wexler make this point, but Lipton (1977) makes the influence of theoretical orientation even clearer by presenting a historical perspective regarding the overemphasis on interpretation in "classical" technique.

Lipton defines "classical" technique, which he prefers to call "modern" technique, as that in which any therapist communications implying a personal relationship or interventions that reflect the personality of the analysts are to be excluded. Lipton includes here an interesting review of Freud's clinical technique as revealed in his treatment of the Rat Man and in his cases late in his career, in the 1930s. He documents that Freud's technique remained the same throughout his career, including more personal communications and a more "real" relationship with his patients. Freud was also careful to analyze the patient's reaction to these "reality" exchanges. Freud's technique was considered acceptable (classical) during the first 40 years of history of psychoanalysis. In his discussion of Freud's technique, Lipton notes that Freud had a spontaneous, open, and friendly relationship with his patients. Freud viewed this personal relationship as separate from the analytic work and not a subject for technique, in contrast to the positive transference of repressed, erotic impulses and the negative transference. Fenichel (1941) remarked on how frequently patients who came to him for a second analysis talked about how natural Fenichel was with them. Clearly, a real relationship was part of Freud's and Fenichel's way of working.

However, we would not agree that the personal relationship is not a subject for technique. It is true that some patients take it for granted and soon form a trusting relationship, so that the personal, real relationship remains a silent aspect of the therapeutic context. But in our experience those patients are exceptional, even in analysis. Most patients require active monitoring and diagnosis of both the real relationship and the transference relationship.

During the 1940s, with the advent of Alexander's (Alexander and French 1946) introduction of the "corrective emotional experience" and his advocacy of manipulative action in addition to interpretation, a considerable controversy developed in American psychoanalysis. Lipton puts forth the idea that today's modern "classical" technique developed as a reaction against Alexander's approach. Sachs (1979) also underscores this idea of the development of modern technique. In 1951 Kris (1951) repudiated Freud's technique in the analysis of the Rat Man. Eissler (1953) expanded the criticism of Alexander and formulated a model of technique that relied exclusively on interpretation; he proposed that any other intervention that the analyst found necessary should be designated as a parameter, a term that soon developed a pejorative connotation. A belief developed that Freud's earlier technique—that is, with the Rat Man—had changed into a later technique more in line with Eissler's proposal in 1953. However, there is no real evidence that Freud's technique had changed—in fact there is evidence to the contrary.

With this unfounded equation between Freud's technique and Eissler's formulation, the newer, more strict technique was designated as "classical," and a significant change in technique came into being without recognition or evaluation. An important part of Eissler's model was an explicit exclusion of the personality of the analyst and the living conditions of the patient. In the period after Eissler's paper was published, there was general acceptance of these ideas, which had major influence on the training of therapists in the mental health profession over many years. The orientation of many therapists trained in this technical model tended to be toward avoidance of recognition of the reality relationship. Therapists became more dehumanized (Arlow 1971). If the therapist communicated in a more personal and less purely "interpretive" mode, he or she did so with a feeling that rules were being broken and would certainly not tell colleagues about it.

DISCUSSION

The patient's psychic organization may require a defensive avoidance of new, affectively alive, real relationships, or aspects of real relationships, in the present. The motive for the avoidance may be a threat of disorganization or loss of an aspect of the self, or of object loss, and not necessarily structural conflict. Access to the crucial structures is not through interpretation of transference but through dealing with resistances to the experience of the real relationship.

In our case examples we have tried to illustrate some different technical uses of the real relationship, which vary with the developmental level of organization of the patient and different stages in the process of the therapy. To the extent that a patient is able to consistently experience the real relationship alongside his transference reactions, and can maintain regulatory and observing functions, the real relationship may be taken for granted and remain relatively silent. We have found such patients to be uncommon. In our view the importance of the real relationship arises not only from its value in dealing with transference reaction. The real relationship is at times itself the vehicle of the therapeutic process (see Examples 1, 2, and 4). At other times attention to the real relationship is necessary to establish the two parallel experiences (real relationship and transference relationship) that are essential in making use of transference interpretation. In either case, the patient's resistance to experiencing the real relationship may be a crucial aspect of the therapeutic process. At times the patient's transference experience of the therapist may overwhelm his reality testing and obliterate his experience of the real relationship, so that all interpretation will be experienced by the patient as a repetition of the past. Example 1 illustrates this situation.

The patient in Example 1 was contending with aspects of her self and her aggression that she experienced as intolerable. She attacked the therapist in a critical, sadistic way, and using her sadistic superego, she treated herself the same way. She expected no help from the therapist, which was also what she felt she deserved. As the therapy proceeded she induced a version of her conflict in the therapist. He felt critical of himself, he worried that his interventions might be somehow sadistic, he felt victimized and helpless to do anything about the aggressive onslaught, and yet he felt urgently that he needed to do something to help. For a time he could not extricate himself because he felt he would seem unresponsive, indifferent, or attacking, like her parents. Her problem had also become his problem. His experience of her struggle was more intense than the "signal" level that occurs with higher levels of organization; her problem had crossed the self-object boundary. She had changed the real relationship by changing him. At times in therapy the therapist needs to find and validate the patient's real qualities in the present; in this instance the first step was for the therapist to find and validate himself.

In his 1979 paper "On Projective Identification," Ogden takes up Melanie Klein's (1946) term and uses it "to refer to a group of fantasies and accompanying object relations having to do with the ridding of the self of unwanted aspects of the self; the depositing of those unwanted 'parts' into another person; and finally, with the 'recovery' of a modified version of what was extruded" (p. 357). In this process, "the recipient of the projection experiences himself in part as he is pictured in the projective fantasy. . . . If the recipients of the projection can deal with the feelings projected 'into' him in a way that differs from the projector's method, a new set of feelings is generated which can be viewed as a 'processed' version of the original projected feelings" (p. 361). This "digested" version can then be internalized by the patient.

In the case example, the therapist's ability to come to terms with coercive superego pressure (which he had begun to experience within himself) and coercive demands from the object, and to say no, provided the patient with a new and far-reaching way out of her predicament. She could now emotionally appreciate her dilemma as a child, which she had previously seen only cognitively. The emotional grasp, which came initially from interaction with the real object and not from verbal transference interpretation, led to a resumption of her development. This included a new ability to experience and observe transference reactions and to distinguish them from the real relationship. She now could move back and forth between the two parallel experiences.

In our experience, patients who have grown up with coercion as a prominent mode of interaction often require some type of interpretation through action, such as setting a limit.

Another aspect of the role of the real relationship comes to light in instances in which self and/or object constancy or differentiation are not solidly established, or regulatory structures in relation to affect or impulse are deficient, or some other substantial ego defect is present. In such cases the patient may need the therapist's help in going through an early phase of internalizing a function, as in Examples 1 and 2. Consolidation of regulatory structure or reality testing or self-observing capacity may need specific attention from the therapist before the patient can use his or her regressive experience in therapy in a therapeutic way.

In Example 2, the patient's structural problem had developmentally earlier roots than the patient's problem in Example 1. She had internalized some limited self-soothing capacity from her early relationship with her nanny, but repeated separations made it unstable. The depth of the patient's regression during the three-week vacation indicated the extent of the instability of her self and object constancies. Failure in the early "holding environment" (Winnicott 1965b) led to what Adler and Buie conceptualized in 1979 as a fundamental problem with aloneness:

> If this aloneness constitutes too much of the infant's experience, he will be unable to negotiate development of libidinal object constancy (Fraiberg 1969; Freud, A., 1960), i.e., as an adult he will not be able to maintain a sense of soothing contact with sustaining introjections because the introjects will be unstable and subject to loss through a form of structural regression. . . . The therapeutic task is to provide the patient with an interpersonal experience over time which will allow him to develop a solid evocative memory for the soothing, sustaining relationship with the therapist. (p. 85)

This patient required a real relationship in which the therapist was available enough to intercept the intense anxiety that occurred when she was threatened by an overwhelming aloneness. For a time this required frequent telephone contact to sustain the patient's internal representation of the therapist and to maintain the "holding environment." The therapist also provided a reassuring source of understanding what had been chaotic and bewildering, as well as a conceptualization that the patient could increasingly use herself to organize her experience. She did this first through fantasied conversation with the therapist, and much later by simply thinking it through herself. Very gradually the patient's sense of herself and her ability to call the therapist to mind stabilized. At the point when she developed the capacity to bear the depression (Zetzel 1965), she differentiated the image of the therapist in her mind from the image of her nanny, and she experienced the pain and grief of the loss that had previously been too overwhelming to face. This opened the way to a major reorganization of her patterns of experiencing herself and dealing with objects. A part of the reorganization involved consolidating her ability to work with transference in therapy and experiencing anger at the therapist for the first time (previously it had been displaced and disavowed).

In this instance the real relationship evolved gradually, beginning with the patient's experience of the therapist almost entirely via her nanny transference. When the therapist emerged as himself, different from her nanny, in the patient's representational world, a resumption of development became possible and necessary. (See Winnicott's "The Use of an Object," 1969, and Adler's 1980 discussion of the real relationship, both of which emphasize the establishing of the therapist as a separate person.) Until then, her defensive structure had aimed above all to prevent any attachment to a real object, because she could not let herself have what she could not bear to lose.

The patient in Example 4, who also required a soothing and "holding" action from the therapist, was different in that she had established a greater degree of object constancy. From the first day she related to the therapist as someone she could count on, probably because she had a consistently available father until she was 6 years old. But an aspect of her regulatory structure was subject to being overwhelmed, specifically by an excruciating, overpowering pain in response to loss. When the therapist supplied the missing soothing, holding, regulatory function, and an organizing conceptualization along with it, she was able to gradually come to terms with the loss of her mother through depression when she was 10 months old. In the process she also seemed to internalize the regulatory function that the therapist had been supplying. She then proceeded to deal with the loss of her father when she was 6 without needing the unusual soothing activity from the therapist.

These are technically very different problems from those in which a transference relationship gradually crowds out the real relationship, which then will reemerge as the transference reactions are understood. In our cases, the technical problem involved both reconstructing the past and constructing the present. It also involved interpreting resistances to experiencing the present, including fears and feelings of loss and abandonment in relation to old self and object images that accompanied each step of progress, from the beginning to the end.

Patients often view themselves from both realistic and unrealistic perspectives. The therapist must recognize and therapeutically attend to both self-representations. The failure to acknowledge and work with the patient's realistic, true self and his valid ego capacities may only add to the patient's doubt about these real aspects of himself and may limit his ability to accept and utilize new interpretations and insights into himself.

The patient described in Example 3 had struggled through an earlier experience in therapy in which careful attention only to unconscious drive impulses and fantasies was of but limited help, because the patient could not differentiate between the real relationship and his reliving the past in the transference. He experienced both as emotionally the same. The negative object representation and primitive, sadistic superego, so prominent in his psychic organization, and an accompanying depreciated self seen as the "victim," had been internally lived out most of his life. When the negative images were projected onto the therapist, the patient's ability to distinguish either the real person of the therapist or the more healthy aspects of his own real self was quite limited. The patient's struggles in recognizing his own self-reality had been even more difficult in the prior therapeutic ambience, in which the therapist's interventions were limited to interpretation of the unconscious, viewing the past only in the light of childhood wishes and fantasies, with little or no focus on healthy aspects of the patient. The therapist had also revealed little of himself as a real person. As the patient began in the current psychotherapy to express his rage more directly toward the "abusers," it was necessary for him to ascertain the therapist's reaction to these feelings. The rageful expression had current transference implications that were later more available for interpretation when the patient became angry at the therapist for being unable to make a change in an appointment time. However, initially there was a need for validation of the patient's feelings in the past. A transference interpretation at this point might have once again been experienced as an accusation.

We are not advocating relationship therapy without recognition of transferences, or just being "nice" to a patient, but we are emphasizing the need to aid a weakened, potentially healthy self (the true self spoken of by Winnicott) to gain expression, in an atmosphere of safety. Of course it will also be necessary to make transference interpretations, but they should be made in a real relationship that is monitored and made explicit in such way that the patient can understand what part of his experience is a manifestation of the past. Otherwise he might experience such interpretations as a repetition of trauma of the past.

In addition to agreeing on the importance of the real relationship as a vehicle of transference expression and interpretation, many authors (Blum 1971; Loewald 1960; Glover 1955; Gill 1982) have stressed that encountering the therapist as a real, new object is part of the effectiveness of a therapeutic experience. Blum states, "Even in adult analysis the role of the analyst as a real new object rather than the object of transference must be considered along with identification with the analyst and analytic attitudes" (p. 51). Appropriate real interaction with patients is inevitable and cannot, and should not, be avoided. We are stressing the importance of attention to these interactions, which may lead to valuable transference manifestations and potential interpretations. Such interactions may also be used to facilitate and enhance a new and therapeutic experience with a new object, leading to both insight and change. Eisnitz (1981) makes a particular technical point regarding the therapist as a new object, in contrast to those of the past, pointing out certain mature shifts in the self-representation made by patients. He states, "If the moves away from the narcissistically secure position are not recognized and acknowledged in the treatment, the patient may feel infantilized, demeaned, and unacknowledged just as in the past" (p. 321).

We have noted resistances that patients may have to the real relationship, but therapists also may have resistances to more real participation in the therapeutic relationship, possibly in part because of their theoretical orientation, as we noted earlier. When a therapist allows himself to be experienced as human and does not try to shelter himself behind "the transference," he is sometimes more vulnerable in being seen as he is. This is not always a comfortable position, and it can be tempting to interpret certain realistic views and observations and resulting feelings patients may have about us as transference, especially when the views and feelings are negative. Those of us who become therapists, reinforcing the attributes of sensitivity and responsiveness to others that are necessary in our work, may also find it easier to respond to others than to reveal our real selves in a personal way.

We are aware that our focus on the importance of the real relationship has a potential for misinterpretation and misuse. There is a danger that therapists might in the process of being "human" act out their own object needs and needs for gratification. Others may also see our emphasis as avoidance of transference or neglect of transference interpretation. Our approach is to evaluate and monitor the real relationship in the context of the therapeutic process of a given patient in order to facilitate that process, which can allow transference interpretation to be more effective and meaningful for the patient.

SUMMARY

In this paper we are stressing the importance of attention to the reality relationship in psychoanalytic psychotherapy for certain patients who have difficulties with object and self constancies and/or defensive use of distorted self and object representations. These difficulties are often accompanied by problems with affect regulation. We believe that this aspect of the therapeutic relationship has importance for a broad range of patients and therapies, including psychoanalysis.

We find the model of the therapist as an impersonal screen onto whom transferences are cast to be both unrealistic and undesirable. An emotionally real relationship in the present facilitates the development of transference that is therapeutically useful; it helps in delineating what part of the patient's experience is "not attributable to the actual situation"; it provides a fresh perspective from which to understand the influences of the past. In addition, it facilitates the patient's internalization of aspects of the therapist's functioning. Traditionally, such internalization has been viewed as limited to the analyst's analyzing function, leading to the capacity for self-analysis, and aspects of the analyst's presumably more benevolent superego. We have tried to illustrate additional aspects of internalization, derived from the real relationship, which may be central to the therapeutic process.

The therapist is drawn by the patient into an experience of variable intensity; at times it may threaten the therapist's equilibrium. While the therapist's transference to the patient might be a major contributor to this experience, we believe that his reactions also occur on a countertransference basis and may be a necessary and productive part of the therapy process.

We feel that interpretation, reconstruction of the past, and, if necessary, construction of the present are all central to the therapeutic work. A new experience has by itself a very limited value, as does "interpretation only" without a new experience in the present.

REFERENCES

Adler G: Transference, real relationship and alliance. Int J Psychoanal 1980; 61:547-557

Adler G, Buie Jr. D: Aloneness and borderline psychopathology: the possible relevance of child development issues. Int J Psychoanal 1979; 69:83-96

Alexander F, French T: Psychoanalytic Therapy. New York, The Ronald Press Company, 1946

Arlow J: The dehumanization of psychoanalysis. Unpublished paper, summarized by Simons RC, Bulletin of the Psychoanalytic Association 1971; 11:6-8

Bird B: Notes on transference: universal phenomenon and hardest part of analysis. J Am Psychoanal Assoc 1972; 20:267-301

Blum H: On the conception and the development of the transference neurosis. J Am Psychoanal Assoc 1971; 19:41-53

Brenner C: Some comments on technical precepts in psychoanalysis. J Am Psychoanal Assoc 1969; 17:333-352

Eisnitz A: The perspective of the self-representation: some clinical implications. J Am Psychoanal Assoc 1981, 29:309-336

Eissler K: The effect of the structure of the ego on psychoanalytic technique. J Am Psychoanal Assoc 1953; 1:104-143

Fairbairn W: On the nature and aims of psycho-analytical treatment. Int J Psychoanal 1959; 40:374-385

Fenichel O: Problems in Psychoanalytic Technique. Albany, NY, Psychoanalytic Quarterly Inc, 1941

Fraiberg S: Libidinal object constancy and mental representation. Psychoanal Study Child 1969; 24:9-47

Fraiberg S: Pathological defenses in childhood. Psychoanal Q 1982; 51:612-635

Freud A: The widening scope of indications for psychoanalysis; discussion. J Am Psychoanal Assoc 1954; 2:607-620

Freud A: Discussion of Dr. John Bowlby's paper. Psychoanal Study Child 1960; 15:53-62

Freud S: An autobiographical study (1925), in Complete Psychological Works, Standard Edition, vol. 20. Translated and edited by Strachey J. London, Hogarth Press, 1959

Freud S: Analysis terminable and interminable (1937), in Complete Psychological Works, Standard Edition, vol. 23. Translated and edited by Strachey J. London, Hogarth Press, 1964

Gill M: Analysis of Transference, vol. 1. New York, International Universities Press, 1982

Glover E: The Technique of Psychoanalysis. New York, International Universities Press, 1955

Gray P: Psychoanalytic technique and the ego's capacity for viewing intrapsychic activity. J Am Psychoanal Assoc 1973; 21:474-494

Greenacre P: The role of transference: practical considerations in relation to psychoanalytic therapy. J Am Psychoanal Assoc 1954; 2:671-684

Greenacre P: Certain technical problems in the transference relationship. J Am Psychoanal Assoc 1959; 7:484-502

Greenson R, Wexler M: The non-transference relationship in the psychoanalytic situation. Int J Psychoanal 1969; 50:27-39

Heiman P: On countertransference. Int J Psychoanal 1950; 31:81-84

Hoffman I: The patient as interpreter of the analyst's experience. Contemporary Psychoanalysis 1983; 19:389-422

Kanzer M: The transference neurosis of the Rat Man. Psychoanal Q 1952; 21:181-189

Kernberg O: Technical considerations in the treatment of borderline personality organization. J Am Psychoanal Assoc 1976; 24:795-829

Klein M: Notes on some schizoid mechanisms (1946), in Envy and Gratitude and Other Works, 1946-1963. New York, Delacorte Press/Seymour Laurence, 1975

Kohut H: The Analysis of the Self. New York, International Universities Press, 1971

Kramer S: The technical significance and application of Mahler's separation–individuation theory. J Am Psychoanal Assoc 1979; 27:241-262

Kris E: Ego psychology and interpretation in psychoanalytic therapy. Psychoanal Q 1951; 20:15-30

Lachman F, Stolorow R: Idealization and grandiosity: developmental considerations and treatment implications. Psychoanal Q 1976; 45:565-587

Langs R: Making interpretations and securing the frame: sources of danger for psychotherapists. International Journal of Psychotherapy 1985

Lipton S: The advantages of Freud's technique as shown in his analysis of the Rat Man. Int J Psychoanal 1977; 58:255-273

Little M: Transference in borderline states. Int J Psychoanal 1966; 47:476-485

Loewald H: On the therapeutic action of psychoanalysis. Int J Psychoanal 1960; 41:16-33

Lowenstein R: Some remarks on defences, autonomous ego and psychoanalytic technique. Int J Psychoanal 1954; 35:188-193

Mahler M: A study of the separation–individuation process and its possible application to borderline phenomena in the psychoanalytic situation. Psychoanal Study Child 1971; 26:403-424

Miller A: The drama of the gifted child and the psychoanalyst's narcissistic disturbance. Int J Psychoanal 1979; 60:47-58

Ogden T: On projective identification. Int J Psychoanal 1979; 60:357-373

Racker H: Transference and Countertransference. New York, International Universities Press, 1968

Sachs D: On the relationship between psychoanalysis and psychoanalytic psychotherapy. Journal of the Philadelphia Association for Psychoanalysis 1979; 6:119-145

Sandler J: Countertransference and role responsiveness. International Review of Psychoanalysis 1976; 3:43-48

Searles H: Collected Papers on Schizophrenia and Related Subjects. New York, International Universities Press, 1965

Stone L: The widening scope of indications for psychoanalysis. J Am Psychoanal Assoc 1954; 2:567-594

Stone L: The Psychoanalytic Situation. New York, International Universities Press, 1961

Winnicott D: Transitional objects and transitional phenomena. Int J Psychoanal 1953; 34:89-97

Winnicott D: Ego distortion in terms of true and false self (1960), in The Maturational Process and the Facilitating Environment. New York, International Universities Press, 1965a

Winnicott D: The theory of the parent–infant relationship (1960), in The

Maturational Processes and the Facilitating Environment. New York, International Universities Press, 1965b

Winnicott D: The use of an object. Int J Psychoanal 1969; 50:711-716

Zetzel E: Panel on "The traditional psychoanalytic technique and its variations." J Am Psychoanal Assoc 1953; 1:526-537

Zetzel E: Depression and the incapacity to bear it, in Drives, Affects, Behavior, vol. 2. New York, International Universities Press, 1965

CHAPTER 4

Masochistic Character Formation and the Reemergence of Traumatic Feeling States

Maria V. Bergmann, Ph.D.

This paper stresses the relationship between masochism and traumatic events. The return of traumatic feeling states is manifested in masochistic character traits and behavior.

The term masochistic character I need not define, as Freud did so in 1924 in the classical paper in which he took the step from masochism as a perversion to moral masochism. One of Freud's great contributions was to see character formation as a possible route toward sublimation of sexual wishes. According to Freud, female masochism resulted from actual exposure to the primal scene, which had a traumatic impact on the girl; or it might develop endopsychically, where there were primal scene fantasies: the masochism would result from identification with the masochistic mother, and experiences or fantasies of a sadistic father would be carried over to other men. The girl would thus experience herself as masochistic and men as sadistic. (Analogous mechanisms are, of course, found in the boy.) Today we would not consider masochism an attribute of normal femininity (Blum 1976; Bernstein 1983).

Psychoanalysis began as a theory viewing neuroses as responses to trauma (seduction theory). After 1900 emphasis shifted from trauma to incompatible endopsychic wishes and sexual prohibitions. Psychoanalysis then became a psychology of symptoms, but slowly it moved into building a theory of character development as well.

Some of Freud's writings on character began in "Three Essays on the Theory of Sexuality" (1905). There Freud stated:

> What we describe as a person's 'character' is built up to a considerable extent from the material of sexual excitations and is composed of instincts that have been fixed since childhood, of constructions achieved by means of sublimation, and of other constructions, employed for effectively holding in check perverse impulses which have been recognized as unutilizable (pp. 238-239).

Thus Freud believed that a person's character is shaped by sexual fixations and perversions; that character binds undischarged sexual excitations; that certain instinct derivatives can be sublimated. Throughout Freud's earlier writings, character is linked to sublimation, which is conceived of as converting instinctual strivings into socially acceptable activities. We do not learn how this conversion takes place, but we get the raw material for character formation. Freud differentiated characterological themes that directly expressed an instinctual wish—those that led to sublimation, and others that led to reaction formations or other defenses.

Peter Blos (1968) has discussed character in ways most relevant for my topic. Blos maintains that a firm character structure is not formed until the end of adolescence. In adolescence there is a realignment of forces, and a more permanent integration of character formation is achieved.

This integrative process tends to eliminate conflict and/or overt anxiety arousal. In normal development, the individuation process of adolescence, which brings about a disengagement from the libidinal and aggressive ties of childhood, strengthens the burgeoning adult structure and also consolidates superego, ego ideal, and narcissistic formations. Blos states that if the adolescent process is unable to overcome the disequilibrium of traumatic residues from childhood, the individual will try to assimilate traumata through characterological stabilization.

A firm character organization prevents the arousal of signal anxiety through codification of conflicts. Once the traumatic core has become part of the character structure, Blos continues, it does not alert the ego via an anxiety signal against ego-dystonic behavior but attempts to create adaptive measures within the character structure instead. Nevertheless, residual trauma presses for actualization.

Specific developmental factors play a major role in the normality or pathology of character formation. As character controls direct expression of instinct derivatives, it aids impulse control. Character formation is a sign of synthetic functions being at work. Literature on character in psychoanalysis is extensive, although to this very day there is still no adequate definition of character.

Under normal conditions, character formation introduces a more stable experience of the self, narcissistic gratification, greater consistency of the internal psychic forces, and predictability of behavior. In childhood, character is formed through stabilizing identifications which become the pillars of structure formation, but traumatizing object relationships may lead to precocious character consolidation. Splits in the development of identifications may lead to fragmentation and later to difficulties in object relationships and to internal conflicts. There are these developmental alternatives: the first aims to repress trauma so that no characterological change will take place. The second aims to build a character structure that will be strong enough to withstand the trauma, or a structure so constructed that it can avoid its recurrence altogether.

What occurs if a traumatic core underlies the character structure? What happens to residual traumatic themes when characterological changes and drive maturation have occurred during adolescence? The implications of Blos's formulations are that character formation is designed to prevent the outbreak of traumatic states going back to childhood, by creating a defensive structure that will hold against the repetition of childhood traumata (see also Glenn 1984). Thus, infantile traumata strongly influence character formation. Extensive characterological adaptation may have been achieved at high cost to psychic well-being but may save the individual from the reemergence of traumatic feeling states in adulthood.

A traumatic core in the child's relationship to early objects does not permit synthesis of the developing psyche and adequate adaptation to the environment. An imbalance is fostered by virtue of the amount of incoming stimuli and the child's relative incapacity to discharge them. Overstimulation invariably becomes sexualized or increases the reservoir of undischarged hostile tendencies in the psychic structure. It leads to regression and prevents adequate adaptation to the environment. While symptoms may appear as well, overstimulation leads to a high degree of potential anxiety, although there may be no opportunity for the growing psyche to develop a protective anxiety signal under traumatizing conditions.

Character formation may aim to control or subdue sadistic or masochistic tendencies. However, if control is successful, the person may use masturbation fantasies with a sadistic and/or masochistic content as a means of discharge. In addition, behavior may develop symbolizing hostile masturbatory practices or wishes, and typically may be found also in perversions.

Undischargeable overstimulation that is sexualized or generates excessive hostility may also be turned back against the self. Further complications arise when the superego becomes aware of the pleasure derived from sadistic or masochistic fantasies. The superego behaves punitively, and guilt feelings ensue: sadistic and masochistic character traits and object relations are created. Although a child may successfully develop characterological defenses to cover hostility, sexual anxiety, and fears of object loss, a high degree of narcissistic vulnerability, psychosexual fixations, or perverse tendencies may remain, leading to trauma-creating object relations during the process of psychic development.

If trauma verifies and gives concrete content to phase-specific character development that is already underway, it then attains the gluing power of fixation. If this can be demonstrated to a patient, such insight is a first step in loosening trauma's pathogenic hold over an individual. Strain trauma is ongoing and a result of continuing psychological interaction between child and environment. Shock trauma is a sudden onslaught on psychic reality—such as death of a parent, physical illness, or abandonment. A traumatic character structure may be built either on strain or on shock trauma. The shock trauma also could be described as "confirmatory trauma," as it enhances tendencies or events that were present *before*, such as those related to surgery or object loss. Under such circumstances, the trauma would be used by psychic forces to validate a trend that was already forming developmentally, before the shock itself. In such cases trauma bestows the validity of an existing psychic reality on preexisting fantasies, and the resultant structure may be seen as a compromise formation.

Obstacles to the development of an autonomous self, stemming from early traumatization, will prevent repression. Whenever this occurs, character formation takes the place of repression. When pressures from early childhood remain active, symptom formation and character formation will appear side by side: whatever cannot be assimilated into symptoms or be repressed appears in the character formation.

Trauma is assimilated when the character is so constructed that a person comes to feel increasingly immune to the return of the trauma, which means that trauma has become one of the bases of the character structure itself.

In the course of a psychoanalysis or psychoanalytic psychotherapy, character traits built up to contain the trauma inevitably become character resistances. As development proceeds, the patient becomes narcissistically attached to the defensive characterological structure he or she has built up. As a result, a patient may *not* be motivated to subject his or her behavior or attitudes to special scrutiny: a patient wants to be rid of symptoms but does not want to shed character traits or character structure that carries the stamp of narcissistically valued personality aspects. Characterological difficulties expressed by overt character resistances are in most cases the result of traumatic events in early childhood. These will be relived during later development in the service of mastery.

There is a difference between reliving on the basis of a traumatic feeling state and reliving as a result of repetition in the service of mastery. The latter form of reliving is illustrated by someone who comes for treatment because he always picks a love mate according to an image of a dominating mother instead of available people who are loving and less demanding. The patient feels compelled to pick the less lovable and more demanding partner, who reminds him of mother. He is aware that unless his reasons for making this kind of unfavorable choice are analyzed, he will continue to make such choices for the rest of his life. This is a manifestation of repetition as we know it in psychoneurosis.

On the other hand, when traumata occur in adult life, they may break down already formed cover structures from childhood and add damaging effects at the time of their occurrence. When the traumatic stimulus recurs—representing what Krystal (1975, p. 111) has called a "utilizable" trauma signal—it is as if an organized fantasy embedded in an anxiety state is being relived in the current environment in concretized, externalized form. The anxiety state frequently leads to masochistic fantasies in which the patient must be victimized in order to survive. In oedipal or incestuous guilt, one can trace the sexualization of suffering. Glenn (1984) has also observed that the erotization of suffering seems to "blunt the effects of trauma" (p. 377).

Persons with a history of overstimulation in childhood and with trau-

matic themes in their object relationships frequently seek out an attachment to painful feelings, as Valenstein (1973) has so convincingly described. Patients with a painful past will have tendencies to develop
masochistic characterological reactions and negative therapeutic reactions because they are attached to their painful feelings. In Valenstein's
description, pain takes on the characteristics of a fixation to early trauma
and, by implication, to early objects who tended the child.

Affects may become the symbolic representations of early objects. An
affective screen may be formed, uncovered in treatment later, which
exposes distorted childhood memories or fantasies with sadomasochistic
themes. Early traumatization disturbs the signal function of affect and
slows down further affect development. Guilt feelings may be split off or
denied as well. Early adaptive techniques push away anxiety and traumatic memories. Particular kinds of character organization and masochistic and sadistic character traits have frequently been employed to
keep out of life forever what has been feared most since childhood but
has since become unconscious. Therapeutic exploration of masochistic
characterological themes threatens the carefully guarded equilibrium,
and there is an underlying anxiety that the trauma will be repeated if
analytic exploration continues.

Thus, transference resistance follows the same route that was initially
used to establish the building blocks for character formation and adaptation. As mentioned above, a strong negative transference and very likely
a negative therapeutic reaction will follow this exploration. A traumatic
feeling state may break through the character structure as a result of a
stressful condition in real life, or in treatment when analytic work has
weakened the system of defenses. In the event of such a weakening of the
defensive structure, the negative therapeutic reaction may best be understood and treated as a result of a breakthrough of traumatic feeling states
from childhood. If treatment is successful, a new motivational system
will be constituted and form an adaptive basis. The new motivational
structure may help the patient to face the sexualization of pain and its
masochistic latter-day manifestations, which were based on pain inflicted during childhood but could hitherto not be separated from pleasure.

THE REAPPEARANCE OF A TRAUMATIC FEELING STATE

Repression is never so complete that a traumatic feeling state may not
emerge under stress to re-create the original trauma. As a rule, a traumatic feeling state is short-lived, very intense; there may be a great deal
of anxiety; there is always hostility to be liberated and discharged. The
hostility seems unwarranted by circumstances, and the occasion that

prompted the recurrence of a traumatic feeling state seems small in comparison to the response.

After a traumatic feeling state is mobilized, there is a sudden awakening, ego functions are remobilized, reality testing returns, and the ego regains control.

Example 1

My first example deals with a patient who responded traumatically to an improved relationship with her husband, which had developed as a result of treatment.

> The patient had grown up while in hiding and had reached puberty in a German ghetto during World War II. She had lost her father, who had had repeated heart attacks after he was persecuted and then imprisoned by the Nazis, and she had been separated from her mother, who was taken to a concentration camp. The mother survived and found her children again after liberation.
>
> The patient was an accomplished physician. She was given to anxiety attacks under very specific situations:
>
> *1)* She felt loving toward and aroused by her husband. She anticipated a particularly happy sexual experience. Suddenly she had an anxiety attack. She felt she could not breathe. She asked for water. She felt she couldn't get any air—that there was not enough air here. Her husband said, "But there *is* air in this room." She insisted they get dressed, and he took her for a walk. Being unable to breathe represented the manner in which the patient's father had died as a result of his Nazi imprisonment; it also represented the death of other family members of the older generation, who had died in the gas ovens.

What was the traumatic experience, and why did it appear at this point? When during treatment the relationship between husband and wife improved, including a much more pleasurable sexual relationship, the patient's tie to her father became threatened. In the past, she had always found other men inferior to her deeply loved and idealized father, to whom she remained faithful after she lost him under traumatic circumstances during her childhood. When the father died, he struggled for breath. Intense conflict ensued because the father was intrapsychically alive, and the patient could not desert him after what he had suffered. Both id and superego forces were involved, and her loyalty to her father won. The anticipation of sexual pleasure and closeness to a man other than the father was experienced as an abandonment of the father and provided the traumatic stimulus.

For this patient, death was sexualized and part of her living reality. She felt it could happen at any moment, particularly when life seemed to be too good. She was afraid, therefore, not only of the loss of her father but also of being punished by her superego for experiencing so much pleasure when her loved ones had suffered so much; she had an unconscious fantasy that she would have to pay for these pleasures with her life. She responded masochistically on the basis of survivors' guilt. Why was this not merely a normal example of a strong oedipal tie that created a conflict in the patient's current love life? The patient identified with her cruelly persecuted father and traumatically relived his suffering. His trauma became hers and led to masochistic reliving at the point when her adult love life improved.

2) The same patient was slated to give a lecture before a large audience. Every time this occurred she had stage fright, although she was sure of the content of her communication, which she would render with conviction. When I asked about her anxiety, she smiled and made a gesture with her entire body as though she wanted to curl up into a ball. She put her arms in front of her face: "My heart keeps pounding when I stand up there, and I always feel like hiding." She had the fantasy that the Nazis were going to come and get her as they had taken away her mother, and that if she hid they wouldn't be able to find her. She said, "I must be reliving when they found my father and he got a heart attack and when they carted off my mother." I asked, "What would happen if you would stand there self-assured, a member of the community, a member of your profession, and deliver your lecture?" She shook her head sadly, and tears filled her eyes. She then would lose everybody; she would be abandoning the family and become a "Nazi." She said, "So I have two choices. I can either be a criminal Jew who will be carted off to death, or be the Nazi." She suddenly laughed, partly with relief, partly with sarcasm, and said, "What a wonderful choice!" I said that it might help her to remember this discovery when she had to speak in public until we could work on it further.

In the foregoing example reemergence of the traumatic feeling state occurred as a result of therapeutic improvement, which had become polarized vis-à-vis the patient's internal conflict, survivors' guilt, fears of punishment, and the need to take on the burden of suffering and dying for those who have been lost. A vastly improved life situation with greater capacity for enjoyment and sublimation brought about the necessity to deal with recurrent traumatic feeling states in a new way.

Magical expectations are usually directed toward real objects to protect the person from recurrent trauma. As these are doomed to fail, the traumatic state returns. The second example relates to the traumatic loss of the patient's mother and with the psychic mechanisms that disturbed a newly found sublimatory capacity.

Example 2

In the following situation the traumatic stimulus occurred as a result of an *external* event.

> A woman who had lost two members of each side of her parental family in Auschwitz went to a small store in New York where she often shopped. In a sudden hold-up, some men charged in with guns and ordered all the customers and clerks into an immobile position. The woman caught on to the situation with astonishing rapidity. By moving almost imperceptibly, although she had been ordered to stand still, she succeeded in getting to the very back of the store, where she was almost invisible. She threw her purse behind a large box in which some goods were stored so that *it* was invisible. The gunmen took the others' belongings, in some cases including their clothing, stormed out, and disappeared in a truck that was waiting for them. They left without finding her.

The woman told this story to me in a first therapeutic consultation, with great anxiety; the incident may have contributed to her decision to seek treatment at this point. I was struck by the fact that the patient was primarily responding to the danger to her life rather than to the theft, although she admitted that from the very first she knew that very likely no one would be killed. Her intelligent, self-protective behavior, based on the speed with which she had sized up the situation, had not prevented her from feeling that her very life was in danger. I said that it was an awful story, horribly frightening, but I wondered why she thought her life was in danger, since she had understood immediately that she was caught in a robbery and not in an attempted mass murder. She shrugged and remained in an anxiety state. I said that I thought that perhaps she was unable to make the differentiation between theft and murder because the scene had suddenly and unconsciously put her into Auschwitz.

Although the patient and I at this point hardly knew each other, the effect of my statement was immediate: She relaxed completely, and tears and a softness replaced the stance of terror and rage. She finally said, "I never understood how *we* escaped and why *they* had to perish."

My interpretation about Auschwitz restored the patient's symbolic capacity and enabled her to separate past from present. The fact that the patient behaved realistically during the store hold-up, but experienced in fantasy the danger to life her family members might have felt in Auschwitz, is evidence of a split between a self that belonged to her present life and one that was shared with the parental past. Survivors' children often feel and experience in their own way the dangers to life experienced by their beloved older relatives. Such feeling states may be relived in the present.

In my patient's unconscious, the successful evasion of the thieves contrasted to parental helplessness. The patient felt how much better her life was than that of the parents, and as a result she felt guilty. In order to evade massive guilt feelings, she attempted to falsify reality by equating the relatively small danger she was in with the far greater danger under which her parents had lived. This fantasy distortion constituted a masochistic stance in order to relieve massive feelings of guilt, for unless the hold-up was equated with mass murder, the patient's escape seemed too easy and unjust.

Example 3

My final example illustrates how traumatic childhood events can convert a person's present life into an arena in which the traumatic past is relived. In this instance the trauma was not repressed but was reworked by a masturbation fantasy that created a precondition for orgasm.

> When the patient was of puberty age, she developed a serious illness of long duration from which she recovered. The illness involved surgery and a prolonged after-cure, which in turn necessitated frequent changes of bandages in order to remove pus exuding from wounds. The patient defended herself against her extraordinary pain by falling in love with her surgeon, who would bring her a little flower when he visited because she had been "such a good girl."
>
> As an adult, the patient relived the forced surgery trauma and the pain and pleasure connected to the person of her surgeon through a masturbation practice. She used white gauze to stimulate her genitals. This was extremely pleasurable. At the point when she feared that she had hurt herself, she had an orgasm. In the fantasy she injured herself rather than being injured by the doctor. When she had a sexual relationship, the men didn't injure her and she did not experience orgasm. We see here the sexualization of a trauma. A sexual fixation, originally toward the surgeon who stood for the father, was still evident in adulthood; the patient could not experience orgasm without concomitant pain.

A patient who suffered from a congenital deformity once entered the hour and said, "When I left yesterday, I suddenly realized that for the first time in my life I felt no anxiety. I began to hate you. I thought that you had deprived me of my most stable and reliable companion. *Where* was my anxiety? I felt very uncomfortable. I am happy to report to you that it returned after a few hours and that I feel well and sick as usual."

CONCLUSION

In this discussion, case material is used to illustrate that a traumatic core underlies masochistic character formation. Infantile traumata that have not undergone repression reemerge in current life as traumatic feeling states. Paradoxically, times of greater health that subsequently separate the fate of the patient from the fate of his parents can also act as a stimulus for reawakening the trauma. Likewise, if in a traumatic situation the patient behaves more realistically than the parents, the original trauma may also be reawakened. In addition, the traumatic state returns when an actual event in life becomes associated with the original trauma. These states need to be understood clinically as a form of reliving of trauma, and that understanding must be put into words in treatment in order to be curative for the patient.

REFERENCES

Bernstein I: Masochistic pathology and female development. J Am Psychoanal Assoc 1983; 31:467-486

Blos P: The second individuation process of adolescence. Psychoanal Study Child 1968; 22:162-186

Blum HP: Masochism, the ego ideal, and the pathology of women. J Am Psychoanal Assoc 1976; 24:157-191

Freud S: Three essays on the theory of sexuality (1905), in Complete Psychological Works, Standard Edition, vol. 7. Translated and edited by Strachey J. London, Hogarth Press, 1953

Freud S: A child is being beaten (1919), in Complete Psychological Works, Standard Edition, vol. 17. Translated and edited by Strachey J. London, Hogarth Press, 1955

Freud S: The economic problem of masochism (1924), in Complete Psychological Works, Standard Edition, vol. 19. Translated and edited by Strachey J. London, Hogarth Press, 1961

Glenn J: Psychic trauma and masochism. J Am Psychoanal Assoc 1984; 32:357-386

Krystal H: Trauma and affect. Psychoanal Study Child 1975; 33:81-116

Krystal H: Trauma and the stimulus barrier. Psychoanalytic Inquiry 1985; 1:131-161

Valenstein AF: On attachment to painful feelings and the negative therapeutic reaction. Psychoanal Study Child 1973; 28:365-391

SECTION 2

Consultation and Supervision: The Teaching and Uses of Psychoanalytic Developmental Theory

Edited by
Wayne A. Myers, M.D.
Eugene Golderg, M.D.

CHAPTER 5

Masochistic Character Pathology in Medical Settings

Steven T. Levy, M.D.
Carol Lyle, M.D.
Steven A. Cohen-Cole, M.D.

Patients with significant character pathology pose many difficulties for physicians and others providing them with medical care. Because character pathology does not fit neatly into an illness model, blending imperceptibly into personality variation, it is not regularly recognized by nonpsychiatrists as an emotional disorder. Nonetheless, patients with character pathology are experienced by physicians and other caretakers as frustrating, difficult, "hard to treat" people. Sometimes difficulties result in major impasses in medical care that lead to psychiatric consultation. This paper will deal specifically with aspects of sadomasochistic character pathology manifest in medical settings, where it frequently results in medical treatment failures. Such failures are in some ways analogous to the negative therapeutic reactions that occur regularly when patients with this kind of pathology undergo psychoanalytic treatment. The dynamics of negative therapeutic reactions will be explored in relation to the conditions of medical treatment, and issues in management will be discussed.

The masochistic character and the nature of masochism have always been of interest to psychoanalysts. Psychoanalytic viewpoints have changed with each major addition to or new perspective in psychoanalytic theory. Freud's position about masochism changed significantly with his hypothesis of the death instinct, leading to the idea of primary masochism (Freud 1924). This conflicted with his earlier view of masochism as sadism secondarily directed inward. Freud (1923) felt masochistic characters were dominated by an unconscious need for punishment that found expression in a life of sacrifice, suffering, and failure. When masochism based upon a need for punishment over oedipal wishes was reinforced by primary masochism, which Freud believed to be related to excess, unbound death instinct, either a constitutional variant or an instinctual vicissitude reflecting problems in early mother–infant interactions (Loewald 1972), the possibility for amelioration of the masochistic pathology was, in Freud's view, very slim. Subsequent analytic formulations have emphasized preoedipal conflicts, separation-individuation problems, distorted internal object relations, pathological identifications with masochistic-depressed mothers, and narcissistic disturbances as crucial to the development of masochistic pathology.

Masochistic character pathology is particularly common among patients who seek medical care excessively. These patients make constant trips to doctors' offices and to hospital emergency rooms. They make up a significant percentage of patients with chronic pain syndromes. They have frequent surgery, often without adequate justification. And most important, they continue to suffer, frustrating those who attempt to help them.

81

Case A

Mrs. R was a 47-year-old married female referred for psychiatric evaluation by her gastroenterologist because of a long and dramatic medical history complicated by psychological "overlay." She had multiple physical illnesses including hypothyroidism, megaloblastic anemia, neurogenic bladder and rectum (related to an unusual connective tissue disorder), and chronic abdominal, bladder, and back pain. She had had 18 major surgical procedures for a variety of pelvic, abdominal, and back problems. When seen by the psychiatrist, she was taking folic acid, thyroid replacement, a stool softener, metaclopramide for gastric retention, cimetidine for abdominal pain, and Maalox for constipation. In addition, she had been on multiple pain medications, including narcotic analgesics. She had been tried on different antidepressant medications and reported some transient improvement.

The patient reported difficulties with her many physicians, some of whom "don't believe I am in pain." She believed all her complaints had clear physical bases and that doctors were often unable to diagnose her "real" problems and unfairly accused her of having pain that was "in my head." She rather proudly pointed to the fact that the doctors were always "proved wrong in the end." She reported great stress in her interpersonal relationships, complained monotonously of constant pain, and noted considerable difficulty in sleeping.

The psychiatrist elected to give her a cautious repeat trial on antidepressants, hoping to help her with her sleeplessness and chronic pain. She was also told that stress in interpersonal relationships made it more difficult to cope with chronic physical problems. Psychotherapy and the opportunity to learn relaxation methods were suggested. She came to one or two appointments, had many new physical complaints, but reported some benefits from the antidepressants and relaxation therapy. She wanted to "learn" how to avoid repeating mistakes she had made in the past in interpersonal relationships. She wanted this learning to take place in a few sessions. She soon decided not to come to appointments regularly but began seeing an osteopath and continued visiting other medical subspecialists.

Descriptions of masochistic characters in the psychoanalytic literature do not sufficiently emphasize somatization and hypochondriasis as typical of this type of pathology, perhaps because those masochistic patients who are seen in analysis tend to somatize less than their counterparts in medical settings. Patients in the latter group are thought to be less psychologically minded, less able to handle the deprivations of analytic treatment, and less able to give up their physical pain and suffering than the former group, whose "pain" remains within the psychological sphere as guilt, recurrent disappointment, habitual failure, and avoidance of pleasurable experiences. However, it should be noted that even the former group of masochistic patients usually come for analysis only in crisis situations, frequently at the urging or insistence of spouses, children, or employers. We do not know whether masochistic patients seen in medical settings, if induced to seek psychoanalytic treatment, would prove to be less analyzable than "nonsomatizing" masochistic patients. Somatization and hypochondriasis often take on the appearance of fixed delusional thinking, giving an impression of severity and permanence that may not be warranted. All masochistic character pathology is difficult to influence by analytic treatment, although the analysis of such patients is sometimes very gratifying, even if always technically demanding and, for long periods, frustrating.

In medical settings, masochistic patients are usually misunderstood and often mistreated, in accordance with their own unconscious requirements and in ways that they themselves orchestrate. Psychoanalytically derived ideas used in medical settings to understand these patients are often outmoded or incomplete formulations dating from early periods in the history of psychoanalysis. Specifically, the "pain" of physical suffering is often seen as consciously or unconsciously pleasurable in a manner analogous to the stimulation the sexual masochist experiences when beaten.

Masochistic patients regularly respond to treatments of known effectiveness—treatments that help other patients—by feeling worse, often in rather dramatic ways that embarrass and irritate the physicians and other caretakers involved in their treatment. It is not unusual for such patients to be accused of enjoying their misery and to be angrily refused further treatment. Nonetheless, many such patients form very lasting relationships with physicians, clinics, and hospitals, relationships that can only be characterized from a surface point of view as mutually hostile and rejecting. It is within such "relationships" that negative therapeutic reactions occur against a background of medical treatment. Such reactions tend to be poorly understood by participants in the interaction, often leading to their mismanagement.

Case B

The psychiatric consultation service in a large general hospital was asked to see a 42-year-old divorced woman who had been hospitalized for the past five weeks for vague neuromuscular weakness. She had been treated frequently in the past for other ill-defined complaints, no definitive diagnosis ever having been made regarding any of her problems. Her physician of many years recognized that there was little likelihood of solving any of the medical problems the patient posed, yet he frequently admitted her to the hospital, ordering elaborate and expensive medical work-ups. He described to the house officers during this admission his heroic efforts to be of use to the patient and her predictable thwarting of these efforts. He seemed resigned to failing once more but prided himself on his patient and even-tempered approach.

As during previous admissions, no diagnosis was made despite intensive neurological work-up. A somewhat elaborately organized program of physical therapy seemed to be helping the patient in her gradual return to full activity. This program emphasized the patient's efforts to aid in her own recovery and the hard work that entailed. As discharge approached, all seemed to be going well until the patient offhandedly remarked that one of the physical therapy trainees seemed unnecessarily "rough on her." She was "overheard" by a supervisor, who defended the student, setting off a chain of accusations, phone calls, and confrontations that led to an immediate deterioration in the patient's condition and eventual angry transfer to another hospital.

MASOCHISM AND SOMATIZATION

There are many sources of the tendency of certain patients with masochistic character pathology to manifest their problems via somatic channels in medical settings. The traditional psychoanalytic view of such somatization is that it reflects a very primitive psychic organization, which produces profound regression to prestructural, somatic expression of affect and instinctual derivatives, particularly in conflictual situations. Thus somatization is viewed as a general characteristic of the depth of these patients' pathology, perhaps rendering them inaccessible to psychological interventions.

It is our impression, one requiring research verification, that the major determinant of somatization in many such patients is more specific than a generalized regression in psychic functioning. It is a powerful identification with a masochistic parent, usually the mother, that determines the "somatic" clinical picture. The mother may have had many of her own somatic problems and complaints intimately bound up with the depression and suffering that characterized her interaction with her children. An identification with this kind of somatizing mother may thus take shape in terms of somatic complaints similar to hers as a major manifestation of masochistic character problems.

Asch (1976) has noted that masochistic patients frequently describe guilty fantasies of having physically wounded or damaged their mothers during pregnancy and delivery. Such fantasies are fostered by family myth and by actual statements by the mother about nearly dying or about being wounded internally in the process of giving birth to her children. The ambivalent nature of the tie between these mothers and their children inevitably leads to particularly intense disappointment, frustration, and vengeful fantasies in the children that are directed at the mothers. The aggression that is normally part of separation-individuation is heavily colored by such vengeful fantasies. The belief in such children that they have already hurt or damaged their mothers makes a breaking of the symbiotic tie to them especially difficult. Often the aggression that is a normal part of separation is turned inward to protect the object from further damage. The turning inward of aggression, in the form of self-mutilating fantasies that are related in kind and in content to the conviction of having physically damaged their mothers, may play a role in later masochistic pathology involving body mutilation (i.e., illness, physical pain, poor compliance with medical treatment, and unnecessary surgery). Forcing themselves into the role of somatic victim acts to reinforce the identification with the mother-victim and, as Asch has suggested, in part may explain the tenacity of the tie to the early object, characteristically maintained at all costs by such patients.

Case C

Mrs. S was a 54-year-old widowed woman followed for about 10 years for poorly controlled hypertension and many complaints of pain, including headache, back pain, and (most recently) chest pain. Her clinic physician believed she was not compliant about taking her antihypertensive medications. The diagnostic tests performed to evaluate her chest pain revealed no evidence of significant atherosclerotic heart disease. Mrs. S's persistent, unrelieved complaints of pain, her suspected noncompliance with treatment, and her frequent emergency room visits frustrated numerous residents rotating through the medical clinic where she sought treatment. As a result, she was transferred to the care of one of the staff physicians to bring experience and continuity to her management.

The eldest of seven children raised on a farm, Mrs. S felt that she shouldered an unduly heavy load in her family. She held her mother responsible for this because "while mother was having babies, I had to do all the work." While she acknowledged resentment over this burden, she worked hard to prove herself the devoted daughter—nursing her mother through illnesses in later life (which were secondary to hypertension as well) and presenting her with "two of everything, like dresses or pairs of shoes" on special occasions. Her mother died of a stroke; a recent visit to her grave to place flowers had precipitated an episode of back pain that lasted several months.

A pattern of relating similar to that with her mother—overt ambivalence toward an object seen as demanding pain and suffering in return for maintaining contact—was evident in her interactions with physicians. While she devalued the residents who treated her, characterizing them as incompetent and unconcerned, she agreed to their requests for repeated diagnostic tests with little resistance. Because of her continued atypical chest pain, she was evaluated a second time with cardiac catheterization, even though the first, recently performed, revealed only "minimal disease." She reported that she "almost died on the table" during her first catheterization, yet agreed to a second soon thereafter. Similarly, she agreed to a second exercise test, even though she experienced "those bad pains" during the first test, because her doctor "just isn't satisfied without it."

There are many aspects of medical settings that make them fertile ground for the acting out of masochistic pathology. To some extent, pain and other kinds of suffering are the routine currency of interpersonal relationships within such settings. Frequently physicians, hospitals, and illness play important historical roles in the lives of masochistic patients. Often it is easy to see how a patient is recreating or clinging to past experiences and relationships via illness and suffering. More difficult to recognize are the reasons the medical community is slow to correctly identify severe masochistic pathology in patients seeking medical treatment. Even among patients for whom psychiatric consultation is requested, the diagnosis of masochism is rarely made. One of the somatoform disorders, a group of descriptive *DSM-III-R (Diagnostic and Statistical Manual of Mental Disorders, Third Edition, Revised)* (American Psychiatric Association 1987) diagnoses comes closest to fitting the patients under discussion. We wish to focus here on two unconscious factors among physicians and other health care providers that may explain in part this clinical blindspot. Both concern aspects of character structure typical of health care providers that interfere with the recognition of masochistic pathology. It is important to note at this juncture that what are being referred to here are character traits and not psychopathology.

Certain obsessional traits are of considerable adaptive value to and therefore common among health care professionals. People with such character structures are often conflicted about dealing with their sadistic impulses. Patients with severe masochistic psychopathology are adept at inducing sadistic treatment from others. Part of medical care regularly involves hurting patients, although such "hurting" is in the service of efforts aimed at helping patients with their medical problems. Whatever old sadistic aims are connected with becoming a health care provider are assumed to be neutralized via sublimation and relatively outside of conscious awareness. Masochistic patients emphasize, often in dramatic ways, how they are hurt in medical settings and force health care providers to be aware of the pain of the medical treatment they provide. To the extent that such patients also frustrate and provoke anger in others, they frequently induce a reaction formation of defensive kindness and exaggerated tolerance that serves to ward off an awareness of troublesome sadistic fantasies and actions, a defensive response typical in obsessional character structure. A byproduct of this response is a tendency to ignore such indirect provocativeness in patients along with the masochism that is responsible for it.

A second issue that plays a significant role in causing the clinical blindspot in question here is the masochistic nature of medical training and practice, which naturally attracts people with certain masochistic character traits. The seemingly endless years of training, the long work days, the "patients come first," sacrificial tenor of medical settings, all have an appeal to individuals with some masochistic tendencies. This is frequently recognizable in the narcissistic gain that regularly is a hidden aspect of masochism, the sense of privilege or specialness that such sacrifice entitles one to. Such a feeling of entitlement is very common among physicians, and to the extent that it has a masochistic core, it may blind them to masochism in others. In fact, those physicians who care for large numbers of difficult-to-treat patients, especially physicians who seem to take pride in and make well known their heroic efforts on behalf of such patients, are particularly likely to misunderstand the dynamic meaning of their patients' masochistic difficulties and the problems that arise in their clinical management. This often leads to the pejorative labeling masochistic patients evoke from their caregivers. Though labels such as "troll," "crock" and "turkey" are frequently also applied to patients with prominent borderline or histrionic character pathology, masochistic patients are most likely of all to receive such designations. The negative labeling is a product of the special effort and subsequent frustration many health care providers feel after attempting to care for masochistic patients (Cohen-Cole and Friedman 1983). These labels provide physicians and others with a rationalization for discontinuing their usual humanistic caregiving activities.

NEGATIVE THERAPEUTIC REACTIONS

The term *negative therapeutic reaction* refers to those instances during psychoanalysis and related therapies when therapeutic developments that would be expected to lead to clinical improvement instead result in a worsening of the patient's symptoms or other problems. The negative therapeutic reaction was first discussed by Freud in *The Ego and the Id* (Freud 1923), although Freud had earlier noted certain character types with dynamic constellations involving the need to fail (Freud 1916) or to respond to insight in a negative way (Freud 1918). Originally Freud thought unacceptable oedipal wishes and the equation of success with oedipal triumph resulted in unconscious guilt that prevented improvement in analysis (Freud 1923). Freud also noted that an unconscious need for punishment could result from an identification with a masochistic primary object, a situation with a better prognosis for successful analytic resolution of the negative therapeutic reaction if the identification could be recognized and made conscious. Many subsequent investigations of the dynamics of negative therapeutic reactions as they occur in the psychoanalytic treatment of masochistic characters have emphasized these patients' identification with their masochistic mothers, their failure to adequately separate from them, and their continuing sadomasochistic struggling in adult relationships as a way of unconsciously recreating childhood objects and sources of love. The price of such love is a life of pain, deprivation, and failure.

During the psychoanalytic treatment of masochistic characters, negative therapeutic reactions occur frequently. Usually they develop when the maternal transference has been established and partially worked through. Often such reactions can be traced to the emergence or near emergence of some positive feeling toward the therapist that threatens the unconscious symbiotic tie to the mother. Any new, positive relationship with the therapist and any clinical improvement associated with it must be repudiated. It is our experience that similar dynamic constellations exist in attenuated form within medical settings. Patients establish very lasting hostile-dependent relationships with physicians that unconsciously reenact the painfully ambivalent, sadomasochistic relationship with the primary object.

There are two elements that contribute to the development of major medical treatment impasses or failures that are dynamically related to the negative therapeutic reaction. One centers around the negativism that is part of the sadomasochistic relationship such patients regularly establish (Olinick 1964). The negativism is an outgrowth of the dynamic constellation existing during these patients' childhoods. In analysis, such patients describe intense attachments to depressed masochistic mothers that threaten to overwhelm all efforts at separation and autonomy. In these relationships, there is a blurring of affection and hostility in each participant's interaction with the other. From the side of the child, the hostility regularly takes the form of profound and persistent negativism, usually appearing in very specific and limited areas. The overall comprehensive understanding of the unconscious meaning of such negativism can lead to better, more successful interventions.

The second element in such medical "negative therapeutic reactions" concerns the patient's attempt to maintain the sadomasochistic relationship currently enacted with the physician or other clinic or hospital personnel. To improve is to lose an acceptable form of interpersonal relationship, however distorted, as well as to openly disobey the internal primary object, who demands pain and suffering in return for inner approval. Thus the treatment failure is a complicated compromise formation in which separateness from the primary object is maintained via negativism, the primary object's inner approval for suffering and self-deprivation is guaranteed, current masochistic gratifications are protected, and the hostile, frustrating relationship with the health care provider and all it stands for is continued. Such a sadomasochistic interaction supports the patient's powerful identification with the primary object in the form of reliving childhood struggles, often alternating the roles of aggressor and victim. It is the emergence of cooperative effort, gratitude, and affection, the turning to a new, more benevolent object, that must be warded off by the negative therapeutic reaction.

Case D

> Ms. C, a 51-year-old LPN with an extensive medical history, was being followed in a hospital-based medical clinic for mild hypertension, in the surgery clinic for an "abdominal mass," and in the psychiatry clinic for depression. By her own account, she had a remarkable surgical history, including two oophorectomies ("twisted ovaries") in her 20s, treatment for cancer of the cervix with radium implants at age 30, a total abdominal hysterectomy in her early 40s, and a subtotal mastectomy in her late 40s. In addition, she had a trauma history including a self-inflicted gunshot wound after the death of her husband and a still bothersome knee injury incurred in a fall several years earlier. She currently suffered from abdominal pain of at least one year's duration. She had been seen by several different physicians in different clinics for this complaint, never allowing consistent follow-up in any one place. She had received contradictory opinions about the presence of an abdominal mass. She had made, and failed to keep, many appointments for diagnostic procedures. Medical records obtained from other hospitals after her hysterectomy revealed no evidence of prior cancer of the cervix or of radium implant treatment.
>
> Ms. C was the youngest of three children raised by middle-class parents. Her mother was now 80 and in "ill health." According to Ms. C, her mother was "nearly senile" and had insulin-dependent diabetes mellitus. Her father had died after prolonged difficulty with "heart trouble." From an early age, illness and death played a central role in her life, beginning first with the diabetic illness and death of her maternal grandfather, to whom she had been deeply attached. The self-described "black sheep" of the family, she married a man 22 years her senior at the age of 13 and moved with him to another state. After giving birth at age 14 to her only son, she decided she'd "had enough of raising brats." Her marital relationship was marked by frequent strife and much ambivalence on her part. She and her husband separated when she was about 30, but remained in contact. According to Ms. C, they had been planning to remarry 11 years ago when he suffered a fatal heart attack. During their separation, she acquired LPN training and worked fairly steadily. After his death, she was quite depressed and shot herself in a suicide attempt the following year. After her hysterectomy, she returned to work and maintained steady employment until the death of her sister from cancer and her brother's "near fatal" illness with a meningioma. Her sister, an alcoholic with a history of psychiatric hospitalizations, was described as "the real nurse" of the family, helping Ms. C through her hysterectomy. Since her sister's death, Ms. C has been unable to work. "I just couldn't stand the sight of a hospital." The following year, Ms. C had a total mastectomy that "the surgeon totally botched—I didn't even pay him for it, and he's never asked why."

Ms. C lives with her mother in a small apartment, maintaining "she depends on me for everything. Without me she'd be in a nursing home." They fight almost constantly, with Ms. C complaining that her mother could never take care of herself. However, she insisted that as long as her mother lived with her, "she'll never have to give herself insulin shots— I'll spare her that." The patient noted that her world was now reduced to her mother and her mother's friends, that she maintained contact with few friends of her own, often attributing this to her mother's intrusiveness. "She's always asking me where I'm going and who I'm with." Ms. C had sought treatment for depression on several occasions, claiming she had from time to time improved when taking antidepressants. During her most recent trial on drugs, which she told her therapist she took "faithfully," noting to others involved in her care that her compliance was less than optimal, she gained little or no relief of sleeplessness, forgetfulness, poor concentration, and lethargy.

Her difficulty with abdominal pain and the sensation of a mass were the focus of her most recent psychiatric and medical treatment. After several months of attempting to explore the meaning of avoiding a complete medical evaluation, as well as urging that she go ahead with the required tests, she was admitted to the psychiatric inpatient service to treat her continuing depression and to obtain medical and surgical consultation. During this hospitalization, physical examination and an abdominal ultrasound were obtained; neither revealed evidence of abdominal pathology. After discharge, she continued to insist upon the presence of her mass, noting "They gave me a blue sheet [consultation] from surgery that says it's there, and I know it is." Several weeks following this hospitalization, she returned to the surgery clinic for the first time in eight months. She reported they gave her a date for admission to the surgery service in order to do an exploratory laparotomy. However, this procedure was postponed because of an episode of syncope one week prior to planned admission. She refused emergency admission for evaluation of the syncope. About this delay, she noted later that she "was thinking of postponing that admission anyway because Mom isn't doing so well." She was rescheduled for surgery, her mood brightened considerably, and she noted that her family had been more attentive than ever. As she summed it up, "Nobody likes to go for surgery, but everything will be much better when I get this behind me."

DISCUSSION

Our general emphasis has been on conceptualizing the interface between the masochistic character and the medical setting in terms of a psycho-analytic object relations view of the masochist's inner mental life (Berliner 1958). Most psychoanalytic examinations of masochism emphasize the instinctual vicissitudes of masochism. Pain as guilty retribution for forbidden pleasures, as a substitute or precondition for sexual excitement, or as a replacement for a mistakenly perceived form of love are psychoanalytic formulations about masochism that serve as the basis for suggestions about the clinical management of masochistic patients in medical settings. The usual advice offered to physicians who refer such patients for psychiatric consultation includes providing regular appointments without requiring the patient to manifest symptoms; avoiding the threat of removal or cure of the patient's pain; minimizing the use of potentially harmful medications, diagnostic studies, or surgical procedures; and emphasizing the patient's responsibility, sacrifice, and endurance in making whatever interventions are necessary (Engel 1959; Lipsitt 1970; Murphy 1982). In a general way, such suggestions make sense. Yet certain questions should be raised about them.

Chronic medical care abusers are not all masochistic characters. Not differentiating various Axis II character types (e.g., masochistic, oral-dependent, passive-aggressive, hysterical) within the Axis I category of Somatoform Disorders may lead to incomplete understanding of the patient and to unwarranted expectations about the outcome of the recommended treatment approach. The heterogeneous group of somatizing patients is usually characterized as dependent on the physician and on the pain or discomfort associated with symptoms. We believe that in the masochistic character, what is paramount in importance is the maintenance of a sadomasochistic relationship with the health care provider, which conforms to the patient's often repeated inner experience of their relationship with the primary object. The suggestion that following the recommendations described above will lead to a gradual reduction in complaints and to a nondestructive, health-promoting ongoing relationship with the physician is incorrect and misleading. While these recommendations emphasize the importance of the patient's need to maintain the relationship with the physician, they largely ignore the quality of the relationship required by the patient. A more psychoanalytically informed understanding of the complexity of the masochistic patient's object relationships allows for more realistic treatment planning and expectations. The goals of such treatment should be to decrease the frequency and malignancy of inappropriate or unnecessary medical and surgical interventions while providing adequate medical treatment, not to create a more cooperative or less troublesome patient. The latter situation is far more threatening to the patient than a reduction in symptoms or discomfort. The physician can expect to be involved in the patient's continuous efforts to recreate early patterns of mutually frustrating sadomasochistic interaction.

The suggestion that health caretakers encourage compliance with treatment regimens by appealing to the masochist's hypertrophied sense of sacrifice requires reconsideration. While taking into account patients' character traits is generally useful in assessing optimal treatment approaches, manipulative appeal to character pathology rarely has a lasting positive outcome. In our experience, patients quickly recognize the ingenuousness of such manipulations. They are usually exquisitely sensitive to interpersonal distortions and are far more experienced and expert in subtly controlling relationships than are their physicians.

It is difficult to accept that the physician's best efforts to be helpful often fail to lead to improvement in the patient's general condition or to the development of a cooperative and appreciative doctor–patient relationship. Here the psychoanalyst's experience in long-term analytic work with sadomasochistic characters is helpful in understanding such a patient's need to perpetuate mutually frustrating relationships at all costs. Helping physicians to know what to expect, clarifying as much as possible the patterns such patients usually follow in seeking medical care, is useful in avoiding counteraggressive behavior directed at the patient when the physician's best efforts to help are deliberately, if unconsciously, frustrated.

When recommendations are made by psychiatrists to nonpsychiatric physicians for the management of somatizing patients, it should be made clear that regular, supportive visits will not automatically ensure an improved or less stormy doctor–patient relationship. In some cases, taking the expectation of cure away from the doctor and patient will decrease mutual frustration. However, the need of masochistic patients to repeat intense negative early object relationship patterns will require a continued and troublesome doctor–patient interaction. This realization may help physicians maintain relationships longer and decrease outside referral, hospitalization, pejorative labeling, and iatrogenic injury.

Case D illustrates the intense unbroken symbiotic tie these patients have to the primary object, in fact and in fantasy. This sadomasochistic tie is omnipresent and constantly repeated in all new intimate relationships that threaten to create cooperation, affection, pleasure, and success. The negativism that represents a historically continuous misguided effort at separation likewise plays a constant role in such new relationships, particularly at moments when a more hopeful, positive, or successful outcome threatens the old and familiar. It is at such times that negative therapeutic reactions in medical settings occur.

REFERENCES

American Psychiatric Association: Diagnostic and Statistical Manual of Mental Disorders, Third Edition, Revised (DSM-III-R). Washington, DC, American Psychiatric Association, 1987

Asch SS: Varieties of negative therapeutic reaction and problems of technique. J Am Psychoanal Assoc 1976; 24:383-407

Berliner B: The role of object relations in moral masochism. Psychoanal Q 1958; 27:38-56

Cohen-Cole SA, Friedman CP: The language problem: integration of psychosocial variables into medical care. Psychosomatics 1983; 24:54-57

Engel GL: Psychogenic pain and the pain-prone patient. Am J Med 1959; 26:899-918

Freud S: Some character types met with in psychoanalytic work (1916), in Complete Psychological Works, Standard Edition, vol. 14. Translated and edited by Strachey J. London, Hogarth Press, 1957

Freud S: From the history of an infantile neurosis (1918), in Complete Psychological Works, Standard Edition, vol. 17. Translated and edited by Strachey J. London, Hogarth Press, 1955

Freud S: The ego and the id (1923), in Complete Psychological Works, Standard Edition, vol. 19. Translated and edited by Strachey J. London, Hogarth Press, 1961

Freud S: The economic problem of masochism (1924), in Complete Psychological Works, Standard Edition, vol. 19. Translated and edited by Strachey J. London, Hogarth Press, 1961

Lipsitt DR: Medical and psychological characteristics of "crocks." Int J Psychiatry Med 1970; 1:15-25

Loewald HW: Freud's conception of the negative therapeutic reaction with comments on instinct theory. J Am Psychoanal Assoc 1972; 20:235-245

Murphy G: The clinical management of hysteria. JAMA 1982; 247:2559-2564

Olinick SL: The negative therapeutic reaction. Int J Psychoanal 1964; 45:540-548

CHAPTER 6

The Child Psychoanalyst as a Traditional School Consultant: A Review of the Application of Developmental, Psychopathologic, and Treatment Concepts

Calvin A. Colarusso, M.D.

Psychology will have achieved what education has a right to expect of it if, on the one hand, it describes the primitive nature of the child and, on the other, opens up new avenues for possible development and offers new techniques for the further expansion of the child's personality. (Anna Freud, 1935, p. 17)

Although their methods and training are quite different, the educator and the child analyst share a basic goal that binds them inextricably together—to promote and facilitate the optimal development of the child. This common goal, which is dictated by the innate needs of the child, has led to an interaction of considerable complexity.

Psychoanalysis has much to offer education, including a general theory of normal development and a comprehensive understanding of the psychopathology of learning disorders. Acting as a school consultant, a child analyst can translate this body of knowledge into practical, educationally useful information that enhances the effectiveness of the educator and furthers the education of the children.

Several tenets, which I shall elaborate throughout this chapter, underlie and organize the child analyst's approach to school consultation. The first one may be stated as follows: *A primary goal of the psychoanalyst as school consultant is to convey to the educator an understanding of the basic nature of the child.* By shedding light on "the raw material of education" (Freud A, 1935, p. 16) analysts help teachers delineate discrepancies between the educational goals set by society and the capacity of the child to reach them. An understanding of normal developmental theory produces increased respect for the potentialities of the child and gives them equal importance in the educational spectrum. "Only when it becomes clear which educational goals are compatible with mental health and which are attainable only at the expense of this health, will greater justice be done the child" (Freud A, 1935, p. 17).

It follows that the psychoanalytic school consultant emphasizes development over psychopathology (Kris 1978; Vanderpol 1979). Such an aim is completely consonant with the goals of education since "education . . . addresses itself to the progressive potentialities in the child, encouraging him or her to negotiate the developmental ladders which lead from total immaturity to relative maturity in the areas of object relationship, self-

I thank the many colleagues in education with whom I have worked over the years for their help, knowledge and friendship, in particular Joseph Tezza and William Wary, former Directors of Pupil Personnel Services in the Bucks and Lehigh County Intermediate Units (both in Pennsylvania), and Glen Pierson, who holds the same position in San Diego County, California. They and the members of their staffs made school consultation a thoroughly enjoyable learning experience for me. I have worked with hundreds of teachers over the years, but I wish to single out Phyllis Green, an extraordinary Master Teacher, a research partner on the Bucks County Project, and a close friend.

95

reliance, impulse control, body management, ego functioning, orientation in the external world, and adaptation to its rules" (Freud A, quoted in Wilson 1977, p. 481).

The following example demonstrates what may happen when developmental considerations are not understood and taken into account by educators. An experienced school psychologist and I were asked to evaluate a 15-year-old seventh grader. After meeting with the assistant principal and concerned teacher, I took a history from the student's mother while the psychologist administered tests to the student. Then I saw the boy while the psychologist obtained further information from his parent. Later both consultants met with the teacher and principal. Languishing in a seventh grade classroom at 15, this student was two years behind his chronological peers. He had been retained twice, once in first grade and once in seventh. Four grade levels behind in reading and math, and at 6'1" towering over his younger, physically immature peers, he was so ashamed that he refused to attempt the academic work and increasingly cut class. This young man went on to drop out of school despite efforts to place him in classroom settings with his chronological and developmental peers and to provide intensive individual tutoring. Ignorance of the developmental implications of multiple retention resulted in an educational situation that proved to be irredeemable. Neither his first nor seventh grade teacher anticipated or understood the tremendous need for peer acceptance and approval in the face of the profoundly unsettling physical and psychological developmental changes of early adolescence. Feeling continually exposed as "dumb" and "stupid," and in an infantilizing situation—"My friends laugh at me because I'm in with all those babies"—the boy fled from a school situation that struck intolerable blows to his self-esteem.

This case offers a vivid illustration of the importance of a knowledge of normal development for the educator. If the teachers had been thinking in developmental terms, the first retention might have been considered more seriously as to its long-range educational and emotional implications, and the second retention would not have occurred at all.

CONSULTANT AND TEACHER

A second tenet is: *To stimulate development in general and formal learning in particular, the analytic consultant provides impetus and support for the teacher and offers new techniques that enhance his or her effectiveness and expand the child's personality.*

The child analytic consultant approaches the teacher as a colleague and an equal. Such respect grows out of in-school observation of the enormous skill and knowledge required to teach effectively, and a recognition of a compatible, common goal—to promote the total development of the child—despite different approaches and training. The analyst for the most part is a silent, impartial observer who tempers his personality in the service of his work; while the teacher, "who is also the subject of transference . . . must play a very personal part in the child's life," accomplishing his educational purposes ". . . chiefly through the imponderables of his attitude" (Homburger 1935, p. 50).

Transference may also become an important aspect of the relationship between consultant and teacher, particularly if a bond develops over time and the consultant approaches the teacher with empathy and understanding for his or her feelings and problems. It is generally agreed among analysts that such transference phenomena should neither be encouraged nor interpreted (Berlin 1966). The consultant should make every attempt to develop an empathic, respectful relationship with his colleague, being careful to act only as a consultant, never attempting to replace the consultee in his job (Kris 1978).

Instead the focus should be on the elaboration of individual and collective techniques that enhance the teacher's effectiveness. Such suggestions can be varied, ranging from a brief exchange in the teacher's lounge, to extended interaction around a particular child, or to the introduction of formal assessment instruments and elaborate teaching strategies. The analyst's knowledge of the educational process may arise from such disparate sources as direct consultative experience (Hitchcock 1977), research conducted in the schools with educators, or even, for example, the psychoanalytic observation of school children in the People's Republic of China (Cohen 1977).

THE BUCKS COUNTY PROJECT

In addition to applying direct and indirect consultative techniques to individual learning problems, the analytic school consultant may use his theoretical orientation and clinical knowledge to develop projects intended to increase the teaching skills and effectiveness of classroom teachers by organizing a framework to improve their understanding and use of analytic concepts, particularly those of normal development. Christ (1977), for example, applied Piaget's theories of normal cognitive development to the cognitive assessment of psychotic children.

Another example is the Bucks County Project. Conceived and initiated by William Stennis (1970, 1971), this multidisciplinary study was developed in Pennsylvania as a Federal ESEA Title III Project under the auspices of the Bucks County Public Schools, Intermediate Unit Number

22. *Using the teacher as the main source of information, the project attempted to elicit the educational, psychological, organic, and social factors that affected the learning of elementary age children and to use this knowledge to improve teaching techniques.* During a four-year period, over 50,000 children and 1,000 teachers were involved.

The project materials are in three forms: a diagnostic questionnaire, a computer print-out that assigns each student to one of three relatively homogeneous developmental groups, and a teaching strategies book that relates the developmental groups to classroom management. Each of the three core elements represents an amalgam of psychoanalytic and educational theory, practice, and goals. The questionnaire distills many areas of psychiatric diagnostic inquiry into 12 questions. The three developmental groups, which were formulated from studying the data clustering obtained from the questionnaire, are analogous to (but not the same as) the diagnostic categories, and the teaching strategies are the educational equivalent of psychiatric treatment modalities.

The Diagnostic Educational Grouping Questionnaire

In designing the questionnaire (see appendix) Stennis and his co-workers were attempting to devise a diagnostic scheme that could be used with equal effectiveness by teachers and behavioral scientists and have widespread applicability in the regular elementary classroom. Such an instrument had to reflect either the progressive or regressive development of the child and link diagnosis to a method of treatment for the behavioral scientist and a method of classroom management for the teacher. Since thorough individual, psychiatric evaluations cannot be performed on large numbers of children in an educational setting, the data would have to be collected by the classroom teacher in a simple, efficient manner.

After extensive statistical validation and field testing a Diagnostic Educational Grouping Questionnaire was devised that distilled into 12 basic questions data from longitudinal classroom observations and thorough neurologic, psychological, and psychiatric evaluations performed on a research study group. Each of the data sources is reflected in one or more of the 12 questions. For example, question 12 explores the child's relationship with parents, while number 10 uses human figure drawings to assess intelligence, fantasy, and organicity. Data on muscle coordination (question 8) and talking (question 3) are evaluated as sensitive indicators of fine and gross motor control and synthesizing and organizing ability, while statements 11 (school work), 7 (behavior), and 6 (peer relationships) evaluate the child's object relationships with teachers and peers and his adaptation to the classroom.

Three Developmental Groups

When I became involved in the third year of the project, the instruments had been developed but not fully field tested. This was accomplished by Phyllis Green, a Master Teacher, and myself through hundreds of interviews with individual teachers who were using the instruments in a controlled study. On the basis of their responses, refinements were made in the instruments. For example, the three developmental groups were originally called Oedipally Conflicted, Developmentally Arrested, and Ego Disturbed. The teachers found those psychiatric terms frightening and confusing. Because the primary intent of the project was educational, and the grouping was meant to help the teachers organize their thinking about students, the names were neutralized to Group I, Group II, and Group III, which met with much less resistance.

Statistically, the percentage breakdown of the three developmental groups in the regular, elementary classroom remained essentially the same during each of the four years of the research project: 60-68 percent fell into Group I, 30-35 percent into Group II, and the remaining 3-10 percent in Group III. (See Table 1.) When seen from a psychiatric diagnostic viewpoint, normal and neurotic children usually fell into Group I; those with developmental arrests and "character" problems into Group II; and those with severe organic and emotional problems, regardless of etiology, into Group III.

In addition to asking for less threatening names for the developmental groups the teachers also wanted fuller descriptions. The challenge for the psychoanalytic and educational consultants was to describe the groups in simple English without using psychiatric jargon. This was presented in the revised manual for teachers, *Strategies for Teaching* (Colarusso and Green 1972), as follows:

Group I "The group one child represents the healthiest stage of personality development. . . . They are successfully achieving the rigorous task of 'growing up' with the least amount of emotional distress. . . . The teacher generally feels that she will be able to successfully teach this group. . . . If distress is present, it is more likely to be seen as inner distress, which is not usually inflicted on adults or peers. . . . When behavior appears recalcitrant, for the most part confrontation of the child with the unacceptable behavior will often, after inquiring into the reasons, give rise to a quick release of feeling in the form of tears. . . . The backgrounds of these children are generally smooth. . . . If there is a history of difficulty . . . it usually happened between the ages of four and six. . . . The parents of these children are in general interested, concerned and cooperative." (pp. 3-5)

Table 1. Sample of Teacher Computer Print-out, Bucks County Project for Diagnostic Educational Grouping

Date:10–15–70
Room No.: 03
Grade: 3   Report No. EGQ034

Student Name	Sex	Age Group*	Developmental Group
STUDENT # 1	M	8 2	Group I
STUDENT # 2	M	9 3	Group I
STUDENT # 3	M	9 3	Group I
STUDENT # 4	F	9 1	Group I
STUDENT # 5	F	8 1	Group I
STUDENT # 6	M	8 2	Group I
STUDENT # 7	F	8 1	Group I
STUDENT # 8	F	8 2	Group I
STUDENT # 9	F	8 1	Group I
STUDENT # 10	M	8 4	Group I
STUDENT # 11	F	7 3	Group I
STUDENT # 12	F	8 2	Group I
STUDENT # 13	M	8 2	Group I
STUDENT # 14	F	8 3	Group I
STUDENT # 15	M	9 3	Group II
STUDENT # 16	F	8 2	Group II
STUDENT # 17	M	8 3	Group II
STUDENT # 18	M	8 3	Group II
STUDENT # 19	M	8 1	Group II
STUDENT # 20	M	7 4	Group II
STUDENT # 21	F	8 3	Group II
STUDENT # 22	M	8 1	Group II
STUDENT # 23	M	9 3	Group II
STUDENT # 24	F	8 3	Group II
STUDENT # 25	M	8 2	Group III

* Chronological age by year and quarter.

Group II   "These are the children who cause the teacher the most frustration. . . . Teachers . . . find . . . their behavior very difficult to tolerate. . . . They see the teacher either as an all-giving mother who will supply endlessly their demands or a giant out to subdue them. . . . These children fear most loss of the love of an important human being. . . . Their thinking, choice of words, and manner is immature. Either gross or fine motor movements often show perceptual motor immaturity. . . . The developmental histories of these children are characterized by a failure to progress in one or more areas of growth. . . . Relationships with people, especially the mother, are often characterized by a demanding struggle."
(pp. 11-14)

Group III   "The Group III child displays the most troubled forms of personality disturbance . . . these children need further referral and evaluation. . . . Their strangeness or difference often evokes a feeling of apprehension within us but . . . often a feeling of compassion as well. . . . It is difficult to find a success area for him. . . . Many of these children show multiple failures at adaptation. . . . Their thinking often shows evidences of fragmentation and disorganization. . . . Relationships with parents, siblings and peers have been rather severely limited, either because these people have in one way or another abandoned the child or because the child is unable to organize his world adequately. . . . Academic successes will likely be limited . . . and should be subordinated to helping the child to develop interpersonal relationships, as well as beginning to learn how to organize his world." (pp. 25-27)

The interviews with the teachers also revealed a desire for more detailed knowledge of normal child development and an interest in more elaborate teaching strategies linked to developmental concepts. Those requests resulted in the rewriting of *Strategies for Teaching* and its division into three parts: 1) A description of each developmental group (presented above) followed by teaching strategies related to that group. 2) A section of short essays on the areas of greatest concern to the teachers, such as classroom seating and control of motility, competition in the classroom, discipline, homework, and so forth. 3) A summary of psychoanalytic developmental theory, emphasizing its expression in the classroom and relation to teaching.

The Teaching Strategies

Here is a sample of the strategies offered for each of the three groups. Once again, it was critically important to translate psychiatric concepts into educational terms. Teacher–Pupil Interaction Strategies are described for Group I, Strategies Dealing with Classroom Seating and Peer Relationships for Group II, and Teaching Suggestions by Subject Matter for Group III, thus providing examples of the three different kinds of strategies.

The suggested strategies were as specific as possible, and could only be effective when used by a teacher who had a thorough knowledge of each student's personality, interests, and background. Teachers were encouraged to use their judgment in *selecting* which specific strategies from among those offered would benefit a particular child.

Teacher–Pupil Interaction Strategies—Group I

1. For the most part these children can learn through oral, aural, or visual–motor learning activities equally well.

2. Repetitive drill of materials that they obviously know is often a waste of time and interferes with motivation.
3. Projects in all curricular areas closely linked to interest areas should be very much encouraged. Both individual and joint projects usually produce positive results.
4. Although definite goals should be set for any assignment, the means should be left as unstructured as possible. Discovery activities work very well for this group as the excitement of discovery is very exhilarating for them. The "open classroom" setting provides an excellent learning atmosphere for these children.
5. Progress goals can often be set jointly by teacher and pupil or by the child himself. "How far do you think you can read this morning?" or "How many problems can you complete?" To offset possible side-effects of the more unstructured approach, make sure that all goals are reached.
6. Provide the opportunity for independent study through learning centers equipped with interesting and challenging materials. Examples: 1) Current events center with magazines and clippings. 2) Social studies/science/language arts centers. 3) A film strip theater. 4) Puppet stage. 5) Study carrels for quiet reading or writing. 6) A tape recorder. 7) Box of collage materials for art design. Interesting educational toys and games should be within the relevant centers. Materials should stress a "learning is fun" philosophy as opposed to a "play" concept.
7. These children are basically competitive yet fearful of its consequences. Thus curriculum activities should *not* encourage or foster excessive competition. Shy children are particularly vulnerable to developmental regression in the face of competition.
8. The "daydreamer" should be encouraged to describe, verbally, in writing or drawing, his thoughts. Keep him attentive by speaking to him, touching his shoulder or standing nearby, surrounding him with more active peers.
9. Impress upon them that intelligence alone will not carry them throughout their educational careers; independent work and study is necessary. (Colarusso and Green 1972, pp. 6-7)

Strategies Dealing with Classroom Seating and Peer Relationships—Group II

1. Because of the Group II child's low tolerance for sensory distractions they benefit greatly from a *carpeted* classroom with *reduced visual and auditory stimuli*. A bland environment is the most conducive surrounding until they have mastered the inner controls and orga-

nized personality structure that concentration demands, exemplified by the Group I child. This Group II child will not function well in the intellectually stimulating classroom of modern day. They are physically and/or emotionally unable to screen out unnecessary distractions, and it is unfair to demand that they do so without providing the setting for them to gradually grow toward this accomplishment.

2. The image of the "old school," "traditional" teacher who sets definite limits and teaches in a rigid style can be of most help to the Group II child. Naturally, he/she must be able to show understanding and provide flexibility as the child progresses emotionally, but the basic approach should remain heavily structured. A free, loose, discovery classroom atmosphere, in which Group I children thrive, can cause further personality regression in Group II children.

3. Because of their need for routine and consistency they do not respond well to the "open classroom" setting. They become unsettled by an environment that is changing or requires making choices. A lack of structure demands built-in flexibility, which these children do not have. Even changes to special class teachers are difficult and they will often lose control. This is less evident in Phys. Ed. class since it also allows the child to let off steam in an acceptable manner.

4. Surround with strong Group I children to help provide external controls, compensating for the lack of inner controls.

5. Because of their need for frequent reassurance seat them near the front of the room. Talk to them and touch them often.

6. Group II children need a friend desperately but often use the most overbearing tactics to gain one. Some techniques to help them are: private talks encouraging better methods of dealing with peers, placing them in the "helping others" situations already mentioned, bringing a toy or game of their own to share at school to attract others at recess; controlling their anger by counting, walking away, or taking deep breaths.

7. Pairs of disruptive Group II children should be separated within the classroom or in some cases placed in separate classrooms. They tend to reinforce the immature behavior and prevent a push toward mature behavior.

8. A study carrell may be necessary for working tasks if the child is extremely distractible. The teacher should stop by frequently, conveying encouragement.

9. Use an older Group I child as a tutor to supervise drill tasks or games. The older child offers a stabilizing influence and also is an object for identification.

10. Art, music and physical education may offer success for these children that they find in no other area. Use their proficiency to build

self-esteem by having them tutor younger children. (Colarusso and Green 1972, pp. 21-22)

Teaching Suggestions by Subject Matter—Group III

1. Before specific subject matter can be introduced, Group III children must be taught *how* to learn. This can best be accomplished by employing all of their *senses* as avenues to learning. Concrete, manipulative materials, simple games, visual aids, tapes, records, films, filmstrips, magazines, pictures, and drawings are the means.
2. *Language arts* activities must be based in conversation. Listening to stories, discussion, role playing, and talking about pictures increases understanding, values, attitudes, and vocabulary.
3. Many strategies suggested for the Group II child are equally appropriate for the Group III child.
4. When the Group III child is ready for reading skills the language experience approach provides the best transition from concrete thinking to letter symbolism.
5. Group III children react to mathematics in one of two ways. Usually they find this subject extremely difficult, too abstract to handle. However, some—especially the more intelligent—do quite well in math because it is devoid of emotional ties and can be dealt with strictly on an intellectual level. On the other hand, these emotionally impaired children may exhibit a total resistance to all of the usual reading programs in spite of intellectual competence. A marked difference in performance between math and reading may also be due to early cultural deprivation. Lack of language usage delays the child's readiness experiences needed for reading skill.
6. *Perceptual training* techniques dealing with body image, spatial relationships, directionality, motor coordination (fine and gross), and visual discrimination must be thoroughly taught in the early years (K-2nd). These children usually show marked deficiencies and will need a longer period of drill and review before mastery. *No specific handwriting, reading, or math skill should begin until this child shows perceptual awareness in these areas, regardless of his/her chronological age, grade level, or intellectual capacity.*
7. These children have an extremely difficult time expressing themselves. You must speak for them, write for them, and draw them out in any way possible. When speaking for them, have them contribute missing words, phrases, or short sentences to finish your thought. Gradually shift the responsibility to them.
8. Often these children show neurological impairment, thus strategies under the Group II section can be successfully used.

9. *Music, art and physical education* can provide excellent therapeutic experiences for Group III children. In some cases, scheduling double sessions in these subjects will better meet their needs than academic tasks. Many of these subject activities can serve to fulfill the readiness deficiencies created by an impoverished childhood. For some, television has been the only means of emotional and intellectual stimulation.

10. Select *language arts* activities which stress fact and realism over fantasy. Group III children will easily drift toward fantasy because it is so much more appealing than their real world. Stories and studies of people who overcame hardship will help them understand and face their problems and give hope that they can be mastered.

11. Encourage an organized, neat desk as an aid to the development of spatial relationships as well as organized thinking.

12. The Group III child's day should initially be completely teacher directed. There should be little or no opportunity for the child to be faced by a decision or choice throughout the school day. All subject matter must be presented with this in mind.

13. Many skills that come automatically to other children do not come as easily for these children. In attempting to work out the solution they usually lose their original goal. They need constant review of the steps leading to the goal. (Colarusso and Green 1972, pp. 30-31)

Dissemination

The fifth and sixth years of the project, funded by the State of Pennsylvania after the federal grant expired, provided the opportunity for another kind of consultation—namely, the dissemination of information about the project through presentations to individual school districts and professional organizations in several states (presentations at the national conventions of the American Association of Guidance Counselors and the American Psychoanalytic Association) (Colarusso and and Green 1973; Green and Colarusso 1973). Materials were requested by 600 school districts and hospitals in 43 states and Canada.

THE USE OF PSYCHOPATHOLOGIC CONCEPTS IN EDUCATIONAL CONSULTING

A third tenet underlying the analyst's consultative work is that *psychoanalytic school consultation is founded on an awareness of the dynamics that underlie learning disorders*. The psychoanalytic study of learning disorders began in the 1920s when "psychoanalysis was revealing that there sometimes seemed to be causal relationships between unconscious emotional conflicts and attitudes and scholastic failures in certain subjects" (Blanchard 1946, p. 166). Early writings (Hincks 1926; Strachey 1930) focused on reading problems. Blanchard (1928, 1929, 1935, 1936) showed that neurotic reading disorders resulted from internalized conflict over handling the unconscious aggressive and sadistic impulses stimulated by reading. Pearson (1952) felt that learning itself could be a source of conflict because it is normally used to compete with contemporary rivals and to advance in a chosen sphere of life and attain ultimate success—that is, power, money, position, and prestige.

Increased understanding of pregenital influences and the mother–child relationship led to further delineation of the learning process (Freud A, 1935; Ekstein and Motto 1969) and the description of a second group of more severe learning problems. Mahler (1942) and later Hellman (1954) elucidated a clinical picture of pseudoimbecility resulting from unresolved pregenital ties to the mother. Buxbaum (1964) called this type of learning disturbance "an all pervasive learning difficulty . . ." based upon a partially symbiotic relationship between mother and child (p. 425). More recent work (Newman et al. 1973) has shed further light on the nature of learning problems by describing how parents may unconsciously select developing ego functions in the child and comply with them, encourage and enhance them, or interfere with them. Such parental attitudes are stamped on the immature, preoedipal ego but may not become apparent until later, sometimes playing a major role in the development of learning difficulties.

To understand the nature of the psychopathology in an individual child, a thorough diagnostic evaluation is required. Within the school, the analyst, alone or aided by school personnel (Kaplan 1961), conducts such a study before suggesting intervention. During the history-taking interviews, in addition to gathering a clear description of the symptoms, the analyst is particularly interested in obtaining a dynamic understanding of their origin and meanings. Thus the developmental history provides an in-depth picture of the life course of this particular individual, measured against a comprehensive theoretical framework of normality and psychopathology. Once a descriptive *(DSM-III-R)*, dynamic (genetic and conflict-centered) and developmental (problems understood in terms of major developmental themes) diagnosis is made, a treatment plan is formulated. *The major purpose of any therapeutic intervention, be it environmental, chemotherapeutic, psychotherapeutic, or educational, is to remove blocks to the still-evolving personality and ensure that the individual's developmental potential is realized as fully as possible* (Conference on Psychoanalytic Education and Research, Commission IX 1974). This basic psychoanalytic objective is in complete resonance with the primary goal of education, which is also to stimulate individual potential to the greatest degree possible.

Specific intervention may take any of a number of forms, including the educationally prophylactic, in-school evaluation of nursery school children (Wilson 1977); the elucidation of teaching strategies geared specifically to the elementary age child's level of mental health and learning ability (Colarusso and Green 1972); or the referral of a teenager with a neurotic learning disorder for psychoanalysis.

SCHOOL AVOIDANCE

School avoidance is a good example of a significant educational problem that is amenable to a psychoanalytic approach. Psychoanalytic developmental theory and understanding of psychopathology in childhood provide a conceptual framework in which to place the well-studied syndromes of school phobia and truancy plus less well-recognized and understood causes of school avoidance. In the literature the tendency has been to call most school avoidance either school phobia or truancy. School phobia may be defined as a syndrome consisting of 1) severe difficulty in attending school, often with prolonged absence; 2) severe emotional upset, without obvious organic cause, on being faced with the prospect of attending school; 3) parental knowledge of absence from school; and 4) the absence of significant antisocial behavior (Berg et al. 1969). Waller and Eisenberg (1980) have defined truancy as "a particular kind of unsanctioned school absence, in which the child is neither at school nor at home; usually the parents have no idea where the child is" (p. 210). According to Hersov and Berg (1980) the majority of cases of school phobia are neurotic in nature, as are many truancy problems.

A psychoanalytic understanding of the multidetermined nature of all behavior, normal and pathologic alike (Waelder 1933), and the experience of psychoanalysts in the schools suggest that a broader based understanding of school avoidance may be useful. In a psychoanalytic framework the causes of refusal to attend school are understood in terms of both psychopathology and developmental themes and conflicts. Lewis (1980) takes such an approach in his discussion of the psychotherapeutic treatment of school refusal, stating "In each case the causes have multiple, biopsychosocial components, necessitating a pluralistic approach to treatment" (p. 251). Among the causes listed by Lewis are: 1) Hostile dependent relationships between parents and children, particularly mothers and sons, leading to acute separation anxiety (Johnson et al. 1941; Coolidge and Brodie 1974). 2) Separation anxiety from other causes (Sperling 1951; Robinson et al. 1955; Bowlby 1960). 3) Unresolved sexual and aggressive feelings toward either parent (Klein 1945). 4) Severe psychopathology such as schizophrenia (Millman 1961) and depression (Campbell 1955; Agras 1959). 5) Family disturbance (Malmquist 1965).

6) Fear of school failure. 7) Fear of teacher or peer (Klein 1945; Hersov 1960). Lewis suggests a comprehensive treatment armamentarium including supportive measures, medication, and family and individual psychotherapy. Child psychoanalysis would be a meaningful addition to that list; indeed, particularly in those cases of learning problems and school avoidance that are primarily neurotic, child analysis may be the treatment of choice (Colarusso 1980).

A relatively neglected area is the understanding and management of *less* severe expressions of school avoidance, which are very common and are well recognized by experienced teachers and school consultants. These crises, enormously important to the individual child and very influential in determining attitudes toward school and learning, are the type usually presented to consultants functioning within the schools. The following examples of school avoidance—some mild, some severe—will demonstrate how a psychoanalytic understanding of development, psychopathology, and treatment can facilitate the understanding and resolution of learning problems and school avoidance.

The Preschool Years—The Oedipal Phase

A common cause of school avoidance in nursery school and kindergarten is separation anxiety (Eisenberg 1958; Johnson et al. 1941; Van Leewen and Tuma 1972). Having just achieved object constancy (Mahler 1974), most children between 4 and 7 are still normally adjusting to spending time away from mother. Individual children develop mastery of these feelings at different rates, yet adults sometimes fail to recognize the normal variations along this developmental line (Freud A, 1965) or to appreciate how momentous and overwhelming an experience such as going to school for the first time can be.

For instance, a sensitive elementary principal told the following story. It was the first day of school, and a bus had just arrived carrying those kindergarten children who lived at a distance. The children tumbled off the bus in various states of apprehension. Thinking that the bus was empty, the principal turned to walk away. Then a small voice called weakly from the doorway. As he turned to meet the frightened gaze of a 5-year-old boy, replete with baseball cap and lunch bucket, he heard, "Hey, mister, is this the school?"

In another example, on the first day of school the author stood in a corridor observing children enter kindergarten for the first time. When the bell rang, two children were still clinging to their mothers. Suddenly the kindergarten teacher appeared, firmly told the apprehensive mothers to leave, and pulled their crying offspring into the room, calling over her shoulder, "Don't worry, they'll get over it. They'll be just fine." Follow-up revealed that one was, and one wasn't. Within a week the first child gradually stopped crying and adjusted to the stern teacher and new setting. The second child, however, was still crying a month later and had begun to run and hide when it was time to go to school. Subsequent evaluation revealed the presence of considerable early maternal deprivation and significant problems with the separation–individuation process. For this borderline child, the adjustment to school was an overwhelming task, certainly not aided by the teacher's insistence on an abrupt separation from mother.

When the analytic viewpoint is applied to the developmental task of attending school for the first time, the educator maintains a flexible attitude. Child and mother should be allowed as much time as needed to help the child comfortably separate and master the experience, developing in the process the internal mental capacity to be away from mother for an extended period of time, to be with strange children and adults in a situation that requires the use of multiple ego functions in new ways. If necessary, mother should be allowed in the classroom, gradually decreasing her presence over days or weeks until the child mastered the experience. Large numbers of relatively healthy children with minor separation problems could be helped by such an approach while the small number of children with severe separation problems—and likely other significant pathology as well—could be identified at the beginning of their school experience, early enough to be treated prophylactically rather than remedially.

The Elementary Years—The Latency Phase

Multiple causes of school avoidance are present at all phases of development. However, during the elementary school years, phobic neuroses, true school phobias, may be the cause of school avoidance.

S, for example, was 7 years of age and in the middle of second grade when brought for evaluation because of rapidly increased episodes of school avoidance. Her complaints, which always occurred on school mornings, were physical—headaches and stomach pains, primarily. When her parents did force her to go to school she frequently ended up in the nurse's office by midmorning. At first glance this youngster might have been thought to exemplify the "masquerade syndrome," a subgroup of the school refusal syndrome identified by Waller and Eisenberg (1980) as children whose difficulty in going to school is masked by medical problems. However, evaluation revealed the presence of a phobic neurosis of acute onset. What the parents were unaware of was S's constant preoccupation with her mother's well-being. S was afraid that robbers would come and kill her mother while she was in school. The only way to ensure Mother's safety was to remain at home. S's neurosis responded well to child analysis. As she came to recognize her own hostility toward her mother (expressed concerns for her mother's safety) and her regressive wishes to be taken care of by her mother (as expressed in the physical complaints), her school avoidance disappeared, long before the underlying oedipal and preoedipal dynamics were fully analyzed.

Junior High School—Early Adolescence

After surveying the literature on school phobia in early adolescence, Berg (1980) concluded, "the clinical literature on school phobia is thus by and large in agreement that most cases, even in early adolescence, manifest an excessive state of dependency in the mother–child relationship and that school phobic youngsters differ quantitatively rather than qualitatively from normal in this respect" (p. 235). From his own work Berg concludes that most school phobias in early adolescence are neurotically determined and not based primarily on significant educational problems.

However, analytic developmental theory suggests that another important cause of school avoidance in early adolescence has to do with feelings about the rapidly changing body. All adolescents struggle with the developmental tasks of integrating thoughts and feelings about their suddenly sexually mature bodies. Obviously the majority accomplish this without serious interference with school performance or attendance. For others, however, the experience can be acutely or chronically debilitating. Knowledge of the adolescent process allows the school consultant to understand and often resolve what seem to be overwhelmingly difficult problems for students and teachers.

For example, an exasperated eighth grade teacher, a young man in his early 20s, spending his second year in the classroom, asked for help in coping with a puzzling situation. An outstanding female student, one who had always loved school, suddenly refused to come to *his* class. Further, when forced to attend, she belligerently refused to participate in classroom discussions, even when threatened with failure. In-school evaluation revealed the nature of the problem and suggested the solution. The student was a beautiful girl of 14. Well-developed, she stood out from most of her female classmates. During a period of classroom observation the consultant watched the girl, when called on by her teacher, stand up, turn red, quietly refuse to speak and hold her notebook across her chest.

In a subsequent individual session she readily described her overwhelming sense of embarrassment when asked to stand up and speak. She could not explain why, nor was she encouraged to try, because her embarrassment seemed to be related to conflicted unconscious wishes to expose her large breasts to the class—and to the young male teacher. The

latter thought led to an impression that teacher and student were struggling with their sexual feelings toward one another. This was confirmed
when the student remarked that she liked the teacher but not his jokes
about her clothes. The teacher, bewildered by the sudden change in his
student's behavior and partially unaware of his own sexual response,
tried to manage both by becoming rigid and demanding about classroom
performance—she would stand up in class and answer when called on or
flunk.

As the analytic consultant processed his observations—that is, the
girl's reaction to her adolescent body and the inhibition of school performance that followed, plus the teacher's sexual response to the student
and the strident classroom response, which defended against the excitement—the following form of intervention was decided upon. 1) Say
nothing directly to the student, who was understood to be in the midst of
a transient developmental crisis. 2) Discuss adolescent development with
the teacher, helping him understand the student's behavior. (When the
subject of adult sexual response to teenagers was approached, the teacher
acknowledged with a sigh of relief his own feelings toward the student.)
3) Even if the teacher had not taken the opportunity to discuss his
emotional response, the academic recommendations would have been the
same—do not call on the student in class, do not penalize her for refusing
to participate verbally, grade her on written performance, continue to be
friendly, but do not make comments about her dress or her body. Follow-
up revealed that the class avoidance had disappeared and both student
(who was doing A work) and teacher were more comfortable.

A contrast to that example of mild school refusal in a relatively healthy
girl follows: R, a borderline prepubertal boy, entered treatment at age 12.
Strange and friendless, he attended school, managed passing grades, and
spent most after-school time in his basement absorbed in fantasies about
Dracula and other ghoulish characters. Suddenly at the beginning of
seventh grade (in a new school), he began missing school on a regular
basis, regressing markedly as he retreated further into his fantasies. As
the analyst began to understand the sudden change in behavior, it gradually became clear that R could not tolerate undressing or showering in
front of the other boys. His attempts to integrate his and their emerging
sexuality were so primitive, so unsuccessful, that the only option was to
flee. Because no amount of understanding or environmental manipulation was likely to quickly affect his urgent need to avoid school, the
analyst arranged for the boy to be permanently excused from gym class
that year, which allowed him to attend his other classes and continue to
progress academically and prevented prolonged school avoidance. This is
an example of a case that might easily have been conceptualized as
primarily involving separation issues. However, intensive treatment re-

vealed that the major etiological factor was a severe ego disturbance with multiple deficits in ego functioning, which resulted in a failure to engage and master the developmental tasks of early adolescence, particularly those relating to emerging sexuality and changes in body image.

Adolescence—Senior High School

School avoidance is also a very common experience in senior high school. As in earlier phases of development, the causes are multi-determined, related to issues of current and past development and prior school experience. In addition to separation issues, other causes are concerns about the body such as obesity or acne, lack of friends, shame over poor academic performance, or apprehension over sexual feelings and actions.

B was an attractive 16-year-old junior. A fair student of average ability, she had always attended school regularly until recently, when she began to avoid school entirely. After a month of such behavior, her puzzled parents asked for an evaluation. Although separation issues were prominent, they were not the only significant etiological factors. The precipitating cause of the school avoidance was an inability to control adolescent sexual impulses. B was a shy, dependent, immature girl with many unresolved feelings about sexuality. When she began to date she was quickly persuaded by two different boys to have sexual intercourse. She literally could not say no, despite the fact that the sexual activity conflicted with her strict religious upbringing and primitive superego. By avoiding school and retreating to her home and the regressive protection and care of her mother, she avoided the boys and her own impulses, paying a high developmental price in the process. A change of schools, requested by the student soon after beginning intensive individual psychotherapy, allowed her to return to school quickly. As treatment proceeded, the identification and interpretation of the separation issues and neurotically determined sexual conflicts led to a facilitation of the adolescent developmental process and improved academic attendance and performance.

SUMMARY

The child psychoanalyst may be characterized as a school consultant in terms of his understanding of and emphasis on normal development, his psychodynamic theory of the nature of learning difficulties, and his conceptualization of the relationship between teacher and consultant— one in which he is respectful of and subordinate to the teacher, the final common pathway between himself and the child. The educator and the analyst–consultant share the same goal, the total development of the child.

In order to achieve this goal, the child analyst in the school constantly strives to work with the educator to remove blocks to the still-evolving personality of the child, be they academic, physical, environmental, or emotional.

REFERENCES

Agras S: The relationship of school phobia to childhood depression. Am J Psychiatry 1959; 116:533-536

Berg I: School refusal in early adolescence, in Out of School. Edited by Berg I, Hersov L. New York, John Wiley & Sons, 1980

Berg I, Nicholas K, Pritchard C: School phobia, its classification and relationship to dependency. J Child Psychol Psychiatry 1969; 10:123-141

Berlin IN: Transference and countertransference in community psychiatry. Arch Gen Psychiatry 1966; 12:165-172

Blanchard P: Reading disabilities in relation to maladjustment. Mental Hygiene 1928; 12:772-788

Blanchard P: Attitudes and educational disabilities. Mental Hygiene 1929; 13:550-563

Blanchard P: Psychogenic factors in some cases of reading disability. Am J Orthopsychiatry 1935; 5:361-374

Blanchard P: Reading disabilities in relation to difficulties of personality and emotional development. Mental Hygiene 1936; 20:384-413

Blanchard P; Psychoanalytic contributions to the problems of reading disabilities. Psychoanal Study Child 1946; 2:163-187

Bowlby J: Separation anxiety. Int J Psychoanal 1960; 41:89-113

Buxbaum E: The parents' role in the etiology of learning disabilities. Psychoanal Study Child 1964; 19:421-447

Campbell JD: Manic-depressive disease in children. JAMA 1955; 158:154-157

Christ AE: Cognitive assessment of the psychotic child: a Piagetian framework. J Am Acad Child Psychiatry 1977; 16:227-237

Cohen TB: Observations on school children in the People's Republic of China. J Am Acad Child Psychiatry 1977; 16:165-173

Colarusso CA: Psychoanalysis of a severe neurotic learning disturbance in a gifted adolescent boy. Bull Menninger Clin 1980; 44:585-602

Colarusso CA, Green P: Strategies for Teaching, second edition. Doylestown, PA, Bucks County Public School Press, 1972

Colarusso CA, Green P: Diagnostic educational grouping with strategies for teaching. The Reiss-Davis Clinic Bulletin 1973; 10:17-25

Conference on Psychoanalytic Education and Research. Commission IX, "Child Analysis." New York, American Psychoanalytic Association, 1974

Coolidge JC, Brodie RD: Observation of mothers of 49 school phobic children. J Am Acad Child Psychiatry 1974; 13:275-285

Eisenberg L: School phobia: a study of communication anxiety. Am J Psychiatry 1958; 114:712-718

Ekstein R, Motto RL: From Learning for Love to Love of Learning. New York, Brunner/Mazel, 1969

Freud A: Psychoanalysis and the training of the young child. Psychoanal Q 1935; 4:15-24

Freud A: Normality and Pathology in Childhood. New York, International Universities Press, 1965

Green P, Colarusso C: Grouping by psyche. Teacher 1973; 90:66-73

Hellman I: Some observations on mothers of children with intellectual inhibitions. Psychoanal Study Child 1964; 9:259-273

Hersov LA: Refusal to go to school. J Child Psychol Psychiatry 1960; 1:135-145

Hersov L, Berg I: Introduction, in Out of School. Edited by Hersov L, Berg I. New York, John Wiley & Sons, 1980

Hincks EM: Disability in Reading and Its Relation to Personality. Cambridge, Harvard University Press, 1926

Hitchcock J: Interventions by the psychoanalyst in the consultant role. Journal of the Philadelphia Association of Psychoanalysis 1977; 4:45-59

Homburger E: Psychoanalysis and the future of education. Psychoanal Q 1935; 4:50-68

Johnson AM, Falstein EI, Szurek SA, et al: School phobia. Am J Orthopsychiatry 1941; 11:702-711

Kaplan AM: The psychoanalyst in the public schools. The Pennsylvania Medical Journal 1961; 64:158-162

Klein E: The reluctance to go to school. Psychoanal Study Child 1945; 1:263-279

Kris D: The school consultant as an object for externalization. Psychoanal Study Child 1978; 33:641-651

Lewis M: Psychotherapeutic treatment in school refusal, in Out of School. Edited by Hersov L, Berg I. New York, John Wiley & Sons, 1980

Mahler MS: Pseudoimbecility: a magic cap of invisibility. Psychoanal Q 1942; 11:149-164

Mahler MS: Symbiosis and individuation: the psychological birth of the human infant. Psychoanal Study Child 1974; 29:89-106

Malmquist CP: School phobia: a problem of family neurosis. J Am Acad Child Psychiatry 1965; 4:293-319

Millman DH: School phobia in older children and adolescents: diagnostic applications and prognosis. Paediatrics 1961; 28:462-471

Newman CJ, Dember CF, Krug O: "He can hurt you but he won't": a psychodynamic study of so-called "gifted underachievers." Psychoanal Study Child 1973; 28:83-129

Pearson GHJ: A survey of learning difficulties in children. Psychoanal Study Child 1952; 7:322-386

Robinson DB, Duncan GM, Johnson AM: Psychotherapy of a mother and daughter with a problem of separation anxiety. Proceedings of the Staff Meetings of Mayo Clinic 1955; 30:141-148

Sperling M: The neurotic child and his mother. Am J Orthopsychiatry 1951; 21:351-362

Stennis W: Diagnostic Educational Grouping with Strategies for Teaching: Final Report 1970-71. Doylestown, PA, Bucks County Public School Press, 1970

Stennis W: Diagnostic Educational Grouping with Strategies for Teaching: Final Report 1970-71. Doylestown, PA, Bucks County Public School Press, 1971

Strachey J: Some unconscious factors in reading. Int J Psychoanal 1930; 11:322-331

Van Leewen K, Tuma JM: Attachment and exploration: a systematic approach to the study of separation–adaptation phenomena in response to nursery school entry. J Am Acad Child Psychiatry 1972; 11:314-340

Vanderpol M: in Basic Handbook of Child Psychiatry, Vol 4. Edited by Noshpitz J. New York, Basic Books, 1979

Waelder R: The psychoanalytic theory of play. Psychoanal Q 1933; 2:208-224

Waller D, Eisenberg L: School refusal in childhood—a psychiatric-paediatric perspective, in Out of School. Edited by Hersov L, Berg I. New York, John Wiley & Sons, 1980

Wilson P: The referral of nursery school children for treatment. Psychoanal Study Child 1977; 32:479-502

APPENDIX
DIAGNOSTIC EDUCATIONAL GROUPING QUESTIONNAIRE*

|⎵⎵⎵⎵|
SCHOOL NO.

|⎵⎵⎵⎵⎵| |⎵⎵| |⎵⎵⎵⎵⎵⎵|
ROOM NO.　GRADE　STUDENT NO.

|⎵⎵⎵⎵⎵⎵⎵⎵⎵⎵⎵⎵⎵⎵⎵⎵⎵⎵⎵|
FIRST NAME & INITIAL

|⎵⎵⎵⎵⎵⎵⎵⎵⎵⎵⎵⎵⎵⎵⎵⎵⎵⎵⎵⎵⎵⎵⎵⎵⎵|
LAST NAME

|⎵⎵⎵| |⎵⎵⎵|　　|⎵⎵|
MO.　YR.　　SEX
　BORN　　M or F

01. Much of the time the child appears
    1. Shy
    2. Immature
    3. Strange
    4. None of these

02. In general the child makes me feel
    1. Happy with him
    2. Angry or frustrated with him
    3. Sorry and a little frightened for him
    4. None of these

03. When the child talks his expression is
    1. Easily understood
    2. Immature
    3. Difficult to follow
    4. None of these

---

*Developed by William Stennis, M.D.

04. Child requires
    1. An average amount of attention
    2. More individual attention than usual
    3. Too much individual attention
    4. None of these

05. The child often appears
    1. Involved successfully or trying hard
    2. Restless
    3. Often in his own world
    4. None of these

06. With other children, the child is
    1. Liked or creates no problem
    2. Often in conflict
    3. Set apart
    4. None of these

07. Much of the time the child's behavior is
    1. Pleasant and likeable
    2. Stubborn and defiant
    3. Clingingly dependent
    4. None of these

08. Muscle coordination is
    1. Adequate
    2. A little uneven
    3. Poor
    4. None of these

09. Emotional growth and development is
    1. Forward and progressive
    2. Standing still
    3. Slipping backward
    4. None of these

10. Human figure drawings are
    1. Age adequate
    2. Immature
    3. Strange
    4. None of these

11. Success in school work is
    1. Usual
    2. Erratic
    3. Infrequent
    4. None of these

12. Parents are
    1. Interested and concerned
    2. Defensive and overconcerned
    3. Disinterested or limited
    4. None of these

CHAPTER 7

A Psychoanalytic Contribution Toward Rearing Emotionally Healthy Children: Education for Parenting

Henri Parens, M.D.

In 1969, two colleagues (Robert C. Prall, M.D, and Elizabeth Scattergood, M.A.) and I set out to develop an Early Child Development Program in our Children's Unit. The program richly served research, training, and service sectors of our unit, and within two years we came upon one of several unexpected findings. When we contracted with a group of pregnant mothers that in exchange for letting us observe their children in a naturalistic research project we would answer to the best of our abilities any questions they had about their children, we felt, in good faith, that we might be able to help them. But we did not expect our help to go as far as it did. We found that the work of parenting can be facilitated much more than we had realized.

During years of naturalistic, longitudinal, mother-child observations we found, as have many health clinicians, that even good mothers and fathers too often do not understand their children's needs and behaviors. As a result, parents frequently cannot evaluate which of their children's demands ought to be gratified and which benevolently frustrated. Perhaps 20 times a day a mother may have to decide between alternatives in handling her child's behavior without an assured feeling that the alternative she selects is a good one for her child at a given time. Of course many parents have an excellent intuitive feel for what is good and not good for their children. This is particularly true of those who can feel within themselves the residua of their own childhood yearnings, as well as their own past growth-promoting and growth-inhibiting experiences.

We were also surprised by the eagerness our original project mothers eventually showed for learning about parenting. This was not their reaction at the outset. Several were in fact quite skeptical—for a variety of reasons—about the possibility that we would be of any substantial help to them at all. Of course, we had committed ourselves to answer as best we could any questions they had about their children's behaviors and their rearing. What happened is this. In an economical and, we now know, an education-wise move, our observational project came to serve the training needs of our child psychiatry fellows, social work students, and psychoanalytic candidates (in child analysis) in child development and behavior while at the same time it was the focus of our research efforts. As we would point to certain cardinal, developmentally relevant behaviors and talk of their psychodynamic and developmental implications, the mothers—who could hear us—would ask me to tell them about

The substance of this paper has been presented in a number of forms, in a number of places. A draft was read at the National Conference on Parenting, November 16-17, 1984, at the Allentown Hospital, Allentown, Pennsylvania.

it too. We were, of course, aware of possible sensitivities; but our task was easy because we started with newborns, and under one year of age most issues tend not to produce much anxiety in the mothers. The mothers would even begin to ask for clarification when, before I had learned the best way to talk to them, I used a technical term they could not make sense of, such as "stranger anxiety." Soon I simply began to talk to the trainees and the mothers at the same time. I sharply decreased my use of technical terms and put most psychoanalytic concepts into lay language—with a good deal of success, I am told.

I discovered two things: 1) that the parents were learning much more than I had anticipated about their own children's development, and about psychodynamic issues and their implications, and 2) that in general we could teach nonprofessionals much more than I had realized. In short, we discovered that we could teach parenting with much success— as a number of my collaborators, colleagues, and students have now been doing since the mid-1970s[1]—and that we had found a method of doing so. Many parents can be excellent students of parenting—indeed, students highly committed to the subject, their own children (see Frank and Rowe 1981).

Let me interrupt my narrative here to briefly describe the research method we employed, which brought these findings to light so vividly for us.

METHODOLOGY

Since 1969, our research approach has been naturalistic, longitudinal, psychoanalytic, direct child observation (see Parens 1979, chap. 4, for a detailed description of our research methodology). Starting in 1970, 15 infants and their mothers were the focus of our research for over seven years. Regretfully, fathers met with us only on rare occasions. The mothers and their children met as a group once or twice weekly for two-hour sessions in a large living room in our Children's Unit. The mothers brought all their children who were not in school, but it was those children whom we had seen since birth who were our primary research subjects. The infants were cared for by their mothers, the project staff

---

[1] In addition to me, staff members who have conducted such groups include Elizabeth Scattergood, M.A., Rogelio Hernit, M.D., Andrina Duff, M.S.S., Elaine Frank, M.S.W., Denise Rowe, B.A., Elsa Malmud, Ph.D., Bernice Schneyer, Ph.D., and Gayle Jessar, M.S.W. Colleagues who have seen the work in progress and were especially impressed with its feasibility include Selma Kramer, M.D., Robert C. Prall, M.D., and Peter G. Bernett, M.D., all psychoanalysts of adults and children. Among those we have trained to instruct such groups, I particularly want to mention Rogelio Hernit, M.D., past Coordinator of this training program.

observing. The preschool children also met in an adjacent Toddler Area, equipped modestly to meet their needs. The children were free to move between the Infant Area, where the mothers tended to stay, and the Toddler Area.

As I mentioned, our "contract" with the families was simply that if they would permit us to observe naturalistically the development of their children, we would attempt to the best of our ability to answer any questions the mothers had pertaining to the meaning of their children's behaviors and to their rearing. Narrative records detailing observations and comments on them referent to areas under study were kept on each research subject. In addition, since the early phase of the research film-data of selected behaviors were collected, and video recordings were also started three years later.

Let me now pick up the thread of what I want to communicate.

PARENTING: A DOMAIN FOR STUDY

What I want to emphasize is this: We found that *there is much factual information on matters essential to healthy child development, which parents lack and which is readily teachable.* For example, we have often found gross misunderstanding of what a child's emotional needs are, of what will and will not spoil children, of what *thumbsucking* is all about, what *transitional objects* do for children, what causes *stranger anxiety* and *separation anxiety*, what the *separation-individuation process* achieves. Many parents know nothing about the *Oedipus complex*, what it does *for* and *to* children, how important it is to the development of morality, social conduct, and the ability to form good love relationships. Many parents do not know whether these ubiquitous phenomena are good, bad, or indifferent; nor do they know how to deal with undesirable as well as desirable elements in them.

Here are a few examples of the kind of phenomena I have in mind. From the time their children were about 6 months old, two of the mothers would "sneak out" when they had to leave their children—say, for an appointment—because they felt they might thereby avoid upsetting their 6-month-olds. They did not know that such disappearing acts—that is, leaving in a way that does not allow the child to become aware of the actual separation—at such a critical period of psychic immaturity, infantile omnipotence, and magical thinking, can endanger the development of *basic trust* (Erikson 1959). Explanations of this matter were at first startling to these mothers, who had never been introduced to such ideas before. As is common, they found no cues to it in their own repressed childhood experiences.

Discussions of thumbsucking, separation anxiety, and stranger reactions took place frequently. Some of the mothers could not distinguish acute anxiety from (healthy) narcissistic orneriness. They did not know when to yield to their children's wishes, or when to frustrate benevolently. Too often they would gratify or frustrate at the wrong time. For example, when they are reprimanded by their mothers, 2-year-olds often become upset. Naturally and usually, the 2-year-old, when upset, seeks comfort from his/her mother. Several good mothers would reject the child's request for comforting. Each mother felt that since she had just scolded the child, the child was now trying to "butter her up"; thus the mother concluded that she would spoil her child by comforting him/her. These mothers agreed that the lesson to be learned would be defeated.

The mothers did not know the error of that thinking and the harm that this approach can bring with it. Nor did the mothers know that *comforting the scolded child can promote growth* in two important ways. 1) Comforting the scolded child can make him/her learn the lesson better because the admonition repeated by the comforting mother tends to be more readily internalized than that of the rejecting mother. The influence of the comforting mother then becomes greater than that of the fantasied bad mother, whom the infant wishes to destroy and externalize, and whose admonitions the child wishes to get rid of. 2) Comforting the scolded child can insure the *fusion* of good with frustrating mother representations, protect against splitting object and self representations, and thereby secure a more advanced stage of object-relatedness and psychic development (Kernberg 1966, 1967; Mahler 1968; Mahler et al. 1975). Indeed, rejecting the child, especially under these conditions, reinforces the especially pathogenic defense of splitting by strengthening the influence of the bad-frustrating mother and bad self-representation. After a number of efforts at explaining these concepts, all but one of the mothers dealt with this matter quite well.

Talk about children's interests in babies and their genitals was introduced by a 3½-year-old girl, who sent a shock wave through several of the mothers by announcing that she wanted to have a baby. Attaining conversational ease with sexual matters is a rather slow process. It is, in fact, the most difficult area for most of the mothers. By contrast, such areas as limit setting, ambivalence, hostility, and temper tantrums are much easier for them to discuss. Nonetheless, talking about sexual matters, when carefully dealt with, can be most beneficial. For example, one of our most skillful and talented mothers had a lovely relationship with her fifth child. Much warmth, compatibility, and comfort characterized their relationship. When Jane was about 2½ years old, we began to see a significant change in their relationship; some of Jane's behavior led to considerable impatience, annoyance, and anger in this same good mother. Four months after we recorded this change in their relationship, the mother walked in once and with a half-smile said: "Anyone want her for a year?" While this was said lightly, it was our cue to begin to explain that Jane was entering her oedipal period. We let Jane and the other children provide us with behavioral data from which we could illustrate, talk about, and gradually explain this salutary phenomenon to the parents. We were impressed with how readily some of the mothers and fathers, because of the feelings stirred in them by their own daughters and sons, could recognize and appreciate this important, insufficiently talked about development. We observed—and the mothers confirmed our observations—that because the mothers could understand their children's behavior better, they could deal with it better; we also thought that they dealt with it less conflictually. Education about the oedipal period is only one of many examples of increased parental comfort with sexual material.

ONE CAN EDUCATE FOR BETTER PARENTING

Thus, gradually we came to recognize that our approach provides a method for educating mothers, fathers, and even children. Our experience underlined the merit of Freud's repeated comment that one of the largest contributions psychoanalysis will make, in addition to its enormously useful clinical applications, will be its "application to . . . the upbringing of the next generation." He described this contribution as "exceedingly important" and "rich in hopes for the future" (1933, p. 146).

I want to say a little more about the method we gradually developed for teaching parenting (Parens et al. 1974; Frank and Rowe 1981). Much like the method used during the research, the technique consists of regular weekly (or twice-weekly) two-hour meetings, in a reasonably comfortable setting, of five to ten mothers, their infants, and their preschool children, with one or two child development professionals and one paraprofessional to help organize activities for the children. Our facility includes a large living room, a small Toddler room, a bathroom, toys and preschool type equipment, and snack and coffee supplies.

The focus of our interest is the child's behavior, with a view to talking about any issue pertinent to that behavior found to be puzzling or troublesome to the mother or to the child. Essentially this approach is *educational, not psychotherapeutic*. Some supportive psychotherapeutic measures are used but only secondarily to the processes devised for educating students who are undertaking the arduous work of being parents. The professionals do not initiate discussion with the mother of her reactions to her child. Neither do they discuss the mother's dynamics nor her transference-like reactions to the professionals or to each other. This method, we have found, differs only along two major axes from the *developmental guidance* developed by Selma Fraiberg (1980). The difference is that we work in a group, and ours is *not* a psychotherapeutic undertaking. We have found this method enormously useful with nonpatient as well as some patient populations. As with Provence and her group (Provence and Naylor 1983), our target population is not a patient population. We adhere primarily to the goal of *imparting information*, like any instructor, since these mothers and children are not patients, but students. When it becomes necessary to borrow from supportive psychotherapy technique, we do so to make the imparting of information more feasible and useful. Of foremost importance, of course, in our method is the requirement that the instructors have a sufficient knowledge of (psychodynamic) child development theory.

Let me note parenthetically that in this presentation I have targeted the mother as the parent involved in our groups. However, it is neither our wish nor our intent to exclude fathers from this educational process. In fact, several colleagues (Rogelio Hernit, M.D., Elsa Malmud, Ph.D., Elaine Frank, M.S.W.) have for a number of years now implemented our educational method with both parents with much success.

Prevention–Early Intervention Parent–Child Groups

This method of education and guidance for parents has as its goal the prevention of, and where indicated the early intervention in, the development of commonly found, experience-derived emotional disorders in children (Parens et al. 1974). As indicated, in the course of our research we found that good mothers, good parents, because of the lack of formal and technical training for parenthood, often do not understand their children's needs and behaviors. Because they do not sufficiently understand what contributes to optimal psychic development—as best we know to date—parents often cannot judge what is a normal demand in their child and have difficulty deciding what to gratify and what to deny. Similarly, they cannot choose the proper alternative in handling problematic behavior. We have seen that many times they interfere with, impede behavior that is not only reasonable but in fact promotes growth. We have found in this work that becoming and being a good-enough parent is greatly facilitated when one has some basic understanding of the complex nature of human psychic development.

As I say in our film (Parens et al. 1974), "More people work as parents, have the job of parenting than do any other kind of work. Yet, it is the one job which requires a great deal of technical knowledge and enormous skills for which no training is required and little education is formally imparted. For centuries we have been forced to do our parenting intuitively. It seems to have gone unrecognized that there is *much teachable knowledge, teachable skill in mothering, in parenting.*"

Here, taken from our film data, are examples of three children to illustrate what happens in such mother-child groups—the enormous opportunities for teaching parents they present, the large opportunities they provide for the prevention of, and, where needed, the early intervention (and even referral for treatment) in the development of many experience-derived emotional disorders in children.

Temmy

When Temmy was 20 weeks of age, she suffered acute anxiety reactions when she entered our project area. The acute reactions, we deduced, were instigated by strangers and the new environment. (Temmy was the only child among our research infants who was not "born into" the group; she came to us at 17 weeks of age.) These anxiety reactions, we felt, interfered with conflict-free sphere development, as exploration of the external environment. Jane, an infant just one day younger than she, by contrast, was a busy explorer, well related for her age (see below), and gave much evidence that her young ego apparatuses were being very well exercised. We already knew that Temmy was attaching quite well to her mother and could easily be comforted by her. We helped the worried and uncertain mother to understand Temmy's anxiety, which we felt resulted from feelings of separateness and stranger reactivity. We told the mother that because it appeared to be such sharp anxiety, if the mother brought Temmy close to her, the anxiety would subside and Temmy would feel better and become comfortable with us and the new environment sooner. Close to the mother, she was able to be interested in and to begin to explore the environment. She molded well into her mother, and the mother could comfort her nicely. Spontaneously, the mother began to make efforts to calm and comfort her and found she could *play* age-appropriately well with her and could make her laugh. This mother turned out to be excellent in playing with her children.

At 7 months, 15 days of age, Temmy made very skillful use of a walker, a device used by the mother because Temmy did not seem able to learn to crawl—we thought perhaps because of a neonatal hip problem. With the walker Temmy became quite mobile. She was able to separate at will from her mother, to "socialize" with peers, to investigate her environment, and then to return to her mother for long periods of closeness. When our professional audiovisual crew came in to do some special filming, her insistent approach to them and their camera showed that her anxiety in the face of strangers and strange situations had abated to a significant degree.

Then at 1 year, 1 month, and 24 days of age, in the process of working through separating from her mother and early in the process of individuation, Temmy found it necessary to use a psychic device to allay the anxiety separation-individuation was causing her. She used what I came to label *proxies* (Parens et al. 1974). She put soft toys onto her mother's lap, demanding that her mother feed them and care for them.

Temmy shared in that caring (offering her bottle to each in turn), and she also shared in being cared for (she took one or two sucks from her own bottle, as if in line with the soft toys). We came to understand this psychic mechanism as the complement of *transitional objects* (Winnicott 1953), which most often stand for the mother as part object of the undifferentiated dyad; the *proxy* stands for the self. Because we could explain to the mother what Temmy's behavior meant, the mother could respond to it in an engaged and very helpful manner. She told us that without our explanation she would have been uncomfortable in complying with her child's requests (induced by separation anxiety) to feed her proxies. When these requests were comfortably gratified, Temmy could leave her mother's side, checking now and then to see if the *proxies*, representatives of herself, were safely close to mother.

Jane

At 15 weeks of age Jane was a very busy infant (Parens and Prall 1974; Parens 1979). Her exploratory activity was vigorous, her energy level high, her persistence and assertiveness notably strong. We predicted from Jane's strong aggressive drive disposition, that she would easily become age-adequately self-assertive, self-confident, and self-reliant. In her early years this was borne out. Unfortunately, we have not yet been able to do a follow-up study.

In such a child, with her good, energetic drive disposition, during the practicing subphase (Mahler 1965) setting appropriate limits, which is required in the rearing of every child, can become a real problem. At 11 months of age Jane wanted to go into the hall. Because there was a cleaning cart there at this time of the morning, her mother did not want her to go out. Jane insisted, and so did the mother. For a number of weeks, this particular battle of wills persisted.

We talked with Jane's mother about Jane's emerging thrust to autonomy. It is more difficult for the mother when she becomes frustrated and irritated with what she experiences as her child's stubbornness rather than as the internal pressure of her child's drives (and wishes). With our explanation the mother could persist in her limit setting with much more patience. She could insist without becoming enraged at her 1-year-old, and in the end she was enormously helpful to her child's own efforts to control such drive pressures. The great pressure within Jane, by leading to unavoidable frustration in her, was difficult for her too. Even more difficult for Jane though was the significant tension that the conflict with her beloved mother created. Defensively and creatively she made a game of the battle of wills, teasing and trying to playfully squeeze herself out or sneak out; but negative effects, anger, and weepiness associated with frustration emerged nonetheless. Without understanding the child's inner pressures and struggle, even a mother as good as this one could become very angry and even resentful of her child.

At 18 months of age Jane continued to be strongly self-assertive and age-adequately self-reliant. She continued to show increasing ego skills in her orderly mastery of the environment, resulting from the combination of innate skills and the well-exercised, age-adequate control she had already developed over the internal pressures of the drives. At 18 months, relatedness with mother, siblings, and others was of very good quality. Interestingly, but not surprisingly, the relationship with her mother came upon hard days during her third year, with entry into her oedipal period (Parens et al. 1976).

Lucy

At 6 months, 23 days, Lucy seemed to us to be quite well endowed, a normal child with regard to instinctual drives and autonomous ego apparatuses and their functions. Her affective expressions appeared adequately developed too for her age and showed pleasant-enough internal feelings; thus, in terms of disposition, her affects were evaluated as normal. Attachment indices (smiling responses, stranger and separation responses, and reunion reactions) were good. At this age Lucy was active, explored well, and asserted herself on the external environment with vigor.

Then by 1 year, 2 days of age (according to our written and film records), Lucy appeared painfully, clinically depressed (see Parens et al. 1974), with her activity notably slowed down. Evidence of it had begun to be recorded at 9 months of age. We tried repeatedly to explain to her mother Lucy's need for emotional closeness, but the overburdened mother could not respond adequately. Lucy's depression had become more and more profound. Because of the continuing difficulties sustained by her caregivers and the ineffectiveness of our explanatory educational efforts, it became necessary to recommend treatment for Lucy and her mother. As emphasized, our group work has been *education and guidance*, not treatment. The treatment that we recommended, however, was carried out within the context of this mother-infant group.

I would like to add a word about the treatment of this anaclitically depressed (Spitz 1946) infant and her mother. At the time the treatment was begun, in the spring of 1971, our approach to an infant as ill as this one was derived from the child guidance model, a model that has served us well for decades with children and adolescents. That is, the child—in this case infant Lucy—was seen by one therapist (Rogelio Hernit, M.D.) and the mother by another (Elizabeth Scattergood, M.A.). Usually, in such cases, the child was seen by a psychiatrist and the mother (parents) by a social worker, and their therapists would collaborate in their respective individual efforts. The treatment of Lucy and her mother was very successful (see below), but today we employ a different approach to most infant cases. We now implement an infant-parent psychotherapy (described by Fraiberg 1980), in which one therapist works with both infant and parent(s), mostly jointly. We have not discarded the child guidance model—some cases still warrant the dual approach to the mother-infant dyad—but we usually find large advantages in the joint treatment approach—for example, optimization of the infant-parent(s) relationship(s) (see also the "tripartite" approach of Mahler 1968; Fraiberg 1980; Provence 1983).

Therapy with Lucy and her mother began when Lucy was 15 months old. A film sequence (Parens et al. 1974, with addendum 1976) at 1 year, 4 months, 19 days, shows Lucy in interaction with her therapist. He tries to draw her out of her depressive withdrawal, and he comforts her when she yields to her depression while attempting to gratify some of her needs for closeness. Improvements came only gradually. Lucy formed a meaningful relationship with her therapist, and the depression lifted very slowly but not before it had made a significant, perhaps indelible, imprint on her character. Later film material shows Lucy much improved. At 3 years of age she was no longer depressed, with all major aspects of ego functioning, object relatedness, and inner emotional state in very good order. This continued well into latency. At the same time that the treatment was carried out, we continued to try to educate the mother as to the nature of her infant's needs and behaviors.

These brief observational notes convey some idea of the types of issues that come up in such parent-infant groups, the large opportunities they present for clarifying children's behaviors, discussing all types of child-rearing issues, and even intervening early in the face of emerging disturbances.

WHY EDUCATE FOR PARENTING?

Central to our concerns is the idea that the child's optimal psychic development requires a relationship to the mother or parenting person(s) in which that mother (parent) is 1) sufficiently *emotionally available* to her child (as Margaret Mahler puts it) and 2) sufficiently *empathic* and *understanding* of her child and his or her needs and behaviors. This fundamental (psychodynamic) view emphasizes the importance of *the qualitative aspects of the child's attachment to the mother (parent) and the mother's (parent's) experiencing of her child.* Ethologists, Lorenz (1935, 1953) in particular, have documented and described the phenomenon of imprinting, a primary object attachment that occurs in many animal species. As more recently reported by Klaus and Kennell (1976), we find aspects of imprinting in human *bonding*, a reciprocal attachment that occurs between mother and infant within hours of birth—very much like that Liddell (1958) reported many years ago in his studies of goats. But as Scott proposed (1963) as an outgrowth of his studies of dogs and cats, there is in *primary socialization*—which goes well beyond bonding—an important more protracted experiential contribution to the development of relationships. As we discussed extensively elsewhere (Parens and Saul 1971), the corollary of imprinting and primary socialization in humans, as elaborated by psychoanalysts, emphasizes an extremely important further consideration, which is the requirement that *the mother (and father) invest sufficiently, emotionally, in her (his) child* in order for the child's emotional investment in the mother (and father) to be assured. The normal human child is primed psychobiologically to attach emotionally to that parent, but for that attachment to be positive enough in character, the parent must sufficiently value her/his child emotionally.

The quality of this reciprocal attachment between infant and parents is vitally important to the child's evolving psychic development. Through the process of identification with the parents, the nature of the attachment influences the development of the child's ego and superego—the internal structures of adaptation and of conscience and ideal self-image. Without a healthy-enough ego the child cannot adapt well and participate constructively in the real, difficult world; and without a healthy-enough superego he either behaves without regard for family and community or is frozen in an avalanche of anxiety.

Therefore, securing an optimal child-parent relationship would be a major step toward the promotion of healthy development or toward the prevention of experience-derived emotional disorders in children. However, as we have seen in our mother-child work, love alone can secure neither an optimal child-mother relationship nor optimal child development. In addition to love and sufficient freedom from emotional disorder, parents require a working understanding of the child's changing needs, of his/her adaptive and emotional functioning, and a degree of knowledge of human psychic development. In addition, they need to acquire methods and skills in child-rearing based on an understanding of that development and on the ability to determine what is growth-promoting and what is growth-inhibiting. In more than 15 years of this work, we have found that the ever-expanding body of child development theories can be taught in varying degrees to people who vary in their education and ability to understand. Our staff has found that psychodynamics can be taught quite successfully to parents under natural living conditions, in interaction with their children—that is, in a *laboratory* rather than in a didactic setting.

As I said earlier, we did not anticipate the impressive extent to which we can help these mothers (parents). In the experience and opinion of our staff,[2] the element that we provided which has made their task as mothers easier, and in a number of instances prevented the crystalliza-

---

[2] Elaine Frank, M.S.W. and Denise Rowe, B.A., are currently evaluating results of a study attempting to document changes in parenting in one of their groups (see also Frank and Rowe 1981).

tion of emotional problems in the children, was our explanations of the meaning of the children's behaviors, of the psychodynamics that motivated them—as these could be inferred and ascertained from observations—and of the consequent parenting behaviors that then seemed desirable or not desirable.

It is of course not necessary to turn the mother into a social worker, psychologist, or psychiatrist in order to give her information, explanations, and meanings of her child's behavior. While there is still much we professionals do not know, there is a great deal of well-organized and highly sophisticated information on child development and child behavior that can be transmitted to parents.

Our method not only facilitates the difficult task of child rearing but is also very useful in increasing the mother's self-esteem and self-confidence as a result of her much improved and more secure parenting performance. Provence and Naylor (1983) also have recently reported such results. This approach brings parenting into clearer perspective and emphasizes the fact that it is a serious and difficult job for which formal training ought to be required.

EDUCATION FOR PARENTING FOR STUDENTS IN GRADE K THROUGH 12

Because our work made us aware that formal preparation for parenting is feasible, we became progressively more convinced that to effect a large thrust toward primary prevention in mental health, such formal parenting education should be instituted in the mainstream of children's education.

In the course of work I shall presently describe, I learned that for about 15 years there has been a vigorous call for education for parenting from national *education* administrators (Currie 1978). In 1973, S. P. Marland, then Assistant Secretary for Education, Department of Health, Education and Welfare, deplored the serious "consequences visited on children whose misfortune it was to be born to parents who lack even a rudimentary understanding of the emotional, nutritional, and early learning needs of the young. The condition is by no means limited to the economically disadvantaged. . . . We must strengthen the capacity of our schools and other community organizations to instruct young men and women—particularly teenagers—in the techniques and responsibilities of motherhood and fatherhood" (1973, p. 3). In 1975, T. H. Bell, Secretary of Education, said that "Parenthood training must be made available to all young people—teenage parents or just parents to be. We educators [must] . . . assure that every youngster graduating from high school is competent to be a parent" (1975).

Then, with noteworthy insight, at a National Education Conference in

1978 in Philadelphia, Stanley Kruger, of the Department of Education, called for the development of education for parenting programs *interdisciplinary* in content and character. He called for the *collaboration of disciplines* whose domains of study and knowledge are relevant to education for parenting.

A unique phenomenon has taken place. There is growing recognition not only of the need for but of the feasibility of formally preparing for parenting. Throughout the United States and Europe numerous parenting education courses are now offered in high schools, neighborhood community centers, and, in some instances, in junior high schools.

These propositions advanced by national education administrators resonated strongly with our own ongoing work and findings. Before I describe further aspects of our own work, let me emphasize two points in Marland and Kruger's recommendations. Marland spoke of "parents who lack even a rudimentary understanding of the *emotional, nutritional,* and early *learning needs* of the young." He and Kruger underscored that adequate parenting requires several sectors of knowledge, among these being understanding the emotional and early learning needs of the young.

Mental Health Aspects of Parenting

We, too, want to emphasize that there are a number of sectors to parenting—for example, the initial child begetting and then homemaking: providing good enough shelter, food, and health care, as well as child rearing. But it is the child rearing upon which I am focusing. Of course emotional factors play a large part in child begetting and homemaking, but they are central to child rearing, that large determiner of the child's and eventually the adult's emotional life. Child rearing, especially, has long concerned mental health professionals.

This is why I repeat that any formal curriculum in parenting has to be steeped in psychological child development, child behavior, and parenting theory. The psychological theory should cover both emotional—especially but not exclusively psychodynamic—and cognitive factors. I will return to these points later.

Kruger, an education administrator, called for the collaboration of disciplines in developing education for parenting programs. What I am describing represents a contribution that can be made to such curricula by mental health professionals, knowledgeable about psychodynamic child development and human behavior. In our own work, we have become acutely aware that education for parenting is a domain where education and the mental health sciences intersect and are on common ground.

Thus far, I have described parenting education for those with young children or for soon-to-be parents. As our work continued, we began to consider education for parenting of primary and secondary school students.

We found not only that the mothers of our project were acquiring a greater understanding of their children and their parenting functions but also that even our 3- and 4-year-old children would often listen most attentively to our discussions with their mothers (parents). In addition, they showed in their play activities a large interest in and, we infer, a preoccupation with (some day) being a parent. As in clinical work with children, we found that one can easily talk with a child about issues of child caring, of children's needs and behaviors, and of the parents' needs and behaviors. As we debated the relevant theory, we began to contemplate formally teaching children a course in human development that would include basic emotional needs, the theory of instinctual drives and motivation of behavior, the development of human adaptive functions and of conscience and ideal-self formation, the emergence of individuality and the process of separation–individuation, and the theory of psychosexual and psychosocial development. We had to evaluate how much of such content was teachable at primary and secondary school levels, and our impression was that much of it could be taught.

Propelled by these considerations, in 1976 a team of three child psychiatrists (two were also psychoanalysts), three social workers, and three school teachers began to work together to develop a curriculum on education for parenting, from which we wanted to develop a graduated curriculum for children from grades K through 12.

After preliminary work both in the research setting and in the classroom, in 1978–79 several members of our parenting curriculum team participated in a pilot project at the Germantown Friends School with students in 3rd, 5th and 6th, and 11th and 12th grades. The student response at all levels was enthusiastic, and the students seemed more interested in the subject than our teachers had anticipated.

Since then, under the leadership of Sara Scattergood, the teachers of our GFS Education for Parenting team have been engaged in a number of local schools, where they have helped develop courses in education for parenting arising out of the variable resources available to each individual school. Having come to this point as an outgrowth of our findings and experiences, we were excited to learn that educators throughout the country were similarly calling for schools to help prepare their students for the universal work of parenting. Many schools are developing such curricula autonomously.

Two special points can be made about the curriculum we envision. First, from both our clinical and direct observational work we know that nursery-kindergarteners and elementary school age children are more openly responsive and interactive in talking about babies, homemaking, and being a parent than are teenagers. This knowledge led us to assume that the younger children would react better to instructional materials about parenting, and that such early instruction would make them more accessible to later education about parenting than youngsters who started such education at junior and high school levels.

In a personal communication on this issue, Anna Freud encouraged our efforts: "I agree with you absolutely that psychoanalytic knowledge can be invaluable if brought to the public in this and other ways, and that at present, not enough is done about this" (letter of October 18, 1978). In that letter she also endorsed our view that the younger child is more receptive to parenting material and that resistances to it are much greater in adolescents. An additional great advantage to starting such teaching in the early grades is related to the fact that more seventh and eighth graders get pregnant than we like to think. That situation might change for the better if the issues were addressed formally and more openly and the children acquired a better early understanding of what parenting entails. Indeed, Sara Scattergood has told me over the years that high school students tend to approach the topic more intellectually and are more removed from emotional engagement in it; elementary school children, she learned to her surprise, become more emotionally involved in the topic at the same time that they develop an acute intellectual interest in it. Thus, we believe that it is most important for such a curriculum to begin in kindergarten, not in junior high school and certainly not just in high school.

Second, judging from the responses in our groups to "live material," we feel that this curriculum should be modeled on the *laboratory* form of teaching. It should especially include live observations of infants and parents in real-life interactions, and even a "hands on" approach (Sara Scattergood, personal communication) to infants and children. Along with didactic lectures, it should also include film presentations and discussions of the children's observations.

We propose that the projected curriculum consist of three major areas of concern: *human behavior and development, child-rearing issues and methods,* and *parenthood.* We are, of course, focusing on the emotional aspects, the psychological aspects of these three areas of concern. We think that they should be based principally but not exclusively on psychodynamic concepts of child development and on the findings of our research experiences with the children and their parents. We hope that once such a curriculum is achieved, it will encourage the development of a cornucopia of grade-adequate instructional materials.

My colleagues and I believe that it is essential that parenting curricula include, in equal weight to other sectors of parenting, that which pertains to the emotional-psychological development of children. However difficult, the effort to develop such curricula is warranted because educated good parenting may well be the widest and most direct avenue to the *prevention* of many crippling, experience-derived emotional disorders in children and hence also in adults. As the work of Fraiberg (1980), Greenspan (1981), and Provence (1983; and with Naylor 1983), and their respective collaborators shows, even the course and consequences of psychiatric disorders that are primarily of organic-genetic origin can be significantly mitigated by more optimal parenting. In addition, having some knowledge of human development, physical and emotional, and knowing important landmarks and events in normal development may lead parents to seek *earlier intervention*—which is at times virtually life-saving—when disordered development becomes apparent. As the participants in our infant groups have told us (Parens et al. 1975), when parents have a clearer view of the tasks and functions of parenting, a better grasp of methods and issues of child rearing, and a better understanding of their children, the job of parenting is facilitated and becomes even more gratifying. Parenting may then, also, come to be recognized as the complex and difficult job it is.

REFERENCES

Bell TH: Parenting and the public schools. Paper presented at the Annual Convention of the National Congress of Parents and Teachers, Atlantic City, June 1975

Currie J: Developing, Implementing and Evaluating the Year of A Curriculum in Human Development and Parenting Education for Juniors and Seniors at Germantown Friends School. Dissertation proposal, University of Pennsylvania, Graduate School of Education, 1978

Erikson EH: Identity and the Life Cycle. Psychological Issues Monograph No. 1. New York, International Universities Press, 1959

Fraiberg S (Ed): Clinical Studies in Infant Mental Health: The First Year of Life. New York, Basic Books, 1980

Frank E, Rowe D: Primary prevention: parent education, mother-infant groups in a general hospital setting. Journal of Preventive Psychiatry 1981; 1:169-178

Freud S: New introductory lectures on psychoanalysis (1933), in Complete Psychological Works, Standard Edition, vol. 22. Translated and edited by Strachey J. London, Hogarth Press, 1964

Greenspan S: Psychopathology and Adaptation in Infancy and Early Childhood. New York, International Universities Press, 1981

Kernberg O: Structural derivatives of object relationships. Int J Psychoanal 1966; 47:236-253

Kernberg O: Borderline personality organization. J Am Psychoanal Assoc 1967; 15:641-685

Klaus MH, Kennell JH: Maternal-Infant Bonding. St. Louis, C. V. Mosby, 1976

Kruger S: Education for Parenthood. Paper presented at a National Conference of Educators, Philadelphia, 1978

Liddell HS: A biological basis for psychopathology, in Problems of Addiction and Habituation. Edited by Hoch PH, Zubin J. New York, Grune and Stratton, 1958

Lorenz K: Companionship in bird life (1935), in Instinctive Behavior. Edited by Schiller CH. New York, International Universities Press, 1957

Lorenz K: Comparative behaviorology, in Discussions on Child Development. Edited by Tanner JM, Inhelder B. New York, International Universities Press, 1953

Mahler MS: On the significance of the normal separation–individuation phase, in Drives, Affects, Behavior, vol. 2. Edited by Schur M. New York, International Universities Press, 1965

Mahler MS: On Human Symbiosis and the Vicissitudes of Individuation, vol. 1: Infantile Psychosis. New York, International Universities Press, 1968

Mahler MS, Pine F, Bergman A: The Psychological Birth of the Human Infant. New York, Basic Books, 1975

Marland SP: Education for parenthood. Children Today 1973; 2:3

Parens H: The Development of Aggression in Early Childhood. New York, Jason Aronson, 1979

Parens H, Prall RC: Film #2: Toward An Epigenesis of Aggression in Early Childhood. Audio-Visual Media Section, Medical College of Pennsylvania, Eastern Pennsylvania Psychiatric Institute, Philadelphia, 1974

Parens H, Saul LJ: Dependence in Man. New York, International Universities Press, 1971

Parens H, Pollock, L, Prall RC: Film #3: Prevention—Early Intervention Mother-Infant Groups. Audio-Visual Media Section, Medical College of Pennsylvania, Eastern Pennsylvania Psychiatric Institute, Philadelphia, 1974

Parens H, Pollock L, Stern J, et al: On the girl's entry into the oedipus complex. J Am Psychoanal Assoc 1976; 24:79-107

Parens H, Scattergood E, Pollock L, et al: The Early Child Development Program: Group Interview with Mothers of Mother-Infant Groups. Video Tape, April 10, 1975. Continuing Medical Education Program. Medical College of Pennsylvania, Eastern Pennsylvania Psychiatric Institute, Audio-Visual Department, Philadelphia, 1975

Provence S (Ed): Infants and Parents: Clinical Case Reports. New York, International Universities Press, 1983

Provence S, Naylor A: Working with Disadvantaged Parents and Their Children. New Haven, Yale University Press, 1983

Scott JP: The Process of Primary Socialization in Canine and Human Infants. Monographs of the Society for Research in Child Development, 28, No. 1, 1963

Spitz R: Anaclitic depression: an inquiry into the genesis of psychiatric conditions in early childhood. Psychoanal Study Child 1946; 2:313-342

Winnicott DW: Transitional objects and transitional phenomena: a study of the first not-me possession. Int J Psychoanal 1953; 34:89-97

CHAPTER 8

Some Issues Involved in the Supervision of Interracial and Transcultural Treatments

Wayne A. Myers, M.D.

In this chapter, I will present clinical data from my work as a supervisor of therapists involved in interracial and transcultural psychotherapies and psychoanalyses. While many of the issues arising in such supervisions are not different from issues seen in the ordinary supervisory situations, one particular phenomenon stands out. What I am referring to here is the use by the patient or the supervisee of racial and cultural differences between the two parties as a resistance to the awareness of either the underlying transference-countertransference affects or the latent psychodynamic content of the material.

It is important to emphasize that the phenomenon to be described here is very frequently seen in psychotherapy practices. Consequently, it is an issue of considerable relevance for training programs, whether these be in psychiatry, psychology, or social work. I will initially present two typical examples of the type of phenomenon to which I am alluding. Following this, I will cite some instances of specifically interracial and transcultural manifestations of what has been referred to in the literature as parallelism or parallel process.

CLINICAL DATA

Example 1

A bright, warm, black male psychoanalytic candidate was working with a white female patient in analysis. After she had been in treatment for nearly five months with him, she began to express feelings of loneliness during periods of separation. Though it seemed apparent to us that her transference wish was to be more closely connected to the analyst and not to be apart from him on weekends and other holidays, she did not directly reveal these thoughts to him. Instead, she dreamt of having mynah bird and offered very few associations to the dream.

When I questioned the candidate about the dream, he too had few thoughts about it, including none in particular about the mynah bird. I then suggested that his patient may have unconsciously represented him in the dream as the mynah bird, to have him near her as a pet. In addition, the mynah bird image incorporated a parody of him as an analyst as mynahs are black, parrotlike birds that retain what is said to them and then repeat it back. Thus, in the dream image of the mynah bird, the patient's transference wish to be with the analyst was contained, as well as her anger toward him (shown in her depiction of him as a parrotlike bird) for not gratifying her desires.

Here we are dealing with the issue of a color representation, the black mynah bird, being used to ward off transference affects, such as anger and wishes for love and closeness with the analyst. If the issue of color resistances is kept in focus in the supervision, then the usual emphases on issues of technique and of countertransference can be dealt with as well.

141

Example 2

A white male psychotherapist of Italian origin, whom I had supervised privately for some time, began to describe to me an impasse that he was experiencing in his treatment of an attractive, black female patient. The young woman had developed a rather intense, eroticized transference toward him. As he related the material to me, he squirmed in his chair, as if he were experiencing considerable discomfort, though he did not specifically verbalize this feeling. I should note here, that in our previous work he had been quite free with me in detailing the sexual feelings directed toward him by his female patients and in describing his own responses to those feelings.

After spending a considerable period of time in describing the patient's amorous desires for him, he abruptly shifted over to a narrative of the presumed "impasse" in the treatment situation. What it ostensibly centered upon was her rage toward him because he charged her for missing their scheduled session on Martin Luther King's birthday. He mentioned that she seemed especially scornful of the fact that he took Columbus Day off, his ethnic holiday, without any hesitation, but he seemed unable or unwilling to grant her equal freedom in her choice of a similarly meaningful ethnic day off.

In his presentation of the material to me, the supervisee began to speculate aloud as to whether or not there might be some validity to her claims that he was a racist. He acknowledged that his family's viewpoint on such matters could hardly be called "liberal" and that perhaps he had not sufficiently divested himself of his earlier identifications with the Archie Bunker-like attitudes of his parents. He went on to state that his father and mother were particularly severe in their condemnations of interracial couples whom they would encounter in their walks around New York City.

I commented to him that a thorough examination of his feelings about blacks would certainly be beneficial to him in a variety of ways, especially in terms of his treatment of his patient. I went on to note, though, that I thought that there were other issues that he might consider in his own treatment as well, such as why he felt so uncomfortable when he was describing the young woman's erotic feelings toward him. I mentioned that his discomfort in this area was something unusual in the history of our work together in supervision.

I further pointed out to him that the "impasse" on which both he and his patient had been focusing was removed from the transference and had allegedly been triggered by a reality rejection, secondary to his presumed racist insensitivity to her feelings as a black woman. I suggested that this explanation may have been more comfortable for both of them to accept, rather than the alternative course of having to confront a possibly more sensitive issue for both of them—his rejection of her because of her intense sexual desires for him.

My supervisee was thoughtful in response to my comments and mentioned that he would take them up in his own treatment. When he returned for our next supervisory session, he noted that what I had said to him had been correct. He had realized in his analysis that he had been blocking off the sexual nature of his countertransference feelings toward his patient, because of the prohibitions by his parents against such desires as those directed toward blacks. Moreover, the parental injunction against miscegenation carried with it strong oedipal overtones, he noted, hence his intense discomfort in our last supervisory session and his need to introduce the reality resistance, the color-culture difference between his patient and him, as the presumed cause of the therapeutic impasse. Having recognized the genetic reasons for his countertransference difficulty, he was able to be more effective in his therapy with the patient thereafter.

PARALLELISM OR PARALLEL PROCESS

One of the more interesting manifestations of color and culture as resistances to the progress of therapy is an entity that has been referred to in the literature as parallelism or parallel process. In such instances, the supervisee enacts with the supervisor a process similar to one that is going on between the supervisee and the patient. I will shortly offer a few examples of this phenomenon occurring in interracial and transcultural supervisions.

Before doing so, let me first note that a number of explanations of the phenomenon have been offered in the literature, most of which are based upon Freud's (1914) observation that patients tend to repeat or relive in action, elements from their past which they are unable to remember and to verbalize. Searles (1955), in one of the early contributions to this field, spoke of a reflection process, whereby the patient enacted an unconscious conflict in the treatment with the supervisee, who then did the same with the supervisor.

The concept of shared identifications between patient and therapist is offered as an explanation for this occurrence, the idea being that the pair share the same unconscious conflicts, anxieties, or value systems. Arlow (1963) also highlighted the concept of shared wishes, defenses, and ideals. Sachs and Shapiro (1976) saw the therapist's unconscious identifications with the patient as occurring when periods of unresolved resistance appeared in the treatment. The authors saw the supervisee's inability to verbalize the nature of the therapeutic impasse as being related to the patient's having to expose areas of narcissistic vulnerability to the therapist; the conflicts are then enacted with the supervisor because of the supervisee's parallel feelings of vulnerability to exposure in the supervisory situation. Doehrman (1976) and Gediman and Wolkenfeld (1980) expanded the parallelism concept to include enactments that proceeded from the supervisory situation back to the therapeutic one, as well as in the other direction. Let me now turn to some clinical examples of this phenomenon.

Example 1

An experienced white private supervisee, who had formed a good
supervisory alliance with me in discussions of previous patients, began to
present material from the treatment of a young Latin male patient. The
sessions described seemed to lack any clearcut unconscious thread or
focus. The only behavior that seemed consistent was the supervisee's
new practice of continually coming in late to our sessions.

As a result of a sense of irritation that I began to feel toward the
supervisee when he offhandedly disregarded my inquiries about his
lateness, I began to wonder whether he might be repeating with me an
interaction that had been going on with his patient. When I asked about
this, he acknowledged that his patient had also been consistently late to
their sessions, despite his attempts to address the issue in the treatment.
The patient had said that punctuality was not a quality held in high
regard in his country, hence he found the therapist's focus on it quite
alien and "pointless."

My supervisee had felt a growing sense of frustration and despair in
working with his patient, because he felt stymied in his attempts to get
the young man to participate in the treatment in a manner that accorded
with his sense of "playing by the rules of the game." His enactment with
me of the authority conflict being played out along transcultural lines
with his barely post-adolescent patient—particularly in his disdainful
treatment of my comments about his lateness, which mimicked his
patient's disdain in the parallel situation—illustrates the specificity of
enactments so characteristically reported by Arlow (1963) and by
Gediman and Wolkenfeld (1980).

Once the supervisee began to see that he was reenacting an important
facet of his interaction with his patient, he was able to work on it more
profitably with the young man. The presumed attitude toward
punctuality and time was recognized as a transcultural resistance, which
served to mask the authority conflict with the patient's father,
reactivated in the transference feelings toward the therapist.

Example 2

In a second instance, a black male supervisee began a psychotherapeutic
treatment with a white male patient. From the beginning of the
supervision, I attempted to highlight the interracial issues that I expected
to arise as resistances in the transference and in the supervision. Despite
my "priming," the supervisee missed a number of the early references to
his color by the patient. Even after I repeatedly pointed out color
resistances in the material from the sessions, the therapist seemed
consistently unable to discover the material on his own.

In the treatment itself, an idealizing type of transference had been
formed wherein the patient (who suffered from impotency problems)
unconsciously ascribed grandiose phallic potential to the therapist
because of his color, with the transference wish being to incorporate the
therapist's presumed phallic potential during the therapy. In this sense,
the patient was similar to one described by Schachter and Butts (1968).
The therapist seemed unable to recognize this material in the overall

output from the sessions and began to feel "impotent" to deal with the interracial resistances that I was pointing out.

In addition, the therapist himself seemed to regard me with a considerable degree of awe. After a while, I began to consider the thought that he was enacting with me what the patient had been enacting with him. In some manner, he expected to extract from me my presumed phallic supervisory wisdom, which would enhance his potency as a therapist. It was not simply that he thought of me as a good supervisor. Rather, he acknowledged that my being white was the essential ingredient in his high estimation of me.

Once we recognized that a racial stereotype was being played out with me parallel to the one that the patient had been enacting with the therapist, the supervisee was able to deal with both me and his patient in a more realistic manner. I might note here that his bringing his feelings about the supervision and the treatment of the patient into his own personal therapy was of great benefit to him.

Example 3

In another example, a young white female supervisee chose to describe her work with an older Chinese female patient, who had been born in Asia, in her supervision. As she presented the material week after week, it became clear that very little of substance had been discussed in the treatment. In particular, her recounting of the sessions with her patient was totally devoid of any affectual material. In addition, no mention had been made of the patient's sexual life or aggressive interactions or fantasies. The supervisee herself, whom I had heard described by colleagues as an attractive young woman, seemed quite drably dressed and colorless in her presentation to me.

When I commented to her that her descriptions of the sessions lacked any references to the patient's instinctual-affective life, the supervisee seemed hurt. When I inquired further about her reaction to my comment, she lashed out at me, informing me that I was breaking the supervisory contract with her and was taking on a therapeutic stance in our sessions. I stopped for a moment and wondered whether or not she might be correct in her assertion. Then I wondered whether she, too, might be acting out with me a complex drama that had earlier been played out with her patient.

I mentioned my theory to her, and she was stubbornly silent for a while. I finally suggested that during her own treatment she might consider looking at what had happened between us. When she returned, she seemed considerably less drab in appearance than she had before.

She informed me that my assumptions had been correct in the prior session. The hurt and anger that she had displayed with me had been played out with her by the patient, when she had pressed the patient for material about the patient's sexual life and about her aggressive fantasies. The patient had informed her that such questions were an intrusion upon her personal life, and that in her culture it was improper to ask such questions.

The supervisee had been stymied in the treatment by this response. Her inhibition about pressuring the patient for further details, however, was not simply based upon her respect of the presumed cultural injunction. Rather, it was predicated upon her own personal reluctance to pressure an older woman, who represented her mother to her, for intimate details of her sexual life. When I had suggested that she examine her interaction with me in the previous session in her own treatment, she had done so and had recognized how blocks in her own life had been responsible for her becoming an accomplice to the patient's transcultural resistance. Armed with this knowledge, her therapy with the patient became considerably more productive.

Example 4

As a final example of parallel process, a young white male supervisee felt hurt by his black patient's continual use of racial epithets in referring to him. He kept trying to shrug off the slurs, saying that they were understandable in view of the patient's history of being maligned by whites. When he additionally noted that his patient had a great sense of humor, even saying that the patient was "quite a card," I became suspicious that his tone and his words might be covering over something else.

I called his attention to the phrase about his patient being "quite a card" and asked him what he meant by it. His face crimsoned with embarrassment. "I think I meant to say that he's a spade," he answered.

What had occurred was another example of a parallelism, for the supervisee who had felt maligned by the racist epithets of the patient had indirectly maligned his patient racially to me. What was important for him to see, however, and then to utilize in his treatment of his patient, was that the racial slurs covered over affectual responses in both instances. The affects in question had arisen in both instances not in interracial situations but in conflicts within their own families. The need to denigrate a sibling, which was at the basis of the patient's attack on the supervisee, had its resonance in the therapist's own life, hence his unconscious identification with the method chosen by the patient.

DISCUSSION

In two prior papers dealing with the subject of interracial treatments (Goldberg et al. 1974; Myers 1977), I have described the tendency of black patients with whom I have worked to attribute any transference frustrations that they have experienced at my hands to the reality differences between us, most notably our skin color difference. As illustrated here, the use of color and culture as a resistance to awareness of the intensity of the transference and to the exploration of historically important psychodynamic themes has often occurred in my supervisions of interracial and transcultural treatments.

In the first of the two examples presented at the beginning of this chapter, the black analyst had to deny the devalued representation of himself as the parrotlike mynah bird in his patient's dream. Here the avoidance of the color reference helped him to minimize his countertransference anger at his patient's having represented him that way in her dream. It also served to diminish his anxiety over his own erotic counterresponse to her wishes for increased closeness to him in the transference. Through his recognition in our supervision of his difficulty in confronting the issue of color as a resistance, he was able to become more effective in dealing with the subject in his treatment of his patient.

In the second example, involving the white therapist and the black female patient with the eroticized transference, the unconscious collusion in their focus on his "racist" rejection of her allowed them to conveniently avoid the more uncomfortable subject of the intense sexual feelings that were being stirred up in both of them. When I made the supervisee aware of his own countertransference contribution to the conjoint resistance, he was able to pursue the subject in his own analysis and thereafter to become a more effective therapist with his patient.

The other instances of interracial and transcultural resistances cited here deal with the subject of parallelism or parallel process. I would like to underscore the extraordinary degree of specificity in the enactments that I have detailed. Possibly this is because the obvious outward differences between patient and therapist serve to heighten the underlying areas of similarity with respect to shared identifications, wishes, and the like; however, future studies in this area would be necessary to explicate the phenomenon further.

What all of the examples most clearly delineate is that the supervisor in such interracial and transcultural situations must constantly be aware of the tendency of supervisees to collude unconsciously with their patients in the utilization of color-culture issues as a resistance. As supervisors, when we are able to keep this difficulty in mind at all times, we can help our supervisees to deal with their denial and to become better therapists.

REFERENCES

Arlow JA: The supervisory situation. J Am Psychoanal Assoc 1963; 11:576-594

Doehrman MJG: Parallel processes in supervision and psychotherapy. Bull Menninger Clin 1976; 40:3-104

Freud S: Remembering, repeating and working through (further recommendations on the technique of psycho-analysis, II) (1914), in Complete Psychological Works, Standard Edition, vol. 12. Translated and edited by Strachey J. London, Hogarth Press, 1958

Gediman HK, Wolkenfeld F. The parallelism phenomenon in psychoanalysis and supervision: its reconsideration as a triadic system. Psychoanal Q 1980; 49:234-255

Goldberg EL, Myers WA, Zeifman I: Some observations on three interracial analyses. Int J Psychoanal 1974; 55:495-501

Myers WA: The significance of the colors black and white in the dreams of black and white patients. J Am Psychoanal Assoc 1977; 25:163-181

Sachs DM, Shapiro SH: On parallel processes in therapy and teaching. Psychoanal Q 1976; 45:394-415

Schachter JS, Butts HF: Transference and countertransference in interracial analyses. J Am Psychoanal Assoc 1968; 16:792-808

Searles HF: The informational value of the supervisor's emotional experiences. Psychiatry 1955; 18:135-146

CHAPTER 9

The Joint Exploration of the Supervisory Relationship as an Aspect of Psychoanalytically Oriented Supervision

Emanuel Berman, Ph.D.

This chapter will discuss the possible benefits and drawbacks of making the explicit joint exploration of the supervisor-supervisee relationship into an integral part of the supervision of psychoanalysis and dynamic psychotherapy. While several risks will be considered, my overall conclusion is highly favorable toward this option, which I consider an element in giving the supervision itself a psychoanalytic orientation.

RATIONALES

There are three major rationales for the introduction of such an exploration.

The first is achieving a better fit between goals and means, between content and form. If we are trying to educate our trainees to be closely attentive to the emotional currents of every analytic or therapeutic session, to notice the subtle nuances of transference and countertransference expressed and experienced at any given moment, then attention to the emotional currents and nuances of the supervisory session provides an immediate, lively model. If instead we stick rigidly to a pre-formed agenda, if we allow supervision to become routinized, we may unwittingly transmit an inflexible mode of interaction that will show up in the trainees' clinical work as well.

These considerations are particularly relevant if our conception of treatment follows what Abrams and Shengold (1978, pp. 402-403) view as the new model of the psychoanalytic situation—namely, a conceptualization of analysis "primarily as an encounter between two people, rather than as a setting whose purpose is the examination of the intrapsychic processes of one of them."

Such a view, when applied to supervision, will lead us to emphasize its nature as an encounter of two three-dimensional individuals. From this perspective, the more traditional emphasis on the didactic and rational aspects of supervision may be seen as part of the "myth of the supervisory situation," equivalent to the myth eloquently described by Racker (1968, p. 132):

> The first distortion of truth in "the myth of the analytic situation" is that analysis is an interaction between a sick person and a healthy one. The truth is that it is an interaction between two personalities, in both of which the ego is under pressure from the id, the superego, and the external world; each personality has its internal and external dependences, anxieties, and pathological defences; each is also a child with his internal parents; and each of these whole personalities—that of the analysand and that of the analyst—responds to every event of the analytic situation.

I wish to thank Yael Leron, Dr. Simon Rubin, Avi Sadeh, and Ruth Segel for their help.

151

The difficulty in accepting the full complexity of the supervisory encounter is mentioned by Gediman and Wolkenfeld (1980, p. 253): "It is as if we as supervisors continued to believe that supervision is governed exclusively by conscious rational processes, even while acknowledging the omnipresence of unconscious phenomena."

A second rationale is the potential informational value of the processes of supervision as a key to a fuller understanding of the analysis being supervised. This idea of "parallel process," introduced by Searles, Arlow, and others, was perhaps the earliest legitimization of the exploration of the supervisory relationship. It has been documented extensively. Undoubtedly it still proves very useful in many cases, but caution is necessary. Ekstein and Wallerstein (1972, p. 196) mention that "parallelism can work in reverse as well," and this point is elaborated by Langs (1979) and by Gediman and Wolkenfeld (1980). Even more critically, Lesser (in Caligor et al. 1984) lists "parallel process" as one of three illusions surrounding supervision (the other two are "the supervisor knows best" and "the supervisor is objective") that help the supervisor to avoid supervisory anxieties.

The difficulty is that the notion of "parallel process" simultaneously calls attention to the supervisory relationship and yet allows for displacement and rationalization of its difficulties. When used defensively, it may amount to a covert message from the supervisor to the supervisee: "The trouble you and I seem to experience is not really our own; it comes from your patient, and if you solve it there, we'll be O.K. too." Such attribution of issues to a third party, and the attempt to structure a dyadic relationship in a roundabout way through that third party, is what family therapists call "triangulation" (see Winokur 1982).

The third rationale is that supervisory work at times gets stuck or sidetracked, and open discussion of the difficulty is crucial to get it going and to make it effective. I will discuss some of the common sources of difficulty later, attempting to take into account both the supervisee's resistance and the supervisor's "counterresistance." The resolution of difficulties may in turn have didactic side benefits. There are similar elements in resistance to therapy and resistance to supervision, and every trainee will benefit from greater insight into the threatening aspects of change, the narcissistic risks of feedback and confrontation, the difficulty of establishing trust, and so forth. The supervisor's capacity and willingness to acknowledge his contributions to the difficulty (be they harshness, vagueness, insufficient attentiveness, or much more complex countertransference patterns) may again serve as a role model to the trainee, helping him to become aware of his own potential contribution to therapeutic stalemates or failures. Again, in this sense supervision itself may be seen as dynamic or as psychoanalytically oriented.

If, on the other hand, difficulties remain latent, supervision runs the risk of developing into a narrow, formal interaction, in which the most powerful emotions present in the room are taboo. Such a stifling situation may become an "as if" supervision.

The same rationales apply to the exploration of group process in group supervision. There we may enjoy the added benefit of the amplification of insight by the consistent response of numerous group members; in other instances, we are better able to analyze parallel process because the respective group members, in their differential responses, dramatize various aspects of the presenter's countertransference, or respond to conflicting aspects of the patient's personality, or reenact different roles that were or are present in the patient's family.

In addition, an effective supervisory group, one in which all participants become active members of a supervisory team, invites and encourages the development of a supervisory capacity in each therapist. This may help to demystify the supervisory process and to provide greater insight into the conflictual aspects of both the supervisee's role and the supervisor's role. The open discussion of group processes helps in crystallizing such insight.

RESISTANCE TO SUPERVISION AND THE NEGATIVE SUPERVISORY REACTION

Resistance to supervision is no less universal than resistance to psychotherapy. Many of its sources were discussed by Ekstein and Wallerstein (1972) under the title of "problems about learning," and I will not attempt to summarize them here.

One widespread source merits particular attention. We may assume, I believe, that a common motive for becoming a therapist is a wish to be helped, loved, and supported. This vocational choice allows such passive wishes a disguised expression by projecting them and maintaining a sense of mastery: it is not I who feels weak and dependent, it is my patient; it is no longer an idealized parental figure who can offer help, it is I. Beginning therapists often verbalize rescue fantasies in varying degrees of openness. In a rescue fantasy, a third party is not needed.

The "appearance" of the supervisor may signify the return of the repressed, the return of the projected, reminding the therapist of his weak, vulnerable position as a novice, still in need of support and instruction. This authority figure, who in fantasy could perform the rescue much more effectively (an oedipal component), may expose the younger therapist as unworthy, incompetent, and even—at the extreme end of the fantasy—as an impostor, using the patients for his own libidinal and narcissistic aims.

Many individual elements, conscious and unconscious, may be combined in forming a particular supervisee's core resistance. For one supervisee, the supervisor may be experienced as demanding endless devotion to the greedy patients, as persecutory in forbidding any deviation from a selfless ego ideal. For another, the supervisor's psychoanalytic orientation may signify a demand for strict neutrality and an infuriating obstacle to the young therapist's eagerness to be warm, supportive, and giving to his needy patients. We can easily recognize transferential elements in such resistances, though the use of such clinically derived concepts is controversial, as I will discuss later.

Resistances may be generally oriented to being in supervision, or they may be specific to a particular supervisor, a particular orientation, or a particular institution. In some instances, an exploration will lead to secret but conscious issues, as in the following example.

> After a few months of supervision, a supervisor felt puzzled by the responses of the trainee. Although claiming to have very little prior experience, he appeared to have very crystallized ways of doing therapy, and whenever alternatives were suggested he became evasive or defensive. When the supervisor shared with him her puzzlement, he confessed that he actually had had a considerable amount of experience working as a disciple of a controversial, charismatic psychotherapist. He had come to the present agency in order to receive formal credentials necessary for licensing in his profession, but he viewed the methods of his "guru" as far superior to any alternative and therefore fought mentally against distracting influences.

Of course, further exploration might have led to the more personal meanings of this situation, but such exploration would depend on the trainee's willingness, which cannot be taken for granted.

Some supervisory resistances are typical "character resistances," part of a more general pattern of rigidity, sloppiness, unreliability, fluctuations of enthusiasm and aloofness, and so forth. Such general issues are of course more a topic of analysis than of supervision, though successful supervision may at times lead to their partial solution in the professional domain. Still, without open exploration the supervisor may err in assessing the situation, as the following vignette shows.

> A supervisee's behavior in sessions was marked by a strict routine, pedantic reading of process notes, and intellectualization. The supervisor tended to see these as character traits, until he brought up his observations. It turned out that the supervisee was in many situations intensely emotional, spontaneous, and impulsive and was very concerned that this might be harmful to her work as a therapist and to her chances of learning. In her fantasy, supervision became a testing ground for a yearned-for capacity for mastery and control. The discussion led to greater flexibility.

A unique manifestation of resistance is the "negative supervisory reaction," which (in ways parallel to the negative therapeutic reaction) leads to a regression in the therapeutic work of the trainee following a seemingly positive development (or even breakthrough) in the supervision. It is an important example of a situation in which an open exploration of the supervisory experience itself becomes invaluable.

Such exploration, bordering at times on a therapeutic process, may eventually lead to the individualized sources of the reaction for the supervisee. Here are examples.

> After some important sessions of supervision, in which the supervisor was able to suggest new ways of dealing with the patient's resistance, improvement in the patient's condition became apparent. The therapist, however, started forgetting supervisory appointments, brought very short notes, and sounded alienated from her work. It turned out that the supervisor's interventions made the therapist realize how poor her past training had been, and how ineffective were the methods she had developed (proudly) during several years of unsupervised work (see Berman 1985). She now felt ashamed of herself and embarrassed to present her work. The supervisor began to recognize that he may have been too active and enthusiastic and insufficiently attentive to the supervisee's anxieties.

> During supervision of a first-year graduate student, several weeks went by in which the student reported a stalemate in the treatment of a difficult patient; finally a completely new interpretation crossed the supervisor's mind, and she suggested it to the supervisee, who greeted it as very convincing. In her next supervisory meeting the supervisee reported that she had used the interpretation, encountering an immediate confirmatory reaction from the patient, who finally felt understood. The therapist reported this in a gloomy tone, however, and soon mentioned thoughts she had of abandoning her training. Further exploration revealed that she could not forgive herself for not thinking of the effective interpretation herself. An omnipotent fantasy was now demolished, activating deep-seated envy and resentment against needing to be supervised, both as a manifestation of incompetence and as a dangerous source of dependence.

In both cases, the open discussion of the source of regression resolved the immediate crisis. The deeper resolution of the emotional issues involved, quite crucial for the trainees' professional futures, remained a long-term goal, to be pursued in personal therapy.

It is very likely that many of the dynamic patterns that have been identified in the literature as leading to negative therapeutic reactions may also lead to negative supervisory reactions. These include unconscious guilt and a need for punishment (Freud); competition with the analyst, a hurt self-esteem, fear of being envied because of success, and experiencing an interpretation as an accusation or proof of dislike (Horney); envy, leading to a need to destroy the envied analyst's competence (Kleinian authors); and negativism (Olinick; these explanations are reviewed by Sandler et al. 1983).

Some recent discussions do not see the negative therapeutic reaction as necessarily stemming from the patient alone. Langs (1976) raises the possibility of an "interactional negative therapeutic reaction," strongly influenced by the analyst's contribution. Stolorow et al. (1983) discuss negative therapeutic reaction as a result of "prolonged, unrecognized transference–countertransference disjunctions and the chronic misunderstandings that result from them" (p. 120). The possible application of such models to supervision requires attention to the supervisor's role.

THE SUPERVISOR'S DILEMMA AND POTENTIAL COUNTERRESISTANCE

No serious discussion of supervisory difficulties can avoid the supervisor's own contribution. Still, such a contribution is often mentioned only in passing. Ekstein and Wallerstein (1972, p. 196) mention the supervisor's unresolved conflicts, but they give them meager attention in comparison to other issues. Fleming and Benedek (1966, p. 70) also talk of "inappropriate emotional responses" in the supervisor but then focus mostly on the supervisor's sensitivity to the anxieties and problems of the supervisee, implicitly portraying the supervisor as a wise, hard-working, and always well-meaning and rational individual. Langs (1979, p. 43) appears to be correct in observing that "even a therapist prepared to surrender an overidealized image of himself in his work with patients clings to the overidealized image of himself as supervisor." Such idealization is another aspect of "the myth of the supervisory situation."

At the core of many of the difficulties of supervisors lies an inherent conflict created by the supervisory situation. In the three-person system, the supervisor may identify at some times with the supervisee in front of him (equivalent to the "concordant identification" the analyst experiences with the analysand; Racker 1968, p. 134), and at other times with the patient described by the supervisee (equivalent to the analyst's "complementary identification" with other persons in the analysand's life, and with the analysand's inner objects).

In analysis or therapy, the way to integrate these conflicting identifications appears clearer. The complementary identification may be very useful in understanding the patient's inner world and the patient's impact on others, but the analyst's ultimate loyalty remains with the patient himself. In supervision, the supervisor's loyalty is more divided (even more so when the supervisee is inexperienced and/or works in the supervisor's own institution). As a result, the supervisor finds himself responsible, at least to some degree, for a situation in which he is not present and which he cannot control. It is a powerful emotional situation in which harm may be done.

Realistically, this is a stressful situation; but it may have additional unconscious implications. Racker (1968, p. 145) convincingly argues that one component of the wish to cure is guilt over aggression, arousing an unconscious need in the analyst "to repair the objects of the aggression and to overcome or deny his guilt." When a patient threatens suicide, for example, "the analyst is threatened with the return of the catastrophe, the encounter with the destroyed object."

In such a difficult moment in the therapeutic situation, the analyst may make increasingly intensified efforts to save the patient, and this may help him ward off the feared encounter. As a supervisor, however, he is in a weaker position, with lesser impact; this situation "often evokes a sense of helplessness and even anxiety when the student's mistakes seem to threaten the patient's safety" (Fleming and Benedek, 1966, p. 58). At the same time, the supervisee may take on the projected role of the aggressor, relieving the supervisor of his own guilt over the process that led to the danger. Such projection can in extreme cases lead to direct accusation by the supervisor, and in more moderate situations to difficulty in maintaining full empathy with the supervisee.

The following vignette is representative.

> The therapist possessed much experience and self-confidence, but in the eyes of his supervisor was not particularly smart. In discussing the treatment of a depressed borderline patient, he quoted some interventions in which he had smugly challenged the patient regarding the seriousness of his suicidal ideation. The supervisor experienced growing anxiety during the session and toward its end forcefully confronted the supervisee with the dangerous impact of such challenges. The therapist now responded with anxiety himself, and subsequently made reasonable efforts to correct his interventions.
>
> This supervisory intervention, which seemed unavoidable to the supervisor, had a price, however: the supervisee became more guarded in future presentations. The identification of the supervisor with the patient "over the therapist's head" ("complementary identification"), and his need to save the endangered patient from the therapist, led to an experience of abandonment in the therapist, which was not easy to correct.

A similar but even more complex situation may occur during the supervision of supervision, where the senior supervisor is one more step removed from the clinical situation (Ekstein, in Wallerstein 1981), in a way even more powerless, and may be in conflict among three competing identifications.

A supervisor in supervisory training presented in his own supervision his work with a beginning therapist treating a vulnerable young homosexual man. Both supervisors found the therapist's work rather weak and possibly marred by unresolved feelings regarding homosexuality. Both were very concerned when the therapist impulsively accepted the patient's stated wish for a (clearly premature) termination. The senior supervisor found himself so critical that he raised the question of dropping the therapist from training; he clearly identified with the patient and experienced a rescue fantasy in which the therapist (whom he never met) played the role of the dragon. The direct supervisor, on the other hand, experienced identification both with the patient and the therapist, and responded to his teacher's suggestion with an effort to rescue the therapist (declared not guilty by reason of inexperience) from the threatening dragon (senior supervisor).

In this case, the direct supervisor's personal contact with the therapist guaranteed a sense of commitment that the senior supervisor had no way of developing. The latter acknowledged that decisions must be reached by those directly working with the trainee and not dictated "from above." The issues of supervising supervision will not be further discussed here, except to say that the exploration of the relationship is equally indicated in that setting.

In some supervisors the burden of responsibility and potential guilt, probably in combination with other factors (Berman 1982), may lead to authoritarian intrusions into the therapy itself, direct contacts with the patient, and turning the therapist into an intermediary. The supervisor's impotence is turned into omnipotence. This, of course, undermines the therapist's autonomous development and may create split transference in the patient.

Narcissistic needs in the supervisor are discussed by De Bell (1963). Gediman and Wolkenfeld (1980) relate the supervisor's authoritarianism to "seeing the supervisee as a potential extension of himself" (p. 246). They also discuss several other components of what I would call the supervisor's counterresistance: "Competitive feelings toward his supervisee and anxieties about the inevitability of the supervisee's eventually becoming his peer" (p. 247); and the supervisor's tendency to be "preoccupied with his teaching reputation as it is displayed to the student body . . . [and] concerned with the image of himself that his student may convey to his analyst" (p. 248). In Racker's terms, the first group of concerns is "direct countertransference" and the second "indirect countertransference." Gediman and Wolkenfeld illustrate much commonality in the deeper concerns of patient, analyst, and supervisor and suggest that such commonalities strengthen multiple identificatory processes.

While the full disclosure of the supervisor's difficulties and emotions to a supervisee may be unnecessary and burdensome, I have no doubt that at certain moments some sharing of countertransferential feelings by the supervisor is helpful. It may facilitate greater openness in the supervisee, make the understanding of complex interactions possible, and serve as a desirable role model. The following examples are quite representative.

> A supervisor noticed a student was tense and apprehensive, and interpreted a transference to himself as a punitive authority. The student confirmed this, and described past encounters that may have contributed to the threat. The supervisor went over the incidents, describing his own experiences at the time they occurred, and articulating some of his emotional reactions to the student. The tension was eased.

> A therapist described abusive behaviors of the patient toward her child, and the supervisor responded by suggesting a directive intervention, of a style not usually favored by her. On second thought, a few minutes later, she told her supervisee that she realized personal emotions may have led her to an inappropriate suggestion. This led to a fuller exploration of the therapist's countertransference as well, and to a joint systematic review of the data about the patient in order to try to understand better her reactions to her child and to figure out what interventions could be effective in improving the situation without damaging the therapeutic alliance.

DIALOGUES ABOUT THE SUPERVISEE, OR A DIALOGUE WITH THE SUPERVISEE?

The supervisor, it appears, has an inherent need to discuss the supervisory relationship, to hear about the supervisee, and to speak about him. When this does not happen in the supervision itself, when it is constricted and "patient oriented," such discussion is likely to happen more outside it. (Similarly, the supervisee may gossip about supervision as an outlet to unexpressed feelings, or obsess about it in analysis.)

If the supervisor is the trainee's former analyst, he knows a lot about him already. If he is not, some authors advocate discussions between supervisor and training analyst (see De Bell 1963). It is interesting that while there has been much discussion regarding the damage that "reporting" (by a training analyst to the training committee) does to the candidate's personal analysis (e.g., Kairys 1964), much less attention has been devoted to the damage such lack of privacy and confidentiality, and the strengthening of the supervisor's omniscient image, may cause to the supervisory process as well (a notable exception is Langs 1979).

Even if we exclude the extreme example of discussions with the supervisee's analyst (it seems quite clear to me that if the supervisor wishes to hear about the analysis, it should be from his supervisee and not from the analyst), the issue of information reaching the supervisor from other sources (e.g., teachers, other supervisors) is still problematic.

Many clinical training programs view the sharing of information regarding supervisees as highly desirable. Forms are devised and collected, meetings arranged, training committees elected. Undoubtedly, the systematic review of supervisors' impressions is crucial for evaluation. A strong example involves the (usually rare) instances in which termination of training appears to be indicated. But what is its impact on the quality of training per se?

On the positive side, one can think of instances where the impressions of one supervisor clarify for a colleague the nature of a confusing impasse in his work with the same trainee. In my experience, however, even more frequent are situations in which group discussion of a trainee creates an impasse where none existed before, such as in the following example.

> In a faculty meeting, a supervisor was surprised to discover that his moderately positive evaluation of a supervisee stood in marked contrast to the harsh judgments of several colleagues. Although defending him during the meeting, the supervisor was left with a burdensome concern about being manipulated by the trainee, being too lenient, and so forth. Over the next few weeks he found himself responding to the supervisee's reports with much more criticism. The trainee, an anxious young man who had earlier experienced this supervisor as his only ally in the program, became even more anxious and isolated, and his clinical performance deteriorated.

An impression of a former supervisor prior to the start of supervision may of course be even more biasing, as discussed by Langs (1979, p. 90) and Shevrin (in Wallerstein 1981). Such influences may reduce the chance for a unique unfolding of a relationship within the new supervisory dyad, which need not resemble any other dyad. (A similar realization led to the disillusionment with the notion of objective "analyzability"; Bachrach 1983.)

Nevertheless, when Langs (1979, p. 91) attributes the harmful sharing of information to the arbitrary wishes of administrators, he seems to be disregarding the supervisor's own eagerness to unload his anxieties, demonstrate his achievements, and "compare notes" with colleagues, hoping to validate his impressions. Such communication can never be outlawed; at the most, one can refrain from its encouragement and institutionalization, except for situations which arouse intense concern.

To the occasional detrimental individual impact of the kind described, one has to add the universal impact of frequent faculty discussions or of a hyperactive training committee on the morale of the trainees as a group. Being thoroughly discussed (even with the best of intentions) is demoralizing and arouses paranoia. Paradoxically, there are instances in which chaotic periods in a program, when administrative weakness leaves each supervisor on his own, which eventually turn out to have been more productive to the individual growth of trainees, thanks to benign neglect.

The most fruitful discussion of supervision, as I am attempting to demonstrate, is the one taking place within the supervision itself. Such a preference tends to make the supervisory relationship into a rather close relationship. How close should it become if its effectiveness is to be optimal?

There appears to be widespread agreement that psychoanalytic supervision may be conducted in a less strict setting than psychoanalysis or psychoanalytically oriented psychotherapy. If transference need not be systematically analyzed, neutrality is not necessary. Even Langs, known to be strict about boundaries in therapy, suggests greater flexibility in supervision (1979, p. 60); and Schlesinger (in Wallerstein 1981, p. 64) describes analytic supervision over lunch. Informality with supervisees may be particularly appealing for psychoanalysts strained by maintaining anonymity and neutrality with their analysands and yearning for more relaxed moments in their day.

Is such informality helpful to the supervisee as well? I believe it is in most instances, but not always. It acquires a unique meaning for each supervisee according to his dynamics, emotional state, and transference implications, as illustrated by these two examples.

> Noticing his supervisee's anxiety, a supervisor attempted to improve the atmosphere by small talk and more personal comments. The trainee's anxiety appeared to increase. A later exploration revealed a fantasy that he was seductive toward her and fear of reciprocal impulses in herself. Formality would have calmed her down much more.

> A trainee got stuck in the middle of a session and finally told her supervisor she was moved by his visible sadness and could not concentrate. After an initial impulse to brush the observation aside or reassure the supervisee of his attention, the supervisor acknowledged his sadness and briefly explained its reasons, feeling that the supervisee's empathy was genuine. Supervision went on, with more openness by the supervisee and greater depth in understanding her own work. After termination, the two became good friends.

The psychoanalytic community at times voices definite skepticism about the combination of supervisory and personal interaction. I have heard of several instances in which psychoanalytic institutes turned down a candidate's request for a particular supervisor (a recognized training analyst), explaining that the two were known to be friends.

Indeed, an already established friendship may make supervision difficult. However, can we be sure that such difficulties can never be surmounted by the two individuals involved? The openness of communication may allow greater depth and subtler understanding. If the two professionals involved believe this can be achieved, should the training committee distrust their judgment?

One wonders whether an additional (not necessarily conscious) motive for a negative position on this issue is the threat posed by supervisor-candidate friendship to the hierarchical structure of the institute. Such hierarchical structure may give the evaluation of trainees (a function clearly damaged by friendship) a disproportionately central weight in comparison to learning proper. The study reported by Wallerstein (1981) does portray the psychoanalytic institute as a setting in which the discussions of faculty about supervisees are much more developed than the supervisor-supervisee dialogue.

CONTROVERSIAL ASPECTS OF THE JOINT EXPLORATION

Several objections have been raised to the explicit exploration of the supervisory relationship, and particularly to the quasi-analytic exploration of transference-countertransference issues. Ekstein and Wallerstein (1972) caution that looking at the interaction in transference-countertransference terms leads to the danger of turning supervision into therapy (e.g., pp. 88, 260).

Of course, supervision and therapy should remain distinct and distinguishable. The belief, heard at times among psychotherapists who are not psychoanalytically oriented, that good supervision can substitute for therapy makes little sense; the setting and time limits of supervision never allow for a full in-depth understanding of the supervisee's life. Nor should they.

Still, I believe there is an *unavoidable overlap* if supervision is to be effective. For example, some discussion of a supervisee's recent divorce may be crucial when he is supervised on a patient with marital difficulties, even though the supervisor has no intention whatsoever to help resolve the supervisee's own conflicts about relationships.

When such a major influence on the countertransference is not brought up, supervision may acquire an "as if" quality. Supervisor and therapist go through the motions of discussing the patient, or even some "safe" aspects of countertransference (e.g., annoyance about resistance, elements of role-responsiveness that can be attributed to the patient and are not personally revealing), while those emotions that for the therapist are most powerful during the sessions (related to personal associations) remain hidden, with no chance of discussing their influence.

An alternative suggested at times in the literature is that once a loaded emotional issue surfaces in supervision (whether countertransference toward the patient, transference toward the supervisor, or—what may be most common—a combination of the two) the supervisor should encourage the supervisee to explore the issue in his analysis. The futility of such recommendations is discussed by Issacharoff (in Caligor et al. 1984, p. 96): "The psychoanalytic process does not necessarily allow for the intrusion of an issue—on command—because it would be convenient in the training process." I find such requests just as unfair as their opposite—the request by a close friend not to reveal some intimate facts in the analysis. I would prefer to explore the issue in the supervision itself to the degree that it is appropriate, and to leave further analytic work to the initiative and timing of the supervisee, within his spontaneous associative process.

The discussion of the supervisory relationship may in itself become an aspect of resistance or counterresistance. One example would be the trainee's use of such exploration as a weapon against his personal analyst. Being both in analysis and in supervision often leads to split transference and to a preoccupation with comparisons. This is intensified when the trainee's friends are in analysis with his supervisor and/or in supervision with his analyst. Langs (1979, p. 347) focuses in this context on instances of inadequacy of either the analyst or the supervisor, but in my experience the situation may be loaded even if both are competent. Sometimes, however, it is precisely the lack of awareness of the competition within the supervisory situation that allows its competitive use, as in the following example.

> An analysand made considerable efforts to emotionally mobilize his analyst into "a male alliance" against his mother and wife. While attempting to interpret this need, the analyst came to realize that it was already being gratified in another setting: the analysand had created the yearned-for alliance with his (male) supervisor, by presenting a highly disturbed and resistant female patient, who annoyed both him and his supervisor.

Langs (1979, p. 62) discusses the possible attempt to use supervision to dilute one's therapy and mentions such manipulations as one reason not to initiate discussions of the supervisory relationship. His position is a complex one: he attributes much importance to the relationship, sees it as considerably influencing the therapy (reverse parallel process is emphasized, with the supervisor's countertransference often responsible for crises in the therapy; p. 198), but prefers to study the supervisory relationship indirectly, by inferring its impact from the patient's responses (p. 31). In my experience, when issues in the relationship are pressing, the avoidance of their direct verbalization and the demand that the supervisee stick to process notes from the therapy may have a stifling impact.

The exploration of the supervisee's transference, however, may be abused in the service of infantilizing or "pathologizing" him. This is particularly true when the discussion is imposed by the supervisor without much attention to the supervisee's wishes, when it is conducted from a position of omniscience and pseudo-objectivity, and when the supervisor avoids exploring his own countertransference. Consider the following example.

> A supervisee reported to his supervisor that he had consulted another faculty member regarding his case. The supervisor noticed a smile on the student's face and interpreted it as an expression of sadistic victory over the supervisor. She further discussed sadistic elements in the student's personality. The student knew there was a point to the supervisor's comment. However, he felt unable to acknowledge it or openly discuss it, feeling too threatened by the condemning supervisor, who would not acknowledge her own sadistic side, evident in the harsh formulation of the interpretation. The tension was never fully resolved.

A supervisor willing to discuss some of his countertransference as well (Langs, 1979, p. 193) has a better chance of achieving a freer discussion of pathological aspects to the supervisee's reactions without becoming intrusive and humiliating. A mutual search into the contributions of both partners to a difficulty is more likely to lead to greater trust and to a relief of tension originating from transferential fears and distortions.

A related issue, raised by Shevrin (in Wallerstein 1981, p. 315), is the hazard that interpretations of transference in supervision may be abused to deny the reality influences of an institutional context—in his case, the power structure of a psychoanalytic institute (compare Berman and Segel 1982). The possibility of such abuse must be recognized, as the serious exploration of the supervisory encounter should be based on a full understanding of its realistic setting (including transferences to the institution by both supervisor and supervisee) rather than on denial of reality factors.

Recent work on transference, such as the work of Gill (1982) or Sandler and Sandler (1983), may supply us with a better model for the exploration of transference within the supervisory situation. The more traditional views of transference emphasized the centrality of genetic reconstruction, which cannot be accomplished in supervision. They often focused on the more intense manifestations of transference, which can be observed mostly within a transference neurosis, more likely to develop in analysis. (For an exception, see Fleming and Benedek 1966, p. 77.) The newer models, on the other hand, emphasize the "present unconscious" and the transference occurring in the "here and now" of the interaction, often expressed within seemingly unrelated communication and in subtle indirect forms to which the analyst must become attentive.

Without entering the debate over the gains and losses involved in these new approaches (and the differences between them), I see them as valid contributions and find the sensitivity they encourage to the emotional nuances of an interpersonal interaction quite applicable to supervision. Attentiveness to the "here and now" of the analysand may be increased by respecting the "here and now" of the supervisee. The supervisor, of course, has no need and no chance to fully illuminate such transference manifestations occurring within supervision. Still, their selective discussion may serve to resolve difficulties (particularly around transference resistance), ease the atmosphere, and at the same time serve as a model.

Finally, we must keep in mind that these new approaches may augment a constant hazard: the possibility of an intense narcissistic absorption of the two partners in their exclusive relationship. In analysis, this can lead to a neglect of serious issues in the analysand's life situation. In supervision, a strong emphasis on the supervisory relationship can lead to forgetting the patient. Similarly, a supervisory group may turn into a T-group and abandon its supervisory goals.

There may certainly be crisis periods when such transformations are productive, and flexibility should be maintained. One criterion of a successful resolution of a supervisory crisis, however, is the gradual return to the natural balance, in which understanding of the analysis or therapy is primary and understanding of the supervision itself is important but secondary.

REFERENCES

Abrams S, Shengold L: Some reflexions on the topic of the 30th congress: affects and the psychoanalytic situation. Int J Psychoanal 1978; 59:395-407

Bachrach HM: On the concept of analyzability. Psychoanal Q 1983; 52:180-204

Berman E: Authority and authoritarianism in group psychotherapy. Int J Group Psychother 1982; 32:189-200

Berman E: Eclecticism and its discontents. Israel Journal of Psychiatry and Related Sciences (in press)

Berman E, Segel R: The captive client: dilemmas of psychotherapy in the psychiatric hospital. Psychotherapy: Theory, Research, Practice 1982; 19:31-42

Caligor L, Bromberg PM, Meltzer JD (Eds): Clinical Perspectives on the Supervision of Psychoanalysis and Psychotherapy. New York, Plenum Press, 1984

De Bell DE: A critical digest of the literature on psychoanalytic supervision. J Am Psychoanal Assoc 1963; 11:546-575

Ekstein R, Wallerstein RS: The Teaching and Learning of Psychotherapy, second edition. New York, International Universities Press, 1972

Fleming J, Benedek TF: Psychoanalytic Supervision (1966). New York, International Universities Press, 1983

Gediman HK, Wolkenfeld F: The parallelism phenomenon in psychoanalysis and supervision: its reconsideration as a triadic system. Psychoanal Q 1980; 49:234-255

Gill M: Analysis of Transference. New York, International Universities Press, 1982

Kairys D: The training analysis: a critical review of the literature and a controversial proposal. Psychoanal Q 1964; 33:485-512

Lane RC: The recalcitrant supervisee: The negative therapeutic reaction. Current Issues in Psychoanalytic Practice 1985; 2:65-79

Langs R: The Therapeutic Interaction. New York, Jason Aronson, 1976

Langs R: The Supervisory Experience. New York, Jason Aronson, 1979

Racker H: Transference and Countertransference (1968). London, Maresfield, 1982

Sandler J, Dare C, Holder A: The Patient and the Analyst (1973). London, Maresfield, 1979

Sandler J, Sandler AM: The 'second censorship,' the 'three box model' and some technical implications. Int J Psychoanal 1983; 64:413-425

Stolorow RD, Brandchaft B, Atwood GF: Intersubjectivity in psychoanalytic treatment. Bull Menninger Clin 1983; 47:117-128

Wallerstein RS (Ed.): Becoming a Psychoanalyst. New York, International Universities Press, 1981

Winokur M: A family systems model for supervision of psychotherapy. Bull Menninger Clin 1982; 46:125-138

Section 3

Conflict and Deficit: The Kernberg/Kohut Controversy in Theory and Practice

Edited by
John Munder Ross, Ph.D.

CHAPTER 10

Kernberg on the Borderline: A Simplified Version

William N. Goldstein, M.D.

The writings of Otto Kernberg (1967, 1975, 1977, 1980a, 1980b, 1981) provide important in-depth, systematic, and comprehensive coverage of the borderline personality within a psychodynamic framework. However, the use of complex terminology and language related to an underlying sophisticated psychoanalytic object relations theory makes these writings difficult for many to read and understand. Despite this, Kernberg's writings are certainly of outstanding value as a source for all those interested in the borderline personality. This would include not only sophisticated psychiatrists and psychoanalysts but also psychiatric residents, medical and psychology students, and the many mental health professionals who do not have the training or desire to easily comprehend Kernberg's writings.

The goal of this chapter is to present Kernberg's ideas and concepts in a simplified yet still comprehensive manner. A different organizational framework from that of Kernberg will be used, and there will be some modifications, clarifications, and additions to Kernberg's original writings. Leaving Kernberg's basic ideas and concepts unaltered, I hope to provide an easy way to understand Kernberg's thinking, in depth, on the borderline (Goldstein 1982, 1985).

THE BORDERLINE AS AN UNDERLYING STRUCTURAL CONFIGURATION

Several influential approaches to the borderline personality appear in the psychiatric literature. A predominant approach, exemplified most clearly by Kernberg, focuses on a view of the borderline based on psychodynamic understanding. This perspective pictures the borderline as a specific, stable, pathological personality organization, characterized by a particular kind of underlying structural configuration. That configuration, which includes recognizable patterns of ego and superego functioning and of instinctual drive organization, is resistant to change except via intensive psychotherapeutic intervention. According to this point of view, the diagnosis of borderline should only be made when the underlying structural configuration can be identified. Symptoms and personality traits are understandable in terms of that structure but are never diagnostic by themselves.

Kernberg holds that there are three levels of pathological psychic functioning, with corresponding distinct structural configurations: the neurotic, the borderline, and the psychotic. Diagnostically, all patients can be classified into one of these groups. Structural diagnosis can serve as a supra-ordinate diagnosis—that is, a first-level diagnosis. Later a more specific secondary diagnosis can be added, providing more descriptive information. The secondary diagnoses under the neurotic structural level would include the "classical" neuroses and what Kernberg terms "higher

169

level character pathology" (1971). The secondary diagnoses under the borderline structural level would mainly include what Kernberg terms "lower level character pathology" (1971). The secondary diagnoses under the psychotic structural level would mainly include the classical psychoses. *DSM-III-R* (American Psychiatric Association 1987) diagnoses could also be utilized as the secondary diagnoses.

CORRELATION WITH OTHER APPROACHES

It is useful to contrast Kernberg's structural diagnosis of the borderline with a second approach prevalent in psychiatry today, especially among researchers. This approach attempts to establish a description of the borderline that is easily defined, reliable, and valid. Primary focus here is on symptoms and traits, particularly those that most clearly differentiate the borderline from other groups of patients. Literature reviews, research designs, and statistical methods are employed to try to identify those traits and symptoms. Typically, large checklists are utilized to make the differentiation. The work of Perry and Klerman (1978, 1980) and of Gunderson (1977; Gunderson and Kolb 1978) is representative of this group. *DSM-III-R* (APA 1987) also falls into this category.

In theory, Kernberg's structural approach is much different from the descriptive one. However, in actual practice, one might not find much difference between the two ways of making the diagnosis. Kernberg (Kernberg et al. 1981) has demonstrated a high correlation between his method and that of Gunderson. I believe that there would likewise be a high correlation between Kernberg's method of diagnosis and *DSM-III-R*. Kernberg (1980b) himself feels that although his approach to the borderline is quite different from that of *DSM-III-R*, the two viewpoints are quite compatible and can complement each other.

For completeness, two other theories about the borderline that contrast with Kernberg's might be noted. One views the borderline as within the spectrum of schizophrenia, genetically related to that disorder. The other views the borderline as within the spectrum of affective disorders, possibly representing a subgroup of affective disorders and possibly being genetically related to those disorders.

CHARACTERISTICS OF THE BORDERLINE STRUCTURAL CONFIGURATION

Returning to the idea of the borderline as a level of psychic functioning with a specific underlying structural configuration, I will elaborate the nature of that structure. The configuration is specific in that it has particular strengths along with underlying weaknesses. Although the specificity characterizes ego and superego functioning and instinctual drive organization, the emphasis in Kernberg's work is predominantly on the ego.

The Ego in the Borderline

Relying on the model of Beres (1956) and Bellak (1958), I will describe the borderline's ego with respect to the various ego functions. Recasting Kernberg's work in terms of this ego psychological approach, one can list the borderline's specific relative ego strengths and underlying ego weaknesses. The relative ego strengths are as follows:

1. the relative intactness of reality testing
2. the relative intactness of thought processes
3. the relative intactness of interpersonal relations
4. the relative intactness of the adaptation to reality

It must be stressed that these four strengths are only relative; they easily break down to various degrees in various situations, to be described later. Because these four relative strengths are superficially prominent, they enable the borderline to present a fairly "normal" appearance. These relative strengths, particularly the first two, most clearly differentiate the borderline from the more psychotic individual.

The underlying ego weaknesses are as follows:

1. the combination of poor impulse control and poor frustration tolerance
2. the proclivity to use primitive ego defenses
3. the syndrome of identity diffusion

In contrast to the strengths, the weaknesses become clearly apparent only with a more in-depth understanding of the individual. Unless the person is in a regressed state, a detailed history or a relationship with him or her over time is usually needed in order to observe the weaknesses. Kernberg's (1977, 1981) structural interview, which I shall briefly discuss later, is also helpful in learning about the weaknesses. Because the weaknesses are beneath the surface, they do not usually detract from the borderline's surface appearance of normality. However, they most clearly differentiate the borderline from the more neurotic individual. A more detailed examination of these ego strengths and weaknesses follows.

The Relative Ego Strengths

Reality testing, on a surface level, and in day-to-day functioning, is basically intact. In his recent writings, Kernberg (1980a, 1981) focuses on the intactness of reality testing as a main factor in the differential diagnoses between the borderline and the psychotic structural configurations. Nevertheless, under stress, and in very close interpersonal situations, there is a tendency for this ego function to regress. A regression under stress can lead to brief psychotic episodes. Some diagnosticians think that a distinction can be drawn between the borderline and the schizophrenic because of the nature of the symptoms during these episodes. However, this distinction is difficult to make, and the symptomatology of the borderline during the episodes is often indistinguishable from that of the schizophrenic. What distinguishes the episodes is their brevity, their reversibility, and their relationship to clear-cut precipitating events. Kernberg particularly notes that such episodes are prone to occur with the use of drugs or alcohol or in relation to a transference regression during intensive psychotherapy. However, any obvious stress and any intense interpersonal interaction can trigger the regression. Kernberg does not state exactly how brief or transient the episodes are, but it is safe to assume that they can be as brief as a few minutes and certainly no longer than a day or two. It should be noted that many borderlines never have such episodes. Thus, transient psychotic episodes under stress sometimes contribute to the diagnosis of borderline but their presence is not mandatory for such a diagnosis.

Thought processes, on the surface, in day-to-day functioning, and in structured situations are predominantly secondary process. However, under acute stress and in unstructured situations (such as projective psychological testing), primary process often emerges. Kernberg feels that projective psychological evaluations will invariably reveal primary process thinking in borderline patients, and he substantiated that hypothesis in a research project (Carr et al. 1979) in which psychological tests were administered to a number of borderline patients. In that project, the pattern of secondary process on the WAIS and primary process on the Rorschach was very clear. Nevertheless, my own personal experience with such evaluations has not been so conclusive, particularly with respect to always finding primary process on the Rorschach. One reason for this disagreement might be the variations in the way different persons use psychological tests to make the diagnosis of borderline. Certainly, however, the tendency for the borderline to reveal primary process thinking on the Rorschach but not the WAIS must be noted.

Interpersonal relations in the borderline often seem intact. Superficially, the borderline seems to "relate" to others, can have many acquaintances, and occasionally can even maintain long-term relationships. However, under close scrutiny, it becomes apparent that the relationships are often characterized by a striking lack of depth, empathy, and concern for the other individual as a person. The other person is seen as someone who can be used to meet the borderline's needs rather than as

a person in his own right. The borderline often vacillates between superficial relationships and intense, dependent relationships that are marred
by primitive defenses. The terms "need-fulfilling relationships," "as-if
relationships," or relationships based on part objects are appropriate
here.

A word might now be said about the difference between interpersonal
relations and object relations. The term *interpersonal relations* is used
here to mean the personal interactions that actually take place between
individuals, either in the present or in the past. The term *object relations*
is used here to mean the internalized derivatives of these interactions.
There are several different versions of object relations theory. Kernberg
(1976), clearly influenced by Jacobson (1964), prefers a restricted approach, stressing the build-up of intrapsychic self and object representations, as reflections of early significant interpersonal relationships. Object relations include object images (object representations) that are built
up in the ego as the result of the way the individual perceives, processes,
and internalizes his past interpersonal experiences. Besides object images
(object representations), the term *object relations* technically includes
self images (self representations). These self images are built up in the
ego as a result of the way the individual perceives, processes, and internalizes his varying past conceptions of his self. Thus interpersonal relations describes interactions, involvements, and experiences between individuals; object relations describes a state within the ego. Kernberg
describes the object relations underlying the interpersonal relations in
the borderline as quite primitive. They involve unintegrated and contradictory self and object images and usually lead to unstable and chaotic
interpersonal relations.

Adaptation to reality is superficially intact, in that the borderline usually looks normal and often manifests adequate achievement in work or
school. However, under close scrutiny, the adaptation often seems less
than optimal. The underlying ego weaknesses usually make it very difficult for the borderline to maintain the adaptation over time. Certain
"exceptional" borderlines can maximize strengths and adapt adequately
over time, particularly in structured settings. These individuals often do
quite well professionally, while typically displaying much more chaos in
their social lives. This exceptional group, more than others, seems to seek
out intensive psychotherapy.

The Underlying Ego Weaknesses: Impulse Control and
Frustration Tolerance

Invariably, the borderline displays the combination of poor frustration
tolerance and poor impulse control. There is an inability to delay, a
demand for immediate gratification, and a proclivity to act out under

stress. To make matters more difficult, these characteristics are not infrequently combined with a sense of entitlement. The difficulties most frequently present themselves clinically by a tendency to get into states of disruptive anger, to use drugs and alcohol to avoid frustration and obtain temporary gratification, and to flee the work or interpersonal situation under stress.

Defenses

Defensive functioning shows a proclivity for the use of the more primitive defenses. Kernberg is very definite in postulating a specific constellation of defenses, centering on splitting (rather than repression) and including primitive idealization, primitive forms of projection and denial, devaluation, and omnipotence. Although others are not so specific here, agreement is uniform about the proclivity of the borderline to use more primitive defenses, including those described by Kernberg. A word of caution is needed here. The term "proclivity" may be taken literally. The borderline does not use primitive defenses all the time. The point is that he tends to use them more than the neurotic in day-to-day functioning, and tends to rely on them most often under stress.

To clarify Kernberg's six borderline defenses, he uses the term "splitting" simply to mean the tendency to see things (external objects) in terms of either all good or all bad. Everything is black or white; there are no gray areas. There is often a concomitant tendency, under frustration, toward complete reversals of the split. What was recently seen as all good suddenly is seen as all bad, or vice versa. Primitive idealization is the positive component of the split, toward an external object. The object is viewed as all good, not for any realistic reason but only because the borderline has the need or wish to see it as all good. Devaluation is the negative component of the split, directed toward an external object or toward the self. Omnipotence is the positive component of the split, as directed toward the self. The primitive forms of denial most often seen in the borderline are of a global nature. Two events or areas are clearly remembered in consciousness, yet one is totally denied or ignored. Or, an event or area is clearly remembered, but there is total denial of its implications and consequences.

Kernberg uses the term "projective identification" to refer to a certain kind of primitive projection. Despite Kernberg's explanation of the term, projective identification tends to be used and understood in various ways. Meissner (1980), in reviewing the usages of projective identification, feels that it is a questionable concept and recommends the abandonment of the term. The term "projective identification" itself is misleading, because it certainly involves processes more primitive than identification.

What Kernberg has in mind by projective identification involves two components. The first is projection itself. The second is fusion of self and object images. Projection in the context of fusion of self and object images includes the characteristics that Kernberg attributes to projective identification. As noted, in close interpersonal situations, the borderline has the tendency to regress in reality testing—that is, he has the tendency in such situations to fuse self and object images. Thus, at those times projections take on the characteristics of projective identification, such as the tendency for the individual to continue to experience the projected impulse as part of the self, and his need to control the object onto which the impulse is projected. I agree with Meissner that the use of the term "projective identification" should be limited or even abandoned. Regarding the borderline, the concept of the proclivity to use projection should suffice. At times when projection and fusion of self and object images take place simultaneously, this can simply be stated.

Identity Diffusion

Kernberg uses Erikson's term "identity diffusion" to describe a core problem in the borderline. This problem is frequently described in other terms—for example, the lack of an integrated self-concept, the lack of sense of self, the lack of a real self, the lack of a stable identity, and the lack of a coherent sense of self. The terms "as-if personality" (Deutsch 1942) and "false self" (Winnicott 1965) are also relevant here. In Mahler's (Mahler et al. 1975) terms, the individual has not attained libidinal object constancy. The lack of an integrated self-concept is most readily noted clinically in the borderline's frequent shifts from group to group as he pursues an elusive identity. The term "chameleon-like" has been used to describe the tendency of the patient to become part of whatever group with which he has contact, then to shift alliances easily and rapidly whenever the next group presents itself. The borderline patient is in constant search for and need of external organizations and groups, with which he quickly identifies in an attempt to overcome his unintegrated self-concept.

Underlying identity diffusion is a poorly integrated concept of the self and a poorly integrated concept of objects. Developmentally, as I will elaborate later, the borderline has not integrated good self images with bad self images; nor has he integrated good object images with bad object images. The borderline's self-concept can remain only as a series of multiple contradictory self images, some good and some bad. At one time one self image is involved, at another time, a different one. A comprehensive image of the self is never integrated in a meaningful way. The same applies to the borderline's concept of objects, which can remain only as a series of multiple contradictory object images, some good and some bad, without the attainment of meaningful comprehensive images of others. Because of his fluctuating self and object concepts, the borderline cannot describe himself or significant others in a meaningful way. There is temporal discontinuity regarding the self and others, along with an over-all distortion of perceptions of the self and others. The diagnostician notices that higher level qualities of object relations are inadequate—that is, the patient has trouble manifesting warmth, concern, tactfulness, empathy, understanding, dedication, and the ability to maintain a rela-tionship under frustration.

Other Structural Characteristics: The Superego and the Id

Although Kernberg notes that superego characteristics are less helpful than ego qualities in the differential diagnosis of the borderline, and that they show marked variation from one individual to another, a lack of superego integration is also typical in the borderline. The ego ideal is often overidealized, based mainly on good self and object images. The conscience often includes sadistic components, based mainly on bad im-ages, and is easily externalized. There is often an inability to experience true guilt, along with difficulties in experiencing true concern.

Kernberg does not focus extensively on id characteristics, particularly when considering the differential diagnosis of the borderline. However, he does point out the prevalence of pregenital aggression as a develop-mental and etiological factor. There is a condensation of pregenital and genital conflicts, with a premature development of oedipal conflicts in the second or third year of life. Various kinds of behavioral patterns that emerge from these phenomena are described by Kernberg. These patterns often seem chaotic initially, because they represent combinations of vari-ous underlying conflicts. On the surface there can be pansexuality and chaos, but underneath, as noted, one finds a combination of genital and pregenital conflicts, under the influence of excessive aggression.

A common characteristic of the borderline is what might be termed the nonadaptive use of aggression, or affective instability. Kernberg does not emphasize this, but it is commonly noted throughout the literature. Thus, descriptions of the borderline frequently include the presence of intense affect, usually depressive or hostile. Anger is underlined as the main affect experienced, accompanied by depressed, lonely, and empty feel-ings. The main point is that aggression is not used in constructive, ego-syntonic, adaptive ways, such as sublimations, work, recreation, and enjoyment. Psychoanalytically, this characteristic is related to a defect in the neutralization of aggression. Thus the aggression often breaks through directly in disruptive ways, such as outbursts of anger and rage;

or the aggression is defended against in maladaptive ways and results in other ego-dystonic affect states, such as depression, boredom, and emptiness. Often there can be rapid and dramatic swings from one affect state to another. Despite Kernberg's failure to emphasize these things, I believe that affective instability, a structural derivative involving both the id and the ego, should be added to the three weaknesses discussed under the ego. In other words, I favor a description of the borderline that includes four main structural weaknesses.

THE DIAGNOSIS OF BORDERLINE

The definitive diagnosis of borderline should only be made in accordance with the structural picture. It is best made only after an in-depth examination of the patient, based both on interviews and history. To aid in structural diagnosis, Kernberg (1977, 1981) has developed a special kind of interview, which he calls the structural interview. This interview, by a series of clarifications, confrontations, and interpretations, focuses in depth on three structural characteristics: reality testing, defensive functioning, and identity diffusion. Kernberg feels that a differential diagnosis between borderline, neurotic, and psychotic structural configurations can be adequately attained by the selective focus on these three characteristics. In fact, Kernberg (Carr et al. 1979) has demonstrated that diagnosis via the structural interview is highly correlated with diagnosis by psychological testing. Obviously, to maximize the efficiency of this approach, a series of structural interviews would be most helpful.

Although the definitive diagnosis of borderline should be made only in accordance with the structural picture, certain symptoms or personality constellations outlined by Kernberg are suggestive of the borderline, in that a significant number of patients with these presentations, under close scrutiny, will turn out to be borderline. Since this clearly is not always the case, one must be cautious here. Kernberg emphasizes that these symptoms and personality constellations are only suggestive, because they can also occur in someone with a basically neurotic structural configuration.

With this in mind, a simplified summary of Kernberg's more understandable suggestive symptoms is as follows:

1. excessive, chronic, free-floating anxiety, particularly when combined with other symptoms
2. multiple neurotic symptoms presented at the same time
3. any neurotic symptom that appears quite bizarre or very disabling
4. multiple perverse trends

Kernberg also states that certain personality types often turn out to be in the borderline group. In essence, many schizoid personalities, many hypomanic personalities, and most paranoid personalities would fit into this group. Most impulse-ridden characters, most infantile characters, most narcissistic personalities, and almost all antisocial personalities would also fit here. Many histrionic personalities of *DSM-III-R*, although certainly not the classically defined hysterical personalities, may be borderlines. Further, as indicated in the description of identity diffusion, one can list higher level character traits that are basically lacking in most borderlines: empathy, humor, creativity, warmth, dedication, tactfulness, concern, understanding, interpersonal depth, and true guilt.

DEVELOPMENTAL THEORY

A sophisticated object relations theory, most clearly presented in Kernberg's second book (1976a), underlies his work. To summarize in a very succinct and oversimplified manner, the infant is thought to organize his experiences according to affect states, initially all good and all bad. At first self and object images (representations) are fused and linked with either a positive or negative affect. With time, there is a linkage of discrete units of self images, discrete units of object images, and discrete affect states. Gradually these units evolve into more complex psychic structure. Mahler (Mahler et al. 1975) now provides a widely acceptable developmental model; its emphasis is somewhat different from Kernberg's, but the two are clearly very compatible. Kernberg's object relations model can be more easily understood when transposed to Mahler's model. In recent writings, Kernberg (1981) himself seems quite disposed to use Mahler's model, even modifying his timetable in accordance with her work. I will here invoke Mahler's model to help us understand Kernberg.

Early Object Relations

Mahler postulates that during the early months of life the child goes through an autistic phase (of approximately one month) during which he is oblivious to anything except himself, followed by a symbiotic phase (up to around 5 to 10 months) in which he views his mother (or primary love object) as an extension of himself. This is followed by a separation-individuation phase (lasting up to age 2 or 3 years) in which the child gradually differentiates and separates himself from his mother and begins to establish his identity as a person in his own right. It is only at the completion of this stage that the child has attained libidinal object constancy (to be defined later). It should be noted that regarding all events of the autistic, symbiotic, and separation-individuation phases, Mahler is speaking of intrapsychic phenomena.

Around the transition from the symbiotic to the separation-individuation phase, the child begins to be able to distinguish himself intrapsychically from his mother. The phenomenon is clinically most obvious when the child develops stranger anxiety, as has been eloquently described by Spitz (1965). This momentous accomplishment, the ability of the child to distinguish himself from his mother, is synonymous with the child's acquiring the capacity to test reality and corresponds to Federn's (1954) concept of establishing ego boundaries and to Kernberg's (1969, 1975) concept of being able to differentiate self images from object images.

The Core Developmental Defect in the Psychotic

In accordance with prevalent psychiatric thinking, Kernberg views a failure in this developmental task—the ability to differentiate self images from object images, to establish ego boundaries, to test reality, and to separate oneself intrapsychically from one's mother—as the core developmental defect in the psychotic individual. The borderline, basically, has been able to accomplish this developmental task; for him the main developmental problem comes later. It should be noted that although the borderline has accomplished the task to a major extent compared to the psychotic, mastery of it usually remains far from total. That would explain the ease with which reality testing in the borderline can break down under stress or in close interpersonal realtionships.

The Origins of Splitting

Kernberg holds that even before the child has accomplished the developmental task of self-object differentiation, from early infancy on, he organizes his experiences according to whether the experiences are perceived as positive or negative. He groups experiences into two categories, good and bad. Thus, he sees his mother as either all good or all bad. She is the good mother whenever she gratifies his needs, soothes him, and is ever present; she is the bad mother whenever she frustrates him or is absent. Even at age 1½, when the child has developed object permanency (Piaget's [1954] concept of a a stable visual representation of the mother whether she is present or absent), he still views her as either a good mother or a bad mother. When she frustrates him or leaves him, the child remembers her very well visually; yet his emotional feelings toward her change, and she is perceived as nongratifying and bad.

This tendency to perceive objects as all-good or all-bad, earlier described by Klein (1946), is called splitting. It is not until the child is between the ages of 2 and 3 (usually closer to 3) that he stops using splitting extensively. In a gradual process described eloquently by McDevitt (1975), the child comes to give up splitting and to obtain libidinal object constancy. Libidinal object constancy is defined as the ability of the child to maintain a relatively nonchanging emotional image of the mother as being basically good but having both good and bad qualities, an emotional image that changes little under frustration or during absence.

The Core Developmental Defect in the Borderline

The attainment of libidinal object constancy is the developmental task that is lacking in the borderline. Although Kernberg does not use the term "libidinal object constancy," he states that the borderline has failed in the task of "the integration of self and object images built up under the influence of libidinal drive derivatives with their corresponding self and object images built up under the influence of aggressive drive derivatives" (1969, 1975). This is equivalent to saying that the borderline has not attained libidinal object constancy and that he still uses splitting extensively.

The tendency of the borderline to utilize splitting is not an all-or-none phenomenon. Just as the psychotic does not always test reality poorly, the borderline does not always split. It is more that the borderline had some difficulty, varying from individual to individual, with completing the developmental task of attaining libidinal object constancy. Depending on the individual, the problem can show itself at one extreme as an ever-present defect in this area, or at the other extreme as a defect that only occurs defensively under stress. Although Kernberg emphasizes the defensive nature of splitting, it seems reasonable to conclude that the vast majority of borderline patients would fall somewhere between the two extremes. Kernberg is also not entirely clear about how splitting, once a developmental defect, later is used as a defense (Meissner 1978).

Hartmann (1955) has described the situation in normal development in which libidinal (good) and aggressive (bad) energies are neutralized and then used for ego and superego formation. Kernberg in turn describes the borderline's tendency to split, which prevents adequate neutralization. This failure not only interferes with ego and superego integration but also with normal modulation and differentiation of affects and with the attainment of an integrated self-concept and stable identity.

Developmental Distinction Between the Psychotic, the Borderline, and the Neurotic

To summarize, one can state that the core developmental defect in the psychotic, originating in the first year of life, is the inability to differentiate self images from object images. The most obvious manifestation is the lack of reality testing. In contrast, the core developmental defect in the borderline, originating between the first and third years of life, is the inability to attain libidinal object constancy. The most obvious manifestation is the tendency to split. Using the theories of Kernberg, we can distinguish the psychotic, borderline, and neurotic developmentally as follows: The psychotic fails in the differentiation of self from object images, does not attain libidinal object constancy, displays identity diffusion, and has a poorly formed ego. The borderline basically is able to differentiate self from object images but has not attained libidinal object constancy. He has a relatively weak ego and displays identity diffusion. The neurotic has no difficulty in self-object differentiation, has attained libidinal object constancy, and has a stable ego and an integrated self-concept. Developmentally, the neurotic's problems originate after age 3 and are related to interpersonal relationships involving himself and significant others.

THE BASIC ETIOLOGIC FACTOR IN THE BORDERLINE

Kernberg sees the basic etiologic factor regarding the borderline patient as related to the presence of an excessive amount of aggressive drive in the earliest (pregenital) years of life. The aggressive drive interferes with the unfolding of the separation-individuation process in such a way that splitting is reinforced and libidinal object constancy is never truly attained. Kernberg has theorized that the excessive drive is either due to congenital factors or is secondary to early frustrations. Although Kernberg leaves unclear the relative importance of congenital versus environmental factors, some (Meissner 1978) feel that his primary emphasis leans more toward constitutional factors.

EARLY INTERPERSONAL RELATIONS IN THE BORDERLINE

Kernberg's theory, as noted, is an object relations theory. The emphasis is on self and object images (representations), themselves internalized derivatives of early interpersonal experiences. With this emphasis in mind, Kernberg does not focus on the early interplay between parents and child (interpersonal relations) that gives rise to the (internalized) object relations. Complementing Kernberg nicely and filling in the gaps of what actually may transpire between the potential borderline child and the parents in the early years of life is the eloquent and detailed work of Masterson (1972, 1976) and Rinsley (1977, 1978). A brief summary of their work will be presented here. The mother, often borderline herself and deriving much gratification from the symbiotic involvement with the child, withdraws her emotional availability when the child begins to make an effort to separate and individuate. This process peaks at the rapprochement subphase (16-25 months) of the separation–individuation period, a timing in accordance with Mahler's (1971) writings. Concomitant with the emotional withdrawal of the mother at this time is the absence and unavailability of the father. The child is presented with the dilemma of being faced with a rejecting, disapproving, and withdrawing (bad) mother if he strives for age-appropriate growth, or an approving, rewarding, and comforting (good) mother if he remains dependent, passive, and compliant. The authors explain how these early interactions between mother and child reinforce the child's tendency toward thinking in terms of two mothers, one all good and one all bad, thus reinforcing splitting. Masterson and Rinsley elaborate on the vicissitudes and consequences, in addition to splitting, of early interpersonal relations of this kind. However, for the purpose of relating their theory to that of Kernberg, a further elaboration of their work need not be undertaken here.

Disagreement with Rinsley's and Masterson's work focuses on several issues. One is lack of evidence that the early interpersonal relations of the potential borderline and his mother are actually in accordance with Masterson's and Rinsley's interpersonal theory. A second is doubt about the specificity of the precise timing postulated regarding interactions in the rapprochement subphase of the separation-individuation period. Because of such questions, some theorists feel that Rinsley's and Masterson's work applies only to a small subgroup of borderline patients.

PSYCHOTHERAPY

Psychotherapy with the borderline is a very controversial area today. Many different approaches, from pure psychoanalysis to supportive psychotherapy, have been advocated. Although many of the early psychoanalytic writers recommended a supportive approach, the current consensus now seems to have shifted to the use of a modified form of psychoanalytically oriented psychotherapy—in particular, Kernberg's version.

Kernberg (1975, 1976b, 1978, 1980a, 1982) has clearly outlined a specific kind of psychoanalytically oriented psychotherapy, which he calls expressive psychotherapy, that he finds useful for many borderline patients. Kernberg's expressive approach is similar to psychoanalysis in that the therapist's neutrality is maintained as much as possible, interpretation and clarification are the primary therapeutic techniques, and the main therapeutic focus is on the exploration of the transference. However, because of the borderline's specific psychopathology, none of these three tasks can be carried out in the same way as in psychoanalysis. Primitive transferences immediately become active in the treatment setting and serve as resistances. These primitive transferences are based on multiple contradictory self and object images, include numerous primitive defenses, and initially can appear quite chaotic. They often result in severe acting out and psychotic distortions within the transference, which can undermine and threaten the overall treatment process. Accordingly, therapeutic focus on these transferences must be rapid and in the here and now. Interpretation and clarification remain the major techniques used to deal with the transferences, but they are often not enough. Interventions involving the structuring of the external life of the patient are often needed. Time-limited hospitalization may become necessary. Interventions of this kind make it impossible for the therapist to constantly remain neutral, but the goal of returning to the neutral position whenever possible is maintained. Because of the need for intense focus on areas where acting out and reality distortions threaten the treatment, exploration of the transference is not as systematic as in psychoanalysis proper. With much psychotherapeutic work, the more primitive transferences are gradually worked through and replaced by more typically "neurotic" transferences. As this happens the treatment becomes more similar to that traditionally used for neurotic patients.

Noting the typically recurring difficulties in the treatment of the borderline by his "expressive" approach, Kernberg (1982) offers a number of guidelines in managing the transference. He advocates a basic strategy of interpreting the negative transference and the primitive aspects of the positive transferences, while "respecting" those aspects of the positive transference that gradually foster the development of the therapeutic alliance. Negative transferences are systematically elaborated initially only in the here and now, without psychogenetic reconstructions. Because interpretation of the primitive defenses gradually brings about structural change, thus strengthening the ego, the typical primitive defensive constellations are interpreted as soon as they enter the transference. Because the borderline often distorts the therapist's interpretations, the patient's understanding of the therapist's interpretations needs to be regularly and systematically examined and clarified. As mentioned, because there is such a tendency for destructive acting out of the transference, limit setting and structuring of the patient's life outside of the hours is often necessary. As the patient advances in psychotherapy and the more primitive transferences are gradually converted to higher level or "neurotic" transferences, these guidelines need to be followed less frequently.

REFERENCES

American Psychiatric Association: Diagnostic and Statistical Manual of Mental Disorders, Third Edition, Revised (DSM-III-R). Washington, DC, American Psychiatric Association, 1987

Bellak L: Schizophrenia: A Review of the Syndrome. New York, Logis Press, 1958

Beres D: Ego deviation and the concept of schizophrenia. Psychoanal Study Child 1956; 2:164-235.

Carr C, Goldstein E, Hunt H, et al: Psychological tests and borderline patients. J Pers Assess 1979; 43:582-590

Deutsch H: Some forms of emotional disturbance and their relationship to schizophrenia. Psychoanal Q 1942; 11:301-321

Federn P: Ego Psychology and the Psychoses. New York, Basic Books, 1954

Goldstein W: Understanding Kernberg on the borderline patient. Journal of the National Association of Private Psychiatric Hospitals 1982; 13:21-26

Goldstein W: An Introduction to the Borderline Conditions. Northvale, NJ, Jason Aronson, 1985

Gunderson J, Kolb J: Discriminating features of borderline patients. Am J Psychiatry 1978; 135:792-796

Hartmann H: Notes on the theory of sublimation. J Am Psychoanal Assoc 1955; 10:9-29

Jacobson E: The Self and the Object World. New York, International Universities Press, 1964

Kernberg O: Borderline personality organization. J Am Psychoanal Assoc 1967; 15:641-685

Kernberg O: A psychoanalytic classification of character pathology. J Am Psychoanal Assoc 1971; 18:800-821

Kernberg O: Borderline Conditions and Pathological Narcissism. New York, Jason Aronson, 1975

Kernberg O: Object Relations Theory and Clinical Psychoanalysis. New York, Jason Aronson, 1976a

Kernberg O: Technical considerations in the treatment of borderline personality organization. J Am Psychoanal Assoc 1976b; 24:795-829

Kernberg O: Structural diagnosis of borderline personality organization, in Borderline Personality Disorders: The Concept, the Syndrome, the Patient. Edited by Hartocollis P. New York, International Universities Press, 1977

Kernberg O: Contrasting approaches to the psychotherapy of borderline conditions, in New Perspectives of Psychotherapy of the Borderline Adult. Edited by Masterson JF. New York, Brunner/Mazel, 1978

Kernberg O: Internal World and External Reality. New York, Jason Aronson, 1980a

Kernberg O: Neurosis, psychosis, and borderline states, in Comprehensive Textbook of Psychiatry, Vol. 3. Third Edition. Edited by Freedman A, Kaplan H, Sadock B. Baltimore, Williams and Wilkins, 1980b.

Kernberg O: Structural interviewing, in The Psychiatric Clinics of North America; Symposium on Borderline Disorders. Philadelphia, W. B. Saunders, 1981

Kernberg O: The psychotherapeutic treatment of borderline personalities, in Psychiatry Update: The American Psychiatric Association Annual Review, Vol. I. Edited by Grinspoon L. Washington, DC, American Psychiatric Press, 1982

Kernberg O, Goldstein E, Carr A, et al: Diagnosing borderline personality: a pilot study using multiple diagnostic methods. J Nerv Ment Dis 1981; 169:225-231

Klein M: Notes on some schizoid mechanisms. Int J Psychoanal 1946; 27:99-110

Mahler M: A study of the separation-individuation process and its possible application to borderline phenomena in the psychoanalytic situation. Psychoanal Study Child 1971; 26:403-424

Mahler M, Pine F, Bergman A: The Psychological Birth of the Human Infant. New York, Basic Books, 1975

Masterson J: Treatment of the Borderline Adolescent: A Developmental Approach. New York, Wiley-Interscience, 1972

Masterson J: Psychotherapy of the Borderline Adult: A Developmental Approach. New York, Brunner-Mazel, 1976

McDevitt J: Separation-individuation and object constancy. J Psychoanal Assoc 1975; 23:713-742

Meissner W: Theoretical assumptions of concepts of the borderline personality. J Am Psychoanal Assoc 1978; 26:559-598

Meissner W: A note on projective identification. J Am Psychoanal Assoc 1980; 28:43-67

Perry J, Klerman G: The borderline patient: a comparative analysis of four sets of diagnostic criteria. Arch Gen Psychiatry 1978; 35:141-150

Perry J, Klerman G: Clinical features of the borderline personality disorder. Am J Psychiatry 1980; 137:165-173

Piaget J: The Construction of Reality in the Child. New York, Basic Books, 1954

Rinsley D: An object relations view of borderline personality, in Borderline Personality Disorders: the Concept, the Syndrome, the Patient.

Edited by Hartocollis P. New York, International Universities Press, 1977

Rinsley D: Borderline psychopathology: a review of aetiology, dynamics, and treatment. International Review of Psychoanalysis 1978; 5:45-54

Spitz R: The First Year of Life: A Psychoanalytic Study of Normal and Deviant Development of Object Relations. New York, International Universities Press, 1965

Winnicott D: The Maturational Processes and the Facilitating Environment. New York, International Universities Press, 1965

CHAPTER 11

A Critical Review of Kernberg's Theory of Borderline Personality Organization

Yale Kramer, M.D.

The following discussion of Otto Kernberg's theory of borderline personality organization was written in the spring of 1978 as part of a longer report made by the Kris Study Group of the New York Psychoanalytic Institute to its members. The Kris Study Groups continue to function in memory of Ernst Kris as a way of perpetuating and honoring his interest in intellectual inquiry and advancement. Kris Study Groups are formed at irregular intervals under the chairmanship of one of the senior faculty members of the New York Psychoanalytic Institute and are made up of those graduate analysts who enjoy the dogged pursuit and clarification of elusive analytic concepts. Taking whatever safety they can from numbers, they often tackle complex issues. Naturally placing a high value on depth and thoroughness, they sometimes convene, like the Council of Trent, for long periods of time. Our group, the Kris Study Group on Borderline States, met for discussion once a month between 1973 and 1977.

Because the subject had become a burning issue by then—not least because of Kernberg's exciting and controversial ideas—the study group was quite popular, and at meetings between 15 and 20 analysts and advanced candidates were almost always present. Although the membership shifted somewhat from year to year, a "hard core" of 10 or 12 members participated for the entire four-year period.[1] The range of experience in the group varied from senior training analysts to recent graduates, with perhaps a modal group of "middle-aged" analysts. The meetings were chaired by Charles Brenner, and each meeting was recorded and summarized by a different member of the group each month.

The natural inclination of the group was to alternate clinical description and theoretical discussion. One of the members of the group might present a case in considerable clinical detail over a period of several months, allowing as much time as necessary for a thorough discussion and exchange of opinion. When interest slackened either a new case was introduced or we shifted our attention to some relevant sector of the literature. Thus during our four-year study we were able to explore the clinical data of five or six cases in depth, supplemented by countless clinical vignettes supplied by various members of the group. Finally, we were able to consider the important contributions to the literature on borderline phenomena in the light of our own collective experience.

---

[1] Participants: Sander Abend, M.D., Klaus Angel, M.D., Leon Balter, M.D., David Beres, M.D., Charles Brenner, M.D., Kenneth Calder, M.D., Gerald Epstein, M.D., Richard Glass, M.D., Herbert Gomberg, M.D., Jay Harris, M.D., Winslow Hunt, M.D., David Hurst, M.D., Daniel Justman, M.D., Robert Kaplan, M.D., Richard Kopff, M.D., Yale Kramer, M.D., Neil Lebowitz, M.D., Edward Nersessian, M.D., Teruko Neuwalder, M.D., Winfred Overholser, M.D., Michael S. Porder, M.D., Bruce Ruddick, M.D., Robert Scharf, M.D., Hilda Shanzer, M.D., Susan Sherkow, M.D., Matthew Tolchin, M.D., Herbert Waldhorn, M.D., Sherwood Waldron, Jr., M.D., Henry Weinstein, M.D., Martin Willick, M.D.

189

More than any other contributions to the field, however, the work of Otto Kernberg was the focus of our study. The reason is self-evident and need not be labored. In the past 10 or 15 years he has written more on borderline states in a complex and thoughtful way than any other author in the field. Because of this we spent many hours examining his ideas and testing them against our own experience.

Nevertheless, many aspects of his work remained unclear to us, which prompted us to invite him to meet with us for an exchange of ideas and opinions. Before the meeting, Kernberg was sent a set of our monthly summaries and the case material that we had reviewed, so that he was oriented to our frame of discourse. On January 22, 1977, we held an all-day meeting that turned out to be both fascinating and illuminating—an example of professional and intellectual discourse at its best. Because of the foresight and enterprise of Sherwood Waldron, the meeting was recorded and later transcribed, resulting in a 153-page manuscript.

The following critical review, then, is based on the discussion of that day-long meeting with Kernberg and on the 40 monthly meetings that the study group had during its four-year convention. Although I must accept responsibility for the organization and focus of the ideas in this review, and for any errors or deficiencies in it, I believe that it reflects—to the extent that one document can reflect the opinions of many people—a consensus of the group. Whatever clinical wisdom the report may possess belongs to all the members of the group who contributed to the discussion.

The original review that was distributed to the New York Psychoanalytic Society on April 25, 1978, has been slightly edited to reflect the different context in which it appears now. In addition I have added a brief postscript to bring it up to date.

The borderline personality organization as described by Otto Kernberg is characterized essentially by what he calls "pathological internal object relations," which give rise to "identity diffusion" and the use of primitive defense mechanisms such as splitting and projective identification, among others. He asserts that individuals with such a syndrome develop their pathological internal object relations very early in life—at least prior to the time of the formation of the psychic structure—and that these pathological object relations result from an overload of aggressive impulses, with which the young child cannot cope. "Splitting mechanisms," he explains, represent the child's defensive attempts at compartmentalizing self and object representations of a loving kind from self and object representations of a hateful kind. In a very condensed and over-simplified form, this is what Kernberg believes. Many of the members of the Kris Study Group who have studied so-called borderline phenomena do not share this view. The differences that finally emerged from our discussion seem sharp on many points and slight on others. What follows is a specification of those points of agreement and disagreement. .

WAS OUR PATIENT POPULATION SIMILAR TO KERNBERG'S?

One of the first questions raised in connection with Kernberg's work was whether we were treating and discussing a patient population similar to his. It was difficult to tell from the clinical vignettes that appear in his work whether his patients and ours suffer from a comparable degree of pathology. This question was finally laid to rest in our discussion with him when he indicated that the cases we submitted to him for discussion fell well within the range of the patients with whom he deals. He indicated to us also that he tends to prefer to take on cases that many analysts would not think suitable for analysis or exploratory psychotherapy; but he ventured a guess that we as a group might undertake such challenging patients, too.

IS "BORDERLINE PERSONALITY ORGANIZATION" A QUALITATIVE OR A QUANTITATIVE CONCEPT?

A related issue that became a central focus of discussion early in our work was whether the concept "borderline" had an essentially quantitative or qualitative meaning. Is there any advantage to be gained from calling a patient a "borderline personality organization" as distinct from calling such a patient sicker than neurotic and not as sick as psychotic? Kernberg, of course, asserts that he is describing a sharply demarcated *class* of patients—those he claims have a specific ego-structure and a qualitatively different type of object relations; furthermore, for Kernberg this has important therapeutic implications, which he claims should give rise to a specific and preferred technique of psychotherapy. Kernberg maintained this position during our discussion with him, and he was questioned specifically on that point. In response Kernberg said, "Why call it borderline? Why not say severe character pathology? I have no objections to that, except that when you say severe, you don't quite highlight the common features that have been described in the literature; but this really may be an element of semantics." Our reply to Kernberg on this point was that what he claims has been described in the literature is precisely what is in question. Kernberg could not validate his position any further, and the group was left with the opinion that he had not produced adequate clinical evidence to validate the existence of common features in the wide variety of character disorders that he claims form a class called "borderline personality organization."

Furthermore, based on its collective experience, the group could not confirm Kernberg's hypothesis that such common features occur; finally, we could see no practical advantage accruing to the use of that term in contrast to terms such as "severe character pathology," which emphasizes quantitative rather than qualitative differences. When we examined our own patients with regard to ego structure, types of defenses, and conflicts observed, we mainly found differences of degree rather than kind.

THE ISSUE OF EVIDENCE

Some members of our group felt that Kernberg's complex theoretical superstructure could not be supported comfortably by the evidence he provides. He offers two kinds of evidence, and both seemed flawed to us. The first kind of evidence comes from his work as a collaborator on the Menninger Foundation Psychotherapy Research Project (Kernberg et al. 1972). Kernberg implies in a general way that some or all of his work on borderlines is based on this empirical study. In fact, in only several places in his monographs and papers does he utilize the Menninger study as supporting evidence. For example, in his discussion of prognosis in borderline personality organization he refers to the variables of anxiety and ego weakness as prognostic indicators and cites the Menninger study as evidence. He makes one or two other references to it in an explicit way in the monograph, but for the most part the relationship between Kernberg's theories about borderline personality organization and this empirical research remain implicit and ambiguous.

We felt that it would be more desirable if Kernberg had specified more clearly in what ways his theory was based on the Menninger study, since the latter does not deal with the question of borderline personality organization as such but rather with the issues of treatment modalities as they relate to a large array of patient variables. Although there may be some overlapping concepts, the Menninger study utilizes a conceptual framework considerably different from that which Kernberg uses in his theory of borderline personality organization; for example, a central concept in the latter, "pathological internalized object relations," never appears in the Menninger study.

The second kind of evidence Kernberg provides is a series of highly condensed and summarized clinical vignettes. Although they often managed to illustrate a point Kernberg was making, we felt the need of one or two full-fledged case reports that would describe in considerable detail the patient's history, the course of his illness, and the vicissitudes of treatment. Kernberg does not provide this in any of his work. Some members of the group felt that the absence of such detailed cases was one of the most serious weaknesses in Kernberg's work.

Kernberg might reply to this criticism that since it is a convention of analytic literature to offer clinical vignettes, why should we draw the line at his work? We would have to answer that there is a difference between using vignettes to illustrate clinical points within the context of a well-established conceptual framework and using vignettes as evidence in the service of a new theoretical departure. The greater and more complex the departure, the more evidence is required to make the new theory compelling. We felt that Kernberg does his work a disservice in thus limiting his evidence to clinical vignettes rather than detailed case reports.

IS THE EVIDENCE OPEN TO ALTERNATIVE INTERPRETATION?

Furthermore, we found that on close inspection the clinical material that Kernberg did provide in his papers and during our discussion with him lent itself to alternative interpretations quite different from his. I would like to cite one example, from among a number of possibilities, of material that Kernberg presented to the group from a case that he had treated. In his work with the patient Kernberg uncovered two transference fantasies. One was a sadomasochistic sexual fantasy, the other a maternal-oral-merger fantasy. Kernberg states that when one was present the other was absent and vice versa, and that the two fantasies appeared alternatively over a period of months. He states further that when he attempted to interpret the meaning of each fantasy to the patient, little or nothing happened in the treatment.

Kernberg understood these clinical events in the following way. He asserted, in terms of his theory, that each of the two fantasies was "like a complete object relation which is highly unrealistic and primitive because it stemmed from the very early period of development—a prestructural" period of development, possibly in the first or second year of life. He asserted further that these two contradictory primitive object relations—one characterized by preoedipal love, the other characterized by preoedipal aggression, and neither of them repressed—were maintained by a dissociating process called splitting, which maintained the two object relations separately for defensive purposes. He said also that the patient maintained these object relations separate and apart for fear that the hate would destroy the love, and that the existence of the two separately organized and split object relations constitutes what he calls "pathological internalized object relations," with many serious developmental implications ultimately resulting in the borderline personality organization.

He asserted further than in order to make therapeutic progress with this patient he had to bring the two separate object relations together by confronting the patient repeatedly with one fantasy when she was manifesting the other, and vice versa. This interpretive step was necessary and gave rise to anxiety in the patient and in addition allowed the treatment to progress.

In our discussion various members of the group were able to formulate an alternative interpretation of the clinical facts that was significantly different from Kernberg's, using clinical ideas more familiar to us. One member, for example, suggested that "some of the anxiety about the sexual relationship in the paternal transference fantasy was that it involved a wish to kill the mother . . . and a fear of retaliation from the mother," and that the maternal dependent fantasy was a defense against the sadomasochistic sexual fantasy. In fact, each of the two fantasies was a defense against the other, and each was manifested depending on what the patient experienced as the greater danger at the time. This is in keeping with the common clinical observation that patients often use drive derivatives of an opposing nature to ward off their opposites; at times patients will ward off aggressive impulses with positive transference manifestations and at other times ward off sexual wishes with hostile transference manifestations.

The important difference between Kernberg's theoretical view and clinical technique and the point of view of the rest of the group was that Kernberg emphasized the dissociation as the predominant defense and therefore tended to emphasize connecting the two fantasies. The group, on the other hand, tended to emphasize the use of one fantasy as a defense against the other, arguing that the defense was motivated by a specific anxiety or danger that has to be interpreted as well—in this case, object loss or loss of love. In our view what was important was the interpretation of the defense and the danger that motivates it. Kernberg, in contrast, emphasizes the bringing together of the two fantasies as the crucial interpretive work.

It was apparent from the discussion of this material that Kernberg's emphasis was both theoretically and technically different from ours. It would be very difficult, however, to determine the degree of the difference without actually reviewing the ongoing clinical details of the case. It would be unjust to Kernberg's skill as a clinician to exaggerate these differences and unfair to his theory to minimize them. Clearly, though, he understands the data differently, he conceptualizes the data differently, and he responds to the data technically in a different way. The degree of the difference and similarities will have to remain moot at this time because we do not have enough data from Kernberg for greater precision.

In other instances in which Kernberg offers clinical evidence in his work, the data he presents can also be alternatively understood using a clinical model that is more traditionally psychoanalytic. In other words, his clinical evidence often lends itself to technical formulations somewhat different from his own.

DOES KERNBERG UNDEREMPHASIZE REPRESSION AS A DEFENSE?

In our discussions with Kernberg, another important difference readily became apparent. Since Kernberg's theory asserts that patients with borderline personality organization tend predominantly to use splitting mechanisms rather than repressive mechanisms because, he says, the pathological events occur at a "prestructural" time in the individual's development he tends to understand the psychological data—thoughts, feelings, actions, symptoms, attitudes—as though they represented the "true" endopsychic state of things. For example, for Kernberg the two fantasies described above represented primitive object relations that began early in the individual's development. Because repression does not seem to play an important part in Kernberg's theory, there is a tendency to blur the distinction between manifest and latent content.

For example, various members of the group might listen to a patient who complained of contradictory feelings about himself associated with feelings of confusion, and understand this complaint as the manifest content of a symptom. This would naturally lead them to search for an understanding of the underlying meaning of the symptom before they made any interpretations to the patient. We think that Kernberg, on the other hand, would tend to understand this symptom as "identity diffusion," which he believes reflects the underlying split in the patient's self-object relations.

In a hypothetical case, Kernberg might interpret paranoid anger in a patient as one half of a split-off object relation with the additional use of projective identification as a mechanism; members of the group, however, might interpret such paranoid anger as a projective defense against unbearable guilt and castration anxiety motivated by unconscious sadomasochistic fantasies.

DEVELOPMENTAL ISSUES

Since so much of Kernberg's theory centers around the use of splitting mechanisms that begin in a "prestructural" phase of development, many questions were raised about psychogenesis and development in connection with his theory and practice. Several interrelated issues emerged in the discussion. One was the question of chronology: At what approximate age did Kernberg think the crucial events occurred that would result in "pathological internalized object relations"? A second concerned how these events were related to the Oedipus crisis. A third asked what Kernberg meant by the term "primitive," which occurs in connection with much of the clinical material he describes.

Kernberg, of course, believes that the pathogenic determinants of the borderline personality organization are largely preoedipal. He tended to hedge a bit when it came to identifying a particular chronological epoch. He appeared to have changed his position, stated in his earlier papers, that the crucial pathogenic events occurred within the first year. Now he seems to believe that a more likely chronology would be around what Mahler calls the "rapprochement subphase." There is a difficulty with that chronological hypothesis, however; if, as Kernberg suggests, the rapprochement subphase is the period during which pathogenic events could activate splitting mechanisms that result in pathological internalized object relations, then one might expect to observe such splitting mechanisms in children who have rapprochement crises. In fact, McDevitt has reported on the case of Donna, a child who suffered an unresolved rapprochement crisis (1979). McDevitt has followed the patient into her eighth year, and instead of splitting mechanisms, he finds character defenses based strongly on repression and reaction formations; he also reports that in other children with rapprochement traumata splitting mechanisms were not strongly in evidence. Since we ourselves found little or no evidence for the genetic assertions in Kernberg's published work, we raised these questions with him during our dialogue.

Kernberg states that patients with borderline personality organization tend to develop what he calls "primitive" transference in the treatment. When we asked him to define what he meant by "primitive," he tended to offer words that seemed to many of us tautological, such as crude, simple, highly unrealistic. It seemed to many of us much more difficult than it was for Kernberg to distinguish between fantasies that were highly unrealistic, moderately unrealistic, or merely unrealistic. In fact, some of the clinical materials that he presents in his papers did not seem to us any more primitive than other material we were used to dealing with. Kernberg and members of the study group agreed that very often one could not ascertain unambiguously from what developmental phase certain clinical material originated. Both he and the group felt that there was so much condensation and intertwining of oedipal and preoedipal material that it was not possible to make a phase-specific "diagnosis" with very much certainty.

Despite such ambiguity, Kernberg tended to make the assumption that the predominant pathology crystallized prior to the oedipal phase. When we questioned him regarding evidence in support of this position, he agreed with us in the case that we presented to him that one could not rule out a pathological regression as a partial resolution to the patient's oedipal conflicts. In other cases, however, he asserted that he was able to reconstruct traumas and fixations prior to the oedipal phase. However, he was not able at that time to support his assertion with clinical evidence.

We noticed in this discussion, too, Kernberg's tendency to assume little or no distinction between manifest and latent content of the so-called primitive transference manifestations. We assume that this does not represent a technical lapse on his part, but is based on his theoretical position that repression does not play an important part in the defensive structure of these patients.

In summary, then, we tended to disagree with Kernberg about the "primitivity" of the clinical material that he described and also to disagree with him that there was any compelling clinical evidence for assuming that these patients suffer predominantly from pathological fixations rather than regressions.

ISSUES OF TECHNIQUE

Structuring

Kernberg's therapeutic suggestions for the treatment of the borderline personality organization emphasize two major techniques which derive from his theoretical position. These techniques apply primarily to the earlier phases of the treatment.

The first major technical suggestion is what Kernberg calls "structuring." By this Kernberg means that he would advise the enlistment of inpatient settings or additional professional aides (psychiatric nurses, social workers, etc.) to prevent the patient from acting out in a dangerous way. This, he suggests, will allow the therapist to function in an analytically neutral way without being susceptible to the patient's provocations. The technique has been used in the past in the treatment of delinquents and addicts in psychoanalytically oriented inpatient settings. Kernberg has revived this therapeutic idea because he believes that borderline states can and should be treated along analytic lines. In the past we would have hesitated to do so for the very reason that such patients tend to act out in possibly dangerous ways, which might be inappropriate for outpatient treatment. It would be highly desirable if Kernberg could share more of the details of how he does it.

Interpreting Splitting

The second of Kernberg's major therapeutic suggestions I have touched on before—namely, his technique for undoing the splitting mechanisms that he encounters in his patients. This involves the diagnosis of contradictory "ego states" and confrontating the patient with these contradictory behavioral patterns. Kernberg claims that the technique results in anxiety at first, followed by more integrated functioning by the patient.

As I indicated before, various members of the study group could not confirm Kernberg's observation of splitting mechanisms in their patients. Where so-called splitting mechanisms seemed to be manifest, we found that we could understand the clinical data more easily as evidence of ambivalence, or as defensive reversals using one drive derivative as a defense against another. Indeed, during the past few years, when some of us have made various attempts to use Kernberg's suggested techniques for undoing the splitting mechanisms in our work with borderline patients, we have not observed the development of anxiety in the patient nor improved integrative functioning. We suggest that without a detailed description of Kernberg's technical operations it is difficult to replicate his methods and to test them definitively.

KERNBERG'S CRITICISM OF OUR TECHNIQUE

In his turn, Kernberg criticized us for not analyzing our patients properly. He suggested that if we had analyzed our cases along the lines that he suggests, we would have indeed found splitting mechanisms. In other words, he argued that we do not observe what he observes because we do not use the method that he uses. What he means specifically is what he calls "a systematic analysis of the transference." To quote Kernberg, discussing one of the cases we submitted to him:

> I start out from common sense and then go into this paranoid transference doggedly from a technically neutral attitude, willing to go to the last resources of a crazy delusional system, without being afraid of it. . . . Now my assumption is that if you had done this with this patient, you might have found intense rage at you, rage attacks, and sadistic efforts to control you, and I would have said, "This patient has projective identification." . . . In this case, I felt that the basic transference was not taken up.

Kernberg would assert this despite the fact that the case was brought to a conclusion with considerable symptomatic and structural change. Kernberg suggested that the analyst could have done it faster and better using his techniques.

Although various members of the group were impressed by Kernberg's claims, we felt that they would be more compelling if supported with more extensive clinical case material. Our own experience indicated that Kernberg tended to overvalue the existence of "systematic paradigms" of transference. Our clinical experience shows us that our patients' major conflicts manifest themselves in a more free-form way; we tend to find that major conflicts appear in the transference, disappear, and reappear in various forms as they are worked through. Many of us felt that the "transference paradigm" is something of a clinical illusion.

We also wondered whether Kernberg's "dogged" pursuit of the transference might be a little *too* dogged, and we wondered also whether such confrontation might underemphasize defensive considerations. It is possible that when a patient's aggression is mobilized by an aggressive act of the analyst, even if it is in the form of a doggedly pursued interpretation, the patient's reactive aggression is not, properly speaking, a "negative transference"—or rather, even if it is, it can no longer be demonstrated to be such.

Finally, this type of dogged pursuit may be masochistically enjoyed by many patients, and specific transferences can hide behind such enjoyment and escape discovery.

WHAT IS PROJECTIVE IDENTIFICATION?

One of the terms that Kernberg uses frequently is "projective identification," a term that has been used by numerous authors in a variety of ways to mean many different things. If we understood Kernberg correctly, he uses it in the following way. An impulse, affect, or attitude is both externalized and at the same time experienced by the patient. The behavior is also accompanied by attempts by the patient to control the projected impulse in the object. After much discussion, various members of the group and Kernberg agreed that the phenomenon could be understood as a "failed projection" . . . that is, the individual has not been able to externalize the impulse completely but remains aware of it in himself. We felt that the mechanism very often occurs in many other types of patients besides borderline states. We did not feel that there was anything unique about this defense, but rather that it was another example of our general finding that all types of defensive mechanisms occur in various combinations over the entire spectrum of psychopathology.

POSSIBLE THEORETICAL INCONSISTENCIES

Finally, if one looks over Kernberg's theory as a whole one sees a complex, multidimensional, and apparently consistent theory that covers psychogenetic, dynamic, descriptive, adaptive, diagnostic, prognostic, and therapeutic issues. However, if one examines the matrix of the theory a little more closely, one sees that Kernberg has borrowed concepts and terms from many different theoretical orientations; those orientations use different models of the mind and are often based on different sets of terms. If they do use the same terms, they sometimes use them in different ways. Many of these orientations are theoretically incompatible, therapeutically incompatible, or conceptually inconsistent. Kernberg uses concepts from Freud, Melanie Klein, Winnicott, Fairbairn, Rosenfeld, Erikson, Jacobson, Mahler, and others. We are not unmindful that there are many valid truths in all of these theoretically disparate systems—some more, some less. However, we are also aware that Erikson's theory of the mind is quite different from Melanie Klein's, and her way of conducting an analysis is quite different from Jacobson's. And these different methods yield different data. In sum, we felt that Kernberg tends to minimize the discrepant aspects of the different theoretical concepts he uses and to underemphasize their inconsistencies.

POSTSCRIPT

This review was presented to the New York Psychoanalytic Society as part of a longer report. Now, a decade after it was written, I have naturally asked myself whether I have changed my mind about the explanatory power or clinical usefulness of Kernberg's ideas. The answer, I am afraid, is no.

No, for two reasons. First, I have tried his ideas—clinical techniques—and for me they do not work. Attempts to confront patients with their split ego states, attempts at integrating split-off opposing transferences, did not result in the generation of anxiety, as Kernberg suggested that they would, nor did confrontations of this sort result in ego integration. But of course others may have had greater success.

Second, perhaps emboldened by the work of the Kris Study Group, I have since then been fortunate enough to treat several patients—all young women—who by virtue of their unusual symptoms and inappropriate behavior would readily fit into the borderline classification. All have been treated along conventional psychoanalytic lines with few or no parameters. These analyses have been long and difficult but have resulted in considerable analytic progress and symptomatic improvement. The major differences between these patients and so-called neurotic patients I have treated are these: They tended to live in ways that were secretly (and sometimes not so secretly) somewhat bizarre. Often their entire life and pattern of interests seemed one tangled web of symptoms. And although the view of these patients was confusing at the beginning of treatment, it did not remain so. It was possible in almost every case, with patient conventional analytic work, to clarify the meaning of these complex behavioral patterns and to understand them as pathological compromise formations that were susceptible of analysis and interpretation.

Contrary to what Kernberg suggests in much of his writing, I did not find that these patients manifested preoedipal conflicts *predominantly.* There were admixtures of both oedipal and preoedipal conflicts in all of these patients—as there are in most neurotic patients—and both sets of conflicts contributed importantly to the pathological picture.

Nor did I find that qualitatively different defense mechanisms were used by these patients. They all used so-called high-level defenses (repression, reaction formation, isolation) as well as so-called primitive defenses (projection and various forms of denial). But since the so-called primitive defenses are seen regularly in neurotic patients, were such defenses more in evidence in borderline patients? In my experience, no. Many severely guilt-ridden neurotic patients use projection very intensively. It is the defense *par excellence* for the management of guilt. And denial-in-fantasy, the commonest form of denial except for children's play, is as universal as breathing—especially in passive-dependent neurotic characters—the opiate of the irreligious.

What was different about these patients was a difference primarily of degree or intensity. They were more anxious, more guilty, and consequently more defensive. They did not use defenses unique to borderline patients but rather combinations of defenses not usually seen in less sick patients. They tended to act out—to play out—their fantasies (denial-in-fantasy), especially the fantasy of specialness (The Exception) or entitlement, more than neurotic patients are apt to do. The tendency to play out the fantasy of specialness was usually associated with phallic-oedipal disappointment, and in one case preoedipal disappointment as well. This defense was almost always combined with 1) the defensive uses of drive derivatives—for example, identification with the aggressor and sadomasochistic enactments; and 2) elaborate, highly rationalized avoidance patterns—for example, compulsive investment in isolating professional training in the service of avoiding heterosexual temptations.

In summary, then, my current experience with so-called borderline patients suggests that Kernberg's view that such patients have a significantly different psychic structure, which is not understandable by or treatable with conventional psychoanalytic concepts and techniques, is incorrect. It suggests, also, that although levels of guilt and anxiety may be higher in such patients, thus giving rise to more intensely fixed defenses—defenses condensed with drive derivatives—it is possible to understand the manifest psychopathology and underlying psychodynamics of most patients who fall into this challenging group using the well-known conflictual model of pathogenesis. The treatments in such cases may be long and difficult, but they are not necessarily longer or more difficult than those with less dramatically disturbed patients with more classically configured neurotic characters.

REFERENCES

Kernberg O, Burnstein E, Coyne L, et al: Psychotherapy and psychoanalysis: final report of the Menninger Foundation's Psychotherapy Research Project. Bull Menninger Clin 1972; 36:1-275

McDevitt J: The role of internalization in the development of object relations during the separation-individuation phase. J Am Psychoanal Assoc 1979; 27:327-343

CHAPTER 12

Self Psychology and Psychoanalytic Psychotherapy

Bertram J. Cohler, Ph.D.
Robert Galatzer-Levy, M.D.

Advances in psychoanalytic theory and technique have led to increasingly effective modes of intervention with psychologically fragile patients. "Object relations" approaches such as those pioneered by Melanie Klein, Fairbairn, and Winnicott, were later modified by Mahler, Modell, Kernberg, Giovacchini, and others, who emphasized that in addition to psychic conflict, other factors were important among patients experiencing difficulty in attaining satisfaction from intimate relationships and in realizing personal goals. Most recently, basing their work on complementary theoretical studies of the development of personal integrity and self-regard together with practical studies of the vicissitudes of understanding in the psychoanalytic situation, Heinz Kohut and his associates have demonstrated particular success in treatment of "difficult" or "fragile" patients, for whom the perspectives of conflict and defense appear to provide incomplete explanations of origin, course, and dynamics of change in psychotherapy. This chapter reviews the contributions of self psychology in order to consider its implications for psychotherapeutic intervention.

PSYCHOANALYSIS AND THE DEVELOPMENTAL APPROACH TO PSYCHOTHERAPY

Psychoanalytic approaches to psychotherapy differ from other approaches in focusing both on present problems and on the origins of those problems. From the beginning of his scientific career, studying neurobiology, Freud emphasized the manner in which the evolutionary past is reflected in present structure and function. Following his reading of Darwin and of Hackel's (1868) discussion of evolution, Freud sought evidence through detailed histological study of the extent to which "ontogeny recapitulates phylogeny" (Bernfield 1949, 1951; Sulloway 1979).

The genetic perspective in metapsychology (Rapaport and Gill 1959), emerging from Freud's pre-psychoanalytic comparative developmental neurobiological study, suggests that persons pass through well-defined, rigidly sequenced, age-specific steps that are manifest in many aspects of personality and are principally determined by shifts in the nature of drive satisfaction, as a function of both maturation and life experiences, including socialization (Ferenczi 1913; Abraham 1924; Erikson 1950/1963; Freud A, 1965). While the genetic point of view appears to allow for the plasticity of instincts, it assumes an invariant schedule of development and a rather limited portrayal of possible outcomes relevant for understanding personality and psychopathology. In particular, it assumes that drives become organized principally around conflicts originating from the family romance, or else that drive energies remain attached to developmentally inappropriate sources. As a consequence, the genetic point of view suggests a distinction between the "genital" and "pregenital" or "preoedipal" disorders that is not supported by clinical observation or response to therapeutic intervention (Modell 1984; Winnicott 1986).

While the genetic point of view appears to offer a means for linking specific forms of psychopathology with presumed genetic determinants, it has been derived largely from outside the "experience-near" perspective of clinical psychotherapeutic study (Kohut 1971). Further, the genetic point of view assumes inevitable connections with the past that are not consistent with findings from either clinical data or systematic, observational, longitudinal study of lives (Abrams 1977; Cohler 1987; Cohler and Freeman in press). Focusing on issues of continuity rather than change over time, and fostering conclusions that often conflict with findings based on developmentally informed clinical and observational study, the genetic point of view fails to provide a means for understanding the transformation of wishes and intents across the course of life, supports a distinction between psychic conflict and personal distress that arises from sources other than presumed drive satisfaction, and leads to artificial distinctions between interpretive and other aspects of psychotherapeutic intervention.

The patient's subjective distress, as well as that of those living with the patient, also provides an important measure of pathology and the need for intervention. Suffering is an indication for treatment, and the diminution of suffering is the major goal of psychoanalytic psychotherapy. However, viewed from the perspective of classical psychoanalytic theory, lives are viewed as constrained only by conflicting, irreconcilable needs and wishes, which must remain frustrated: neurotic misery is replaced with ordinary human suffering.

The self psychology image of mental health differs from that of classical analysis. Relations with others and with social institutions, mature reality testing, the significance and role of both erotic and aggressive desires, and the value of self-knowledge all are understood differently from the perspectives of self psychology and classical psychoanalysis. Freud believed that the infant's initial cathexis of body parts (autoeroticism) was replaced by a cathexis of the entire (bodily) self; because of the incapacity to achieve homeostasis in isolation, the growing child is forced to turn to other people to satisfy biological drives (Freud 1911). This results in a developmental phase during which other individuals function as aspects of the self.

In contrast with more traditional psychoanalytic perspectives, psychology of the self emphasizes development of the *experiences* of others as centers of initiative leading to the construction of the self. From Freud's initial statement in the narcissism paper (1914), it was assumed that narcissistic libido represents a continuing source of difficulty in maintaining satisfying relationships. This perspective has been most clearly explicated in Mahler's description of the process of separation–individuation. Self psychology describes a line of development of narcissism not intrinsically linked to libidinal development aimed at independent objects.

Theoretically, the model proposed by Freud depends upon the concept of psychic energy. Like physical energy, psychic energy is conserved, being neither created nor destroyed: narcissistic energy is unavailable for object cathexis. However, there is no evidence that any quantity with the properties of psychic energy can be meaningfully associated with psychological functioning. The concept of psychic energy leads to enormous theoretical difficulties and has been discarded by virtually all analytic theoreticians (Rosenblatt and Thickstun 1977; Klein 1976; Swanson 1977; Galatzer-Levy 1984). Freud's model predicts that when the self is highly cathected, objects are decathected. However, in fact, when people are happy with themselves they are most interested in others. Furthermore, people who have satisfying relations with others also feel better about themselves.

Kohut (1971, 1977) maintains that narcissism, or self-regard, emerges from a developmental line characterized by increasing stability, permanence, and flexibility in the use of others as a psychological resource. This developmental line of interdependent self does not appear to be well represented by perspective maintaining that the goal of psychological development is increased psychological autonomy and self-reliance. The developmental line of psychological *inter*dependence has been best described by Sander (1962, 1964), Stechler and Kaplan (1980), and particularly by Stern (1985) in his discussion of the origins of the "evoked companion" or "evoked other," associated with the emergence of the core self.

Basing his conclusions on the examination of reenactments in the course of psychoanalysis (see below), Kohut (1977) has shown the importance of being able to use other persons in order to maintain narcissistic equilibrium as an expectable psychological function throughout life. This function is also a function of the self; experientially, the others who help one to perform the function are parts of the self. Kohut introduced the somewhat awkward term "selfobject" to describe such functions: selfobject functions change across the course of life but remain important as a source of psychological well being.

From the perspective of self psychology, psychological health assumes continued reliance upon others as a source of solace and support. Over time, the selfobject's physical presence is needed less often, as psychologically significant features of the other are assimilated as an attribute of self. Psychopathology is reflected in the continuing use of others as archaic, urgently required selfobjects, in feelings of fragmentation when physically separated from the object, or in the compulsive need to seek recognition from others. An understanding of the systematic elaboration of the development of selfobjects over the course of life, as a phenomenon characteristic of all persons regardless of the manner in which others are used in psychological health and illness, remains one of the major tasks for developmental self psychology.

MANIFESTATIONS OF SELF PATHOLOGY

Self psychology provides both a means of understanding and a means of intervening psychologically for personal distress characterized by feelings of depletion, lack of spontaneity, and a sense of incongruence. This approach to the study and treatment of psychopathology is based on observations reported by clinical theorists as diverse as Winnicott, Kahn, Modell, André Green, Gedo, and Kohut, who have shown that there is a group of patients who benefit from the psychoanalytic situation if particular aspects of the treatment setting itself are made explicit as a part of the therapeutic process (Stone 1957, 1961). Earlier described by Eissler (1953) as parameters, these aspects of the setting were long considered outside of the analyst's interpretive activity; however, reports by Zetzel (1959) and Greenson (1967), together with Stone's contribution, showed that the therapeutic or working alliance was important as the "silent carrier" that fostered the interpretive activity of the psychoanalytic process. All patients respond to disruptions in the usual arrangements of therapeutic process. However, a distinct group of patients consistently shows unusual sensitivity to slight fluctuations in the therapist's introspective (empathic) efforts to experience, understand, and respond to the patient's distress, and to fluctuations in such arrangements as fees, schedules, and weekends and holidays. In response to such expectable variation in aspects of setting, these patients feel increasingly depleted or fragmented, or protect themselves from recognition of such feelings.

THE PSYCHONEUROSES AND PSYCHOPATHOLOGY OF THE SELF

These clinical observations suggested that the interpretation of conflict alone was not useful to these patients because it failed to attend to issues related to alliance and situation (Kohut 1971, 1977). The same observations showed that failure to understand and appreciate patients' idealizations of the therapist, including the effort to feel as if they were a part of the therapist, limited the patients' ability to profit from treatment. Descriptively, patients with increased sensitivity to issues of setting or alliance, usually show one or more of three characteristic symptom patterns.[1] Patients in the first group complain of pervasive feelings of emptiness, triviality, meaninglessness, and personal disorganization, which are independent of their accomplishments. A second group suffers from chronic states of reaction to experiences that they believe damaged their self-regard; a characteristic response is chronic and episodic rage. A third group shows intense, disruptive, driven states of desire, reflected in compulsive sexuality, addictive behaviors, and psychological enslavements.

Defenses such as disavowal, denial, or disowning aspects of the self (Basch 1983) are commonly observed in disorders of the self. Disavowal represents the splitting of the *conscious* experiences of self and object in order to protect against painful realization that would result from juxtaposing contradictory aspects of a mental representation. Driven behavior is understood as a desperate effort to protect against the experiences of fragmentation and feelings of lack of vitality and aliveness. Failure of this protective activity may lead to even more primitive defenses and/or more or less direct expression of states of distress of the self.

These three types of self pathology are often observed in one person. Efforts have been made to understand self pathology in terms of structural conflict (Brenner 1982; Wallerstein 1983), but the disarray of self-regard may be more parsimoniously understood in terms of psychology of the self as formulated not only by Kohut but also by G. Klein (1976), Stechler and Kaplan (1980), and Stern (1985). Certainly, problems in maintaining self-esteem may be one outcome of failure to resolve the family romance or nuclear neurosis (Freud 1909, 1910). However, unlike the fragile self-regard of persons with self pathology, these conflicts are played out in terms of complex triangular relationships and respond to interpretations of unacknowledged wishes in the transference.

From the perspective of psychic conflict, based on the concept of the nuclear neurosis, lowered self-regard is viewed as a defensive regression from competitive positions. For example, the patient may unconsciously communicate to others and himself, "I am no (competitive) threat to you. In fact I am without genital interests—all I want, in fact need, is to be soothed like a tiny infant." However, self psychology, emphasizing difficulties in establishing and maintaining a vigorous and cohesive self, may be more useful in understanding states of depletion, fragmentation, and rage. In contrast with perspectives based on psychic conflict, the self psychology perspective is particularly parsimonious. The many deriva-

---

[1] Kohut and Wolf (1978) organize the same group of pathologies in a different fashion, using the type of disorder of the self as their major axis of description, rather than the reaction to that disorder, as used here.

tives of sexual and aggressive drives, the defenses against them, and the richness of symbolic transformations possible allow one to explain virtually any human condition (Brenner 1978, 1982): a theory that explains everything, explains nothing.

Elements of psychic conflict are of course observed in people whose dominant pathology involves archaic mental states, feeling of impending fragmentation, lack of spontaneity, and a sense of living a false life. It is important to recognize the conflict perspective and to provide appropriate means of therapeutic intervention relevant both for issues associated with psychic conflict and for those associated with deficits in maintenance of integrity of self. It is also important to recognize that developmental arrests or fixations, characteristically associated with psychic conflict, may be regressively used in order to protect against recognition of competitive wishes. Ideally, therefore, psychotherapeutic intervention addresses issues in *both* spheres of disturbance, attending to the multidetermined nature of wishes and intents.

Disorders of the self characteristically lead to a profound sense of depletion and lack of integrity. Interpretations of defense against psychic conflict appear to have less impact for people with serious pathology of the self than for those whose difficulties may be traced primarily to the nuclear neurosis. Although both states may be present, at least to some extent, in all people (Gedo 1979, 1981; Masterson 1985), patients with profound self pathology show concern with issues of despair, depletion, and fragmentation, present to such an extent that explanations based on regression from the nuclear neurosis are not complete in accounting for the patient's psychological fragility. As indicated in the descriptions below, reactions to the sense of depletion take different forms in the three symptom patterns of self pathology.

Depletion Disorder

In this first group of patients, evidence of self pathology especially includes a sense of inner depletion and hypochondriasis. Depression has many sources, from organic illness to guilt-motivated attacks on the self (Anthony and Benedek 1975). In depletion depression, ideas of punishment and badness are largely absent. The experience is of painful triviality, dullness, and ennui; nothing seems valuable, important, exciting, or worth enthusiasm.

Hypochondriasis is an expression, in bodily terms, of the feeling that something is profoundly wrong with one. As with many self disorders, psychopathology is associated with archaic forms of experience transformed into "language" consistent with adulthood. A major childhood task is the integration of body sensations as a part of the self. Relative failure in this area supports the experience of self disturbance as bodily disorder; language and symbolic representation are also disturbed. Meaningful words for important experiences are unavailable.

Rage Disorders

The second major group of patients with self disorders consists of those in whom rage is the preponderant issue (Kohut 1972). Rage appears to be a primary reaction to narcissistic injury. Brief experiences with rage commonly occur in response to bodily dysfunction—for example, the intense, diffuse, objectless rage when one stubs one's toe. Rage at the loss of valued bodily functions, often observed among older persons showing signs of cognitive deficit, was well portrayed by Goldstein (1948) in describing the "catastrophic reaction" observed among persons experiencing brain damage. Depending on the capacity to compensate for the narcissistic injury, rage may become the central or organizing feature of the personality. The search for revenge usually involves a similar chronic state of intense narcissistic rage.

Narcissistic rage can be transformed, defended against, and integrated with other psychological functions. For example, it may fuse with assertiveness, in efforts to avoid external situations that bring on rage-inducing shame. Chronic states of narcissistic rage are usually rationalized—otherwise the continued association of the rage with the shame-inducing experience produces constant awareness of shame. Defenses such as splitting and projection are commonly used. Frequently the narcissistic rage is apparent in attempts to stabilize the self. Perverse sexuality, aimed primarily at reestablishing and invigorating the self, often has major sadistic elements that integrate narcissistic rage into the sexual behavior.[2]

Disorders of Action

A third group of self disorders includes efforts to defend against experiences of flaws in the self. The sense of imminent danger to personal survival leads to unusual intensity, reflected in driven efforts to obtain a

---

[2] Rage is so important in perversions that Stoller (1975) plausibly argues that all perversions are transformations of aggression. The unpleasantness of a pervert toward his object is understood from a self-psychological viewpoint in a more complex way. As discussed below, the sexual object is used to fill some self function and therefore must be controlled absolutely, certainly without interest in its independent will or wishes. This need for absolute control is psychologically quite different from aggression toward the object, though the object may well experience it as aggression (see section on countertransference responses to selfobject transferences). In addition, perversions often include enactments of the narcissistic rage.

sense of vitality and integrity. The functions of compulsive actions as attempts at self restitution often are transparent. Details of the symptom choice may be quite complex, and unacknowledged through disavowal. Among the states most usefully understood from a self psychology point of view are hypomanic states, substance abuse, addictive interpersonal relations, and sexual perversions.

Hypomanic states involve denial of loss of self-cohesion, or enfeeblement. The hypomanic state expresses the patient's wish to be grand, powerful, and alive. Symptoms such as squandering money can be understood as the wish for infinite riches, contrasted with feelings of psychic impoverishment. Galatzer-Levy's (1987) report of psychoanalytic treatment of a bipolar disorder, influenced by concepts based on self psychology, suggests that the manic episodes of bipolar disorder show the same psychological meaning but occur in a context of severely disturbed symbolic function.

In substance abuse, the drug is used for its combination of pharmacological and psychological effects to compensate for aspects of self that function inadequately. For example, cocaine provides a sense of grandeur and enthusiasm to people who cannot otherwise generate riveting goals or adequate enjoyment of their skills and talents. Similarly, narcotics and barbiturates calm overstimulated people, and marijuana and alcohol are used in varying doses in order to provide stimulation and/or soothing. Certain eating disturbances appear to involve a similar mechanism: alternating binge eating and vomiting may be in the service of maintaining a balance between under and overstimulation, while anorexia nervosa may be an attempt to obtain some bodily sensation and maintain feelings of being alive.

In addictive interpersonal relations, other people similarly become essential because of their selfobject function, providing a sense of completeness and vitality. As already noted, the use of other people as selfobjects is normal throughout life. It is not such use itself but rather the manner in which others are used—as archaic and poorly integrated aspects of the self—that indicates pathology. A young man's preoccupation with a girlfriend or a student's intense idealization of an instructor are normal developments of young adult life. These idealized experiences of others are integrated with other goals and ambitions (e.g., object-related attachment to the woman and interest in the development of a career). The fate of normal idealization is a gradual, often painful, but essentially nontraumatic disillusionment, as a result of which valued aspects of the selfobject become part of self. Situations suggesting psychopathology include those where interest in the girlfriend or teacher precludes all other interests, becoming a source of psychological enslavement.

Archaic selfobject relations are often highly eroticized. For example,

Anne Reich (1953, 1960) vividly described preoccupation in women whose apparently heterosexual object choice involved the use of men as archaic selfobjects. Relations in which others are addictively used as extensions of the self, or in which sexuality is promiscuous or perverse, are often efforts to stabilize or invigorate the self.

Disorders of the self may also appear as overt perversions. In these disorders, magical rituals are enacted whose purpose is creation of personal stability. The urgency, need for unending repetition, and apparent loss of judgment commonly seen in perversions reflect their centrality for the integrity of the person—they are often matters of psychological life and death. Kohut (1971) called the use of manifest sexuality for narcissistic purposes as sexualization. Because of the particularly significant nature of bodily activities for symbolizing the self, the similarity of erotic activities to early experiences of soothing and basic care, and the integration of physiological urges with psychological needs, sexual behavior is a particularly satisfactory route for the enactment of self concerns.

Perverse acts are often unaccompanied by affect; as Goldberg (1975) has hypothesized, this reflects replacement of affective experience associatively connected to earlier failure in order to realize solace with the perverse act. Disavowal, and the separation from those early experiences, leads to a sense of personal deficit for which a solution is sought through the perverse act. This solution becomes ineffective when, as a result of psychotherapeutic intervention, the connection between present action and earlier experience is understood, and other, more satisfactory means of achieving the same result—usually temporarily in relation to the therapist—can be found. Psychotherapy assists the patient in appreciating the connection, so that perverse behavior loses its driven, tyrannical quality.

CONTRASTING CONCEPTS OF DEFENSE IN TREATMENT OF THE NEUROSES AND SELF PATHOLOGY

Understanding self pathology involves exploration of primitive defensive processes manifest in these disorders, such as disavowal, denial, and splitting. While Freud clearly recognized the significance of these forms of psychological protection, most psychoanalytic study has been devoted to repressive defenses that protect against psychic conflict. Self disorders differ from neuroses not only in their central pathology but also in the symbolic processes employed. Because of their earlier origin, and the greater urgency of their motivation, these symbolic processes tend to include denial, disavowal, and splitting. Typically archaic elements of the self are available to consciousness but remain unintegrated and unaffected by other conscious experience. While distortions in reality testing may be used in order to protect the self, this activity differs from neurotic distortions, which are compromise formations designed to permit partial satisfaction and simultaneously disguise unacceptable wishes.

Freud (1900) has shown that dreams, jokes, symptoms, parapraxes, and transferences bring unacceptable wishes closer to consciousness. Innocuous experiences of daily life are used as nodal points connecting unconscious wishes with thoughts and actions, permitting partial discharge. Applying the concept of associative memory (Rapaport 1942) to dreams, Freud demonstrated that symbols are related to underlying meanings. Sometimes it is possible to accurately guess the meaning of a symbol. However, the only reliable way to interpret dreams is to examine the associative net in which the symbol occurred. As Waelder (1936) has noted, any one-dimensional understanding of symbols is incomplete. Symbols are multiply determined and reflect unconscious, conflictual factors, as well as efforts designed to maintain self-regard. In self pathology, increased efforts at protecting oneself from the distress accompanying recognition of the meaning of the dream take the form of splitting off and denying dysphoric affect and experiences incongruent with self-image, rather than repression, which is the characteristic defense of the neuroses.

In Kohut's later formulations of self psychology (Kohut 1984; Tolpin and Kohut 1980), failure of selfobject functions, stemming from earliest childhood, became the basis of all psychopathology. For example, the oedipal situation was seen not as the result of the inevitable, universal conflicts arising as a result of unacceptable wishes of the "family romance" (Freud A, 1951), but as the product of environmental failures that transformed vigorous, joyful assertiveness into sexualized desire, narcissistic rage, and resultant anxieties.

This position echoes Freud's own early struggle with the question of real versus imagined seduction. After a period of uncertainty (Masson 1984), by 1900 Freud was clear that the basis of oedipal difficulties lay in the child's wishes and fears stemming from the realization of inevitable rivalry with each parent for an exclusive relationship with the other (Parsons 1955). In Kohut's later work, concerns with issues of jealousy, rivalry, and failure of assertiveness, associated with oedipal-level pathology, reflect the failure of oedipal-level selfobjects to respond adequately to spontaneous developments in the child. Often this occurs in the context of a self already enfeebled by earlier feelings of failure, based on disappointing experience of the selfobject as a source of solace and support.

This focus upon presumed "real" failures in caretaking as the source of later problems regarding self-regard presents many of the same problems as Freud's initial concern with the seduction hypothesis. When all psychopathology is assumed to arise from failures of empathy, self-psychology retreats to a kind of explanation that is as reductionistic as an explanation rooted in psychic conflict and emphasizing the nuclear neurosis as the origin of all psychopathology. As formulated by self psychology, resolution of the nuclear neurosis proceeds not through analysis of the transference, which fosters awareness and resolution of previously unconscious conflicts, but rather through allowing a new experience with a more adequate oedipal-level selfobject. Any such explanation as the *only* origin of intense sexual wishes and psychic conflict is alien to clinical experience, the process of psychological development (Stern 1985), and clinical common sense. Oedipal conflict may be exacerbated by selfobject failures, leading to sexualization of the self and intensifying the conflict engendered by the oedipal phase, so that self-psychological issues must often be addressed in the treatment of pathology that has psychic conflict as its prime determinant. However, it remains heuristically useful to maintain distinctions between these two forms of personal distress, and we will restrict this discussion of psychotherapeutic intervention to disorders of the self.

CHARACTERISTIC TRANSFERENCES AND COUNTERTRANSFERENCES IN TREATMENT OF PSYCHOPATHOLOGY OF THE SELF

When persons are unable to realize needs for coherence and vitality, they often turn to the surrounding environment, seeking to psychologically evoke missing attributes of self, or selfobjects. In treatment, often after working through considerable resistance, the patient begins to use the therapist in an effort to complete missing aspects of self—that is, as a selfobject. Since the analysis of these situations serves a function analogous to the analysis of transference in the neuroses, Kohut (1971) used the term "transference-like" for idealizing and mirroring modes of relating to the therapist.

This use of the term transference differs from that generally understood within psychoanalysis (for a review of contemporary uses of the term, see Gill 1982). Derived from Freud's (1900) topographic use of the concept of transference of unconscious wishes onto preconscious residues, "transference" explained the mechanism by which disguised representations of repressed wishes could find their way to consciousness (Kohut and Seitz 1963). "Transference" in the clinical situation refers to the emergence of previously unconscious and unacknowledged wishes, enacted in characteristic modes of experiencing others. The transference includes aspects of past experience that may become manifest in amalgam with current experience. In the transference neurosis the other person is experienced as independent but endowed as the object of both love and hatred. Wishes that are often of great intensity are directed toward the transference object. These wishes are disguised and distorted in compromise formation, barred from consciousness by repression and by secondary defenses that support repression.

Varieties of Selfobject Transference

As contrasted with reenactment based on psychic conflict (Brenner 1982), selfobject reenactments reflect continuing search for realization of personal integrity and spontaneity; the construction of caretaking images during early childhood as not "good enough" (Winnicott 1960) results in constant attempts to experience self as stable, vigorous, and cohesive.[3] Construction of the therapist as an aspect of self, rather than an independent individual, fosters a situation in which both the therapist's efforts to understand the patient's distress and interpretations regarding the meaning of this distress now become experienced as a part of a healing process leading to increased sense of personal congruence and capacity for self-soothing.

The therapist's effort to make sense of the patient's suffering, experienced by the patient as action of himself or herself, becomes indispensable for the patient's psychological survival. At the same time, it is difficult for the patient to acknowledge the significance of the therapist. The patient protects himself against the awareness of the therapist's importance,[4] both because of the sense of disappointment stemming from re-

---

[3] This difference becomes particularly important when the material of the transference is used to reconstruct childhood experience. If transferences in the neuroses are indeed the product of current happenings and unconsciously motivated ways of perceiving, then it should be possible by factoring out the current external reality to discover the unconscious processes at work. Insofar as these are continuations of infantile experience, it is possible then to reconstruct those experiences from the transference. This theoretical possibility does not apply to selfobject transferences. All that we can say is that infantile needs are revivified, but on the basis of these central transferences we can say little about other attempts to meet those needs. This is because, as discussed above, the self is capable of meeting its needs in many ways. The fact that patients in treatment can find good solutions to these needs says nothing about the normal mechanisms a developing infant or child might use.

[4] The term need (as opposed to a wish) is used here in three related senses—a need is something essential to continued normal development, a need is something essential to the continued cohesion and vitality of the self, a need is a subjective experience of need. Since neurotic patients frequently describe their wishes and defensive maneuvers as needs, thereby both indicating the urgency of the underlying wish and denying that it is a wish, accepting the patient's view that something is a "need" may be collusion with the patient's defensive operations. As discussed below, it is not the patient's avowal of need but the nature of the transference manifestations that differentiates selfobject from object-related transferences.

peated past failure in the use of others for self-soothing and because of the potential interference (represented by therapeutic intervention) with the means the patient has found for stabilizing a fragile sense of self. Usually denial, disavowal, and splitting are the principal defenses employed.

Kohut (1971) divided the selfobject transferences into two major groups: "idealizing transference," involving the functioning of the selfobject as part of the ideal self; and "mirror transference," involving the stabilization of the grandiose self. Generally the selfobject transferences are silent when they are functioning effectively. In this silent phase they provide the patient with missing functions necessary to sustain the self. The "silence" is in marked contrast to the fully engaged transference neurosis, in which ever more explicit and explicitly frustrated transference longings lead to intense distress. For the patient whose psychopathology is primarily related to disorder of self, distress is felt only when the selfobject fails. Two typical such failures are disruptions in continuity (e.g., weekend or vacation interruption) or felt breaks in empathy (e.g., the therapist's inevitable failure to appreciate the significance of a particular external event.)[5]

The Idealizing Transference. In the idealizing transference, the therapist is viewed as the incarnation of strength, goodness, and power. Through his reaction to the idealized therapist, the patient feels vigorous, good, and whole. Conscious wishes to be like the therapist are commonly used means of resolving the idealizing transference. Initially, idealization tends to be generalized, including such aspects of the therapist as appearance, manner of speech, and office decor. As a result of working through, the idealization becomes increasingly specific and related to the patient's needs.

There are several ways in which idealizing transferences can be mishandled. Failure to work with idealizing transferences often stems from inadequate recognition of the function of idealization. Overstimulated by idealization, some therapists confront patients with "reality" or question the need to idealize. Idealizations are often mistakenly and prematurely interpreted, usually as a resistance against hostility. These efforts interfere in the emergence and resolution of the transference and may lead to

---

[5] Kohut's initial distinction between the various selfobject transferences is conceptually useful but inconsistent with clinical observations. The transferences tend to merge, with one or another aspect dominating at a given moment. To be an adequate mirror of grandiosity, the mirroring person must be admirable. Similarly, merger with an idealized object results in feelings of grandeur.

interruption of treatment as the patient searches for idealizable objects elsewhere.

Another major error is to use the idealization to make oneself a model for the patient. For example, Flaherty (1982) recommends that adolescent girls identify with the female therapists' solutions in resolving potential conflicts between women's career goals and plans for marriage and parenthood. While these identifications may later be worked through, with the therapist playing a developmentally useful role, it is also possible that the patient may be left with aspirations that are not her own, leading to increased problems in maintaining a sense of personal integrity. Some therapists find the patient's idealization ego-syntonic. They believe they actually possess the marvelous qualities ascribed to them—for example, empathy of a quality the patient can find nowhere else, or wisdom about leading the good life, derived from analytic insights or personal experience. A belief of this kind interferes with the recognition and resolution of idealizing transferences. Therapists who familiarize themselves with their own responses to idealization can often recognize its presence through responses to the patient's material.

Recognition and use of the nondefensive idealizing transference demonstrates the significance of psychology of the self as a framework for understanding possibly effective transactions in psychotherapy. Therapists who believe that all transferences are aspects of the nuclear neurosis are also bound to interpret manifest idealization as a disguised means (compromise formation) of enacting competitive wishes. Self-psychological perspectives point to the possibility of motives other than defense against feelings of competition as the basis for particular enactments in psychotherapy.

The Mirror Transference.   In the mirror transference, the patient delegates to the therapist the task of supporting and encouraging grandiose expectations for self. Kohut (1971) described three overlapping forms of mirror transference—merger transference, alter-ego transference, and mirror transference proper. In the merger transference the patient's grandiose self is supported by the idea of a single entity, the analyst-patient. The alter-ego transference is characterized by the fantasy that patient and analyst share a world view as twins who are well and good because they are the same. In the mirror transference proper, the patient feels well because of the therapist's appreciative response to his grandiosity. He can experience his own glory confidently, as it is reflected back to him by the therapist. Again, during periods of better functioning, these transferences are generally silent. They come into focus only with self-object failure.

Countertransferences in the Treatment of
Psychopathology of the Self

Commonly, therapists respond to mirroring transference with discomfort at being treated as a part of another's self, with no independent will. Boredom and fatigue are common when the therapist is chronically (and often coercively) treated as though his purpose is to satisfy the patient's selfobject needs. Among the ways therapists deal with the distress of being treated as an extension of the patient is therapeutic activism—for example, elaborate interpretation, confrontations, or suggestions, which demonstrate to the therapist that he is still alive and can act and think independently of the patient's wishes (Reich 1951, 1960). It is not uncommon for the therapist, with the conscious motive of improving patients' interpersonal relations, to sermonize about the importance of treating others as people in their own right. Pejorative diagnostic terms, such as "borderline" or "primitive object relations," are attached to patients who demand that the therapist function as a selfobject.

Another group of countertransference responses involves manifest fears that the patient's grandiosity will become unmanageable or intolerable. Interpretations are then replaced with emergency educational measures or prohibitions designed to protect the patient from damaging himself and others. Generally, such measures only lead the patient to feel out of control and evoke increased disorganization. The most effective therapeutic strategy, in such instances, involves recognition and acceptance of the patient's need for mirroring. As a consequence, the patient is able to increase the capacity for understanding reasons for the need for selfobjects, leading to lowered urgency of action.

The therapist's own incompletely analyzed grandiosity may be stimulated by that of the patient. In such an instance, the therapist may try to convince the patient that the therapist appreciates external reality better than the patient; in other circumstances, the therapist may become anxious about the patient's grandiosity and admonish him to proceed carefully.[6] Afraid of becoming enmeshed in the patient's material, and experiencing psychotic (i.e., unrestrainedly grandiose or egocentric) processes in himself, the therapist may feel an urgent need to suppress the patient's primitive ideation, believing that it endangers the patient.

---

[6] There is a group of patients whose psychological state might be likened to a chronic tantrum, and who need to be firmly and calmly "held" psychologically because they continue to create escalating difficulties for themselves. Such patients sometimes feel considerable relief when forbidden to engage in self-destructive enactments. The therapist's position here differs from the countertransference determined response earlier described, since the patient usually has a long history of genuinely dangerous behavior, and the therapist does not experience a pressing urgency when making these interventions.

In a third group of responses, distortions based on reenactment of the therapist's own problems in maintenance of sense of self, one can recognize efforts at directly satisfying the patient's transference needs, in their infantile forms, within treatment. Selfobject transferences put a strain on therapists' vulnerabilities to overstimulation and lack of mirroring responses. It is essential for the therapist to have adequately worked through problems associated with these issues; otherwise, enactment of felt deficits in attaining regulation of tension, and of feelings of lack of support in this regard since early childhood, may become a chronic impediment to clinical work. Such senior theorists of psychoanalytic psychotherapy as Ferenczi, Winnicott, and Bettelheim regard "holding" as an essential element of work with psychologically fragile patients. Such therapeutic activity as actually holding (Little 1985), feeding (Sechehaye 1951), or providing "appropriate presents" to child patients is intended to provide supplies believed absent from the patients' earlier life. The belief that the therapist can provide "reparenting" reflects the therapist's wish, often determined by a fantasy that his own defective development can be remedied in similar fashion, to undo past deprivations.[7]

Treatment of Self Disorders and Management of the Therapeutic Alliance

It should be emphasized that both in analysis and analytically oriented therapy, selfobject transferences (like other transferences) are promoted simply by the analyst's ordinary empathy and courtesy toward the patient. As recognized by Zetzel (1957), Stone (1961, 1964), and Greenson (1967), the therapeutic alliance represents a critical element in the therapeutic process. A major contribution of self psychology to the theory of technique has been to refocus attention on the alliance and to explore its psychology. It should be noted that the focus on development and psychopathology of the self does not provide any rationale for therapeutic activity that is different from that based on psychic conflict. In particular, there is little justification for prematurely interfering with the patient's evolving effort at self-understanding, or confronting the patient with "reality."

Iatrogenic traumatization is common when the antiseptic "model tech-

---

[7] Our experience with therapists who become sexually involved with patients suggests that such activities are often an attempt to provide magically and concretely for narcissistic needs of the patient. At the same time they reflect the therapist's rage at the patient, which leads to the enactment's taking a destructive form and to a sexualized attempt to reassert the vigor of the therapist's self in a context where the therapist (often seriously narcissistically depleted) feels that the patient is not sufficiently responsive.

nique" recommended by Eissler (1953) replaces the ordinary therapeutic situation (Stone 1984). Such actions as remaining silent in response to questions, refusing to look at photographs, or interpreting socially appropriate greetings as resistance neither enhance nor clarify spontaneously developing transference. Rather they obscure the patient's spontaneous transference reactions, replacing them with responses to recurring retraumatization or rudeness.

True selfobject transferences emerge against great resistance. Rapidly forming, essentially normal forms of selfobject relatedness, often seen at the beginning of treatment, reflect engagement in therapy. Such responses are often confused with selfobject transferences, with the result that a misdiagnosis of self pathology is made. It should be noted that intermittent use of the therapist as a selfobject does not constitute a selfobject transference. While such use needs to be understood and appreciated by the therapist, it is best to reserve the term *selfobject transference* for those situations where the central configuration of the treatment involves the patient's use of the therapist as a selfobject in order to replace deficits in the self.

CONCLUSION

Self psychology has clarified the distinctive nature of psychoanalytic understanding and increased our understanding of the problems for which people seek psychotherapy. Through increased focus on issues of meaning and integrity as important determinants of dispositions and intents, and through detailed clinical observation of the means by which patients experience the care and support afforded by others, self psychology has contributed to a life-course human science in which intrapsychologic processes can be systematically studied. The theories of self psychology extend the essential contributions of psychoanalysis both to the human sciences and to psychotherapy. The prediction of lives over time, as well as the understanding of appropriate intervention, must be founded on recognition and explication of the variety of states that can shape personal and collective actions.

REFERENCES

Abraham K: A short study on the development of the libido, viewed in the light of mental disorders (1924), in Selected Papers on Psychoanalysis. New York, Basic Books, 1953

Abrams S: The genetic point of view: antecedents and transformations. J Am Psychoanal Assoc 1977; 25:417-425

Anthony EJ, Benedek T: Depression and Human Existence. Boston, Little, Brown, 1975

Basch M: The perception of reality and the disavowal of meaning. The Annual of Psychoanalysis (Chicago) 1983; 11:125-153

Basch M: Selfobjects and selfobject transference: theoretical implications, in Kohut's Legacy: Contributions to Self Psychology. Edited by Stepansky P, Goldberg A. Hillsdale, NJ, The Analytic Press–Lawrence Erlbaum, 1984

Bernfeld S: Freud's scientific beginnings. Imago 1949; 6:163-196

Bernfeld S: Sigmund Freud, M.D., 1882-1885. Int J Psychoanal 1951; 32:204-217

Brenner C: The Mind in Conflict. New York, International Universities Press, 1982

Cohler B: Approaches to the study of development in psychiatric education, in The Role of Psychoanalysis in Psychiatric Education: Past, Present and Future. Edited by Weissman S, Thurnblad R. New York, International Universities Press, 1987

Cohler B, Freeman M: Psychoanalysis and the developmental narrative, in The Course of Life, revised edition. Edited by Pollock G, Greenspan S. New York, International Universities Press (in press)

Eissler KR: Effect of the structure of the ego on psychoanalytic technique. J Am Psychoanal Assoc 1953; 1:104-143

Erikson E: Childhood and Society, revised edition. New York, Norton, 1963

Ferenczi S: Stages in the development of a sense of reality (1913), in First Contributions to Psychoanalysis. New York, Brunner/Mazel, 1980

Flaherty L: To love and/or to work: the ideological dilemma of young women. Adolesc Psychiatry 1982; 10:41-51

Freud A: Observations on child development. Psychoanal Study Child 1951; 6:18-30

Freud A: Normality and Pathology in Childhood: Assessments of Development. New York, International Universities Press, 1965

Freud S: The interpretation of dreams (1900-1901), in Complete Psychological Works, Standard Edition, vols. 4-5. Translated and edited by Strachey J. London, Hogarth Press, 1958

Freud S: Family romances (1909), in Complete Psychological Works, Standard Edition, vol. 9. Translated and edited by Strachey J. London, Hogarth Press, 1959

Freud S: Five lectures on psychoanalysis (1910), in Complete Psychological Works, Standard Edition, vol. 11. Translated and edited by Strachey J. London, Hogarth Press, 1957

Freud S: Formulations regarding the two principles of mental functioning (1911), in Complete Psychological Works, Standard Editon, vol. 12. Translated and edited by Strachey J. London, Hogarth Press, 1958

Freud S: On narcissism: an introduction (1914), in Complete Psychological Works, Standard Edition, vol. 14. Translated and edited by Strachey J. London, Hogarth Press, 1957

Galatzer-Levy R: Psychic energy: a historical perspective. The Annual of Psychoanalysis 1976; 4:41-64

Galatzer-Levy R: Perspectives on the regulatory principles of mental functioning. Psychoanalysis of Contemporary Thought 1984; 6:255-289

Galatzer-Levy R: Analytic experiences with manic-depressive patients, in Progress in Self-Psychology, vol. 3. New York, Guilford Press, 1987

Gedo J: Beyond Interpretation: Toward a Revised Theory of Psychoanalysis. New York, International Universities Press, 1979

Gedo J: Advances in Clinical Psychoanalysis. New York, Guilford Press, 1981

Gill M: Analysis of the Transference, Vol. I: Theory and Technique. New York, International Universities Press, 1982

Goldberg A: The evolution of psychoanalytic concepts of depression, in Depression and Human Existence. Edited by Anthony EJ, Benedek T. Boston, Little, Brown, 1975

Goldstein K: After-Effects of Brain Injuries in War. New York, Grune & Stratton, 1942

Greenson R: The working alliance and the transference neurosis. Psychoanal Q 1965; 34:155-181

Greenson R: The Technique and Practice of Psychoanalysis. New York, International Universities Press, 1967

Hackel E: Natural History of Creation. (Naturaliche Schopfungsgesichte) (1868). Berlin, George Reimer, 1968

Klein G: Psychoanalytic Theory: An Exploration of Essentials. New York, International Universities Press, 1976

Kohut H: The Analysis of the Self. New York, International Universities Press, 1971

Kohut H: Thoughts on narcissism and narcissistic rage (1972), in The Search for the Self: Selected Writings of Heinz Kohut, 1950–1978. Edited by Ornstein P. New York, International Universities Press, 1978

Kohut H: The Restoration of the Self. New York, International Universities Press, 1977

Kohut H: How Does Psychoanalysis Cure? Chicago, University of Chicago Press, 1984

Kohut H, Seitz P: Concepts and theories of psychoanalysis (1963), in The Search for the Self: Selected Writings of Heinz Kohut, 1950–1978. Edited by Ornstein P., New York, International Universities Press, 1978

Kohut H, Wolf E: The disorders of the self and their treatment: an outline. Int J Psychoanal 1978; 59:413-425

Little M: Winnicott working in areas where psychotic anxieties predominate: a personal record, in Free Associations: Psychoanalysis, Groups, Politics, Culture, Number 3. London, Free Association Books, 1985

Masson J: The Assault on Truth: Freud's Suppression of the Seduction Theory. New York, Farrar, Straus, and Giroux, 1984

Masterson J: The Real Self: A Developmental Self, and Object Relations Approach. New York, Brunner/Mazel, 1985

Modell A: Psychoanalysis in a New Context. New York, International Universities Press, 1984

Parsons T: Family structure and the socialization of the child, in Family, Socialization and Interaction Processes. Edited by Parsons T, Bales RF. New York, Free Press–Macmillan, 1955

Rapaport D: Emotions and Memory (1942). New York, Science Editions, 1961

Rapaport D, Gill M: The points of view and assumptions of metapyschology (1959), in The Collected Papers of David Rapaport. Edited by Gill M. New York, Basic Books, 1967

Reich A: On countertransference. Int J Psychoanal 1951; 32:25-31

Reich A: Further remarks on countertransference. Int J Psychoanal 1960; 41:127-159

Rosenblatt A, Thickstun J: Energy, information and motivation: a revision of psychoanalytic theory. J Am Psychoanal Assoc 1977, 25:537-558

Sander L: Issues in early mother–child interaction. J Am Acad Child Psychiatry 1962; 2:141-166

Sander L: Adaptive relationships in early mother–child interaction. J Am Acad Child Psychiatry 1964; 3:221-263

Sander L: To begin with—reflections on ontogeny (1964), in Reflections on Self Psychology. Edited by Lichtenberg J, Kaplan S. New York, International Universities Press, 1983

Sechehaye M: Symbolic Realization: A New Method of Psychotherapy Applied to a Case of Schizophrenia. New York, International Universities Press, 1951

Stechler G, Kaplan S: The development of the self. Psychoanal Study Child 1980; 35:85-105

Stern D: The Interpersonal World of the Infant. New York, Basic Books, 1985

Stoller R: Perversion: The Erotic Form of Hatred. New York, Pantheon, 1975

Stone L: The widening scope of indications for psychoanalysis. J Am Psychoanal Assoc 1954; 2:567-594

Stone L: The Psychoanalytic Situation. New York, International Universities Press, 1961

Stone L: Notes on the noninterpretive elements in the psychoanalytic situation and process (1981), in Transference and Its Context. New York, Jason Aronson, 1984

Sulloway F: Freud, Biologist of the Mind. New York, Basic Books, 1979

Swanson D: The psychic energy concept—a critique. J Am Psychoanal Assoc 1977; 25:603-634

Tolpin M, Kohut H: The disorders of the self: the psychopathology of the first years of life, in The Course of Life, vol. I: Infancy and Early Childhood. Edited by Greenspan S, Pollock G. Washington, DC, US Government Printing Office, 1980

Waelder R: The principle of multiple function. Psychoanal Q 1936; 5:45-62

Wallerstein R: Self psychology and "classical" psychoanalytic psychology: the nature of their relationship, in The Future of Psychoanalysis: Essays in Honor of Heinz Kohut. Edited by Goldberg A. New York, International Universities Press, 1983

Winnicott DW: Ego distortion in terms of true and false self (1960), in The Maturational Process and the Facilitating Environment. Edited by Winnicott DW. New York, International Universities Press, 1965

Winnicott DW: Holding and Interpretation: Fragment of an Analysis. Edited and with an introduction by Khan M. New York, Grove Press, 1986

Zetzel E: The analytic situation and the analytic process (1958a), in The Capacity for Emotional Growth. Edited by Zetzel E. New York, International Universities Press, 1970

Zetzel E: Therapeutic alliance in the analysis of hysteria (1958b), in The Capacity for Emotional Growth. Edited by Zetzel E. New York, International Universities Press, 1970

CHAPTER 13

Some Reflections on the Theory of Psychopathology and Personality Development in Kohut's Self Psychology

Salman Akhtar, M.D.

The contributions of self psychology belong to five areas: personality development, psychopathology, analytic technique, study of sociopolitical processes, and philosophical implications regarding the nature of the man. This chapter is an attempt to evaluate critically the contributions of self psychology in two of these areas, namely, personality development and psychopathology. Stated differently, the focus here is on "theoretical" rather than "clinical" or "applied" contributions of self psychology. While this delineation of the paper's scope may serve a useful orienting purpose, two other clarifications seem necessary. The first refers to my use of the term *self psychology*. Unless I otherwise specify, the designation will always be used in its "broader sense" (Kohut 1977)—that is, as referring to a psychology that views self as a supraordinate constellation, with the drives and defenses as its constituents. This view is in contrast to the "narrow sense" of self psychology (Kohut 1971), which regards self as a content of the mental apparatus, that is, as mental representations within the id, ego, and superego. The second clarification pertains to my approach. Although I will be underlining and emphasizing the limitations and shortcomings of self psychology, I do not mean to imply that it has made no worthwhile contributions. Indeed, it has made "significant and enduring additions" (Wallerstein 1983) to psychoanalytic depth psychology. A partial list of these includes the descriptions of mirror and idealizing transferences and their corresponding countertransferences (Kohut 1971), the phenomenology of narcissistic rage (Kohut 1972), and the behavioral typologies of various narcissistic characters (Kohut and Wolf 1978). I also include in this list Goldberg's eloquent nosological contribution, the chronic "misfits" (Goldberg 1983), and the fact that the proponents of self psychology have made the traditional analysts more mindful of the importance of the empathic posture on the analyst's part.

However, these significant contributions will not be the focus of my discussion. I will restrict myself to a critical evaluation of certain aspects of the personality and psychopathology theory in self psychology. Among the important theoretical areas that I am not considering here are 1) the self psychology view of a developmental line for narcissism that is separate from object relations, 2) the consideration of aggression as an interpersonal artifact rather than as an inevitable evolutionary legacy, 3) the minimization of the organizing role of superego in self psychology, 4) the need, or the lack of need, of self as a supraordinate concept, and 5) finally, the issue of separateness versus complementarity between self psychology and mainstream psychoanalysis. The regret I feel in having to eliminate these important areas from my essay here is balanced by the reassur-

The author wishes to thank Alexis Burland, M.D., Albert Kaplan, M.D., Sydney Pulver, M.D., and Thomas Wolman, M.D., for their helpful review of earlier drafts of this paper.

227

ing awareness that rich discussions of these matters are available in contemporary psychoanalytic literature (e.g., Blum 1982; Kernberg 1974, 1982; Rangell 1982; Segel 1981; Treurniet 1983; Wallerstein 1981, 1983).

In what follows, I will attempt to highlight what I consider are three major shortcomings in the self psychology approach to the understanding of psychopathology and personality development: 1) a tendency toward linear reductionism by which all narcissistic, borderline, perverse, addictive, and psychotic conditions are seen as emanating from the single etiologic factor of faulty parental empathy; 2) a striking disregard toward the body self, the sexual self, and the constitutional, innate origins of the self and its pathology; and 3) a hypothesis that certain kinds of psychopathology do not emanate from intrapsychic conflict but from a state of psychological deficit. These three are, in my opinion, major problems in a depth psychological approach, and I will attempt to show the sources and results of these erroneous assumptions. Before embarking on this course, I would like to add a brief section on another peculiarity of Kohut's writings (and to a certain extent of his followers as well)—his complete inability to acknowledge the relevant contributions of other investigators.

KOHUT'S HISTORICAL SOLIPSISM

The first and foremost aspect that strikes one about the literature of self psychology is that contributions made by other investigators are constantly ignored or deemphasized. The disturbing professional and historical solipsism of self psychology takes three forms: exaggerated claims to originality, failure to recognize contradictory evidence, and the use of "straw man" arguments.

Claims to Originality

With regard to instances in which a claim of originality is implied although the idea or at least the roots of it existed prior to the birth of self psychology, one example would be Kohut's emphasis upon the importance of the quality of mothering and its influence on the developing ego. He does not mention Freud's (1923) clear recognition of the significance of the real nature of the object in the development of the ego. He wrote that "the character of the ego is a precipitate of abandoned object-cathexes and . . . it contains the history of those object-choices" (p. 29). Nor does Kohut mention Hartmann (1952), who stated that the ego requires a "secure relation not only to the drives but also to the objects" (p. 15) for its proper development. Even more striking is that in the *Restoration of the Self* (Kohut 1977), the acknowledgment of Mahler's work is limited to the mention of her name in the preface. Thus the entire body of research on separation–individuation by Mahler and her colleagues (1972, 1975) is completely ignored, and so is their careful elaboration of the importance of the "optimal emotional availability" (Mahler 1972, p. 410) of the mother to her growing toddler. As a result of this historical sleight of hand, Kohut (and subsequently his followers) succeeds in creating an illusion of originality and uniqueness around some of his propositions. However, the findings of self psychology in this regard are "original [only] in emphasis, not in substance" (Rothstein 1980, p. 426).

Another example of such historical disregard is the way Winnicott's contributions (1965, 1971) are treated in the self psychology literature. Winnicott's concepts of "true" and "false selves" seem to closely parallel Kohut's notions (1977) of the joyful "nuclear self" and the "compensatory structures" elaborated to mask defects in the self. Winnicott's emphasis upon the dual-unity of the mother and baby finds expression in the Kohutian concept of the self-object. Even the mirroring metaphor, introduced by Kohut in *The Analysis of the Self* (1971), finds detailed mention in a paper of Winnicott's (1967) entitled "The mirror-role of mother and family in child development." In this paper, Winnicott emphasizes the role the mother plays in mirroring the child's self to him and the effects that a chronic experience with lack of such mirroring can have on a developing personality. Finally, Kohut suggests that the mother needs not only to mirror enthusiastically her growing child's grandiosity but gradually to shift her mirroring responses to increasingly age-specific tasks and skills. Kohut sees this as facilitating the internalization of the supportive and empathic capabilities and as leading to a deeper and more cohesive self. Winnicott similarly says that the "mother's eventual task is gradually to disillusion the infant" (1953, p. 95). Despite these overlaps in their outlooks, Kohut mentions Winnicott's contribution only in an inconsequential footnote in his 1971 book and in the preface of his 1977 one.

I could enumerate other instances of lack of recognition of precursors,[1]

---

[1] This is true not only of the contributions from within mainstream psychoanalysis but also from the alternate schools of depth psychology. I have elsewhere (Akhtar 1982) hinted at the similarities, for instance, between Sullivan and Kohut. "Both Sullivan and Kohut focused their interest upon the self. Both disregarded instincts. Both minimized the unconscious. Both showed inattention to oedipal issues. Finally, both . . . advocate[d] what seems to be an exaggerated emphasis on the interpersonal and empathic aspects of psychotherapy" (p. 278). In a subsequent publication, Ticho (1982) astutely extended such comparison to include Adler, Jung, and Horney as well. He pointed out the similarities between Kohut and the latter authors. "They speak of the unity of the self, the real self, the ideal self. They describe the self as the core and substance of the individual. They criticize Freud for dividing the psyche into parts. They feel the focusing on parts results in the patient as a whole becoming lost to view. They were afraid that seeing the person in so mechanistic a way would undermine the patient's capacity to develop an autonomous self" (p. 851).

but I will restrict myself to one last example of this sort: the complete absence of Fairbairn's work (1952, 1963) from the bibliography of the two Kohut monographs. Fairbairn is not widely read in this country, and under different circumstances such an omission might have gone unnoticed. In Kohut's case, however, the debt is considerably greater than can be comfortably negated. Robbins (1980), in a paper suggesting that the contemporary Kernberg–Kohut controversy is a replication of the earlier Klein–Fairbairn schism, emphasizes the similarities between Fairbairn and Kohut.

> Both de-emphasize the role of the pleasure principle and the importance of libido and aggression in normal functioning. Both make the self and its object relations the primary unit of inquiry, and consider the nascent self to be the first meaningful psychic constellation. Both consider the self to be a dynamic structure with libidinal and aggressive aspects. Both believe that self-development commences with a state of merger or primary identification. Both believe that satisfactory object relations rather than libidinal gratification promotes growth; that is, they conceptualize the crucial importance of the mother of holding, in contrast to the mother of psychosexual gratification. Both describe how frustration in the primary relationship leads to structuralization of the psyche, including, simultaneously, horizontal (repression) and vertical splitting. Both believe that significant empathic failures or disappointments by the primary object lead to splitting of the dynamic structure, separation of rage, regressive auto-erotic fragmentation, and fantasy restitution. Both view regression as a separate pathway, not a reversal of developmental steps previously traversed. Both seem to believe that it is the timing, the intensity of frustration of the wish to merge with the object which determines whether the results will be pathological regressive fragmentation and splitting, or growth and differentiation of the self. (pp. 486–487)

It must be emphasized that such historical aloofness is not restricted to Kohut himself and can be discerned in the writing of most proponents of self psychology. An example of this is Goldberg's (1978) failure to acknowledge the contributions of Annie Reich (1953, 1960) while discussing a woman patient who required a "relationship with an idealized man to maintain a feeling of inner security and self value" (p. 307). This, like all the other examples I have given so far, illustrates the propensity of Kohut and his followers to ignore contributions of others that have striking similarities with their own.

Failure to Recognize Contradictory Evidence

The second variety of omission in Kohut's writing, his failure to take into account the work of investigators who have presented contradictory evidence, can be illustrated by certain aspects of Mahler's work (1968,

1975). Kohut ignores Mahler's persuasive recognition of the role of body in the emergence of the sense of self, and her emphasis upon innate differences in the behavior of boys and girls. Her attempts to weave together drive and object sides of the equation, her regard for the role of autonomous functions of the ego, and her emphasis upon the changing function of the primary object are all contributions that could challenge Kohut's formulations, but he does not consider them. He also chooses to pay little attention to the object-relations approach to the self and its pathological distortions in borderline and narcissistic conditions, as elaborated in the works of Jacobson (1964), Kernberg (1975, 1976), and Volkan (1976, 1982) among others. Similarly, when it comes to the origins of the self, one can notice omissions of infant research data that could put to considerable test the purely psychogenic view espoused by self psychology. Kohut disregards the works of Thomas and Chess (1963, 1968, 1980a, 1980b), Emde et al. (1976), Stern (1976), Brazelton (1981), and Greenspan (1981), to name just a few. Noticing these kinds of omissions in *The Restoration of the Self*, Stein (1979) tersely states that while this "would be perfectly excusable in a lecture, perhaps in a brief scientific article. It represents a serious . . . omission in a volume that puts forward a radical version of, even a departure from, psychoanalytic theory" (p. 677).

Use of "Straw Man" Arguments

With regard to the third kind of historical distortion, well-known "straw man" argumentative device, two examples should suffice. In the first, Kohut selects Franz Alexander (e.g., Kohut 1977, pp. 69, 72) as a representative of "classical drive theory," whereas numerous other possible representatives would not have suited his purposes as well. In the second, he is surprisingly diligent in distinguishing his views from those of Melanie Klein. For instance, when Kohut speaks of his "conceptualization of a self at the beginning of life," he feels compelled to add that this view is "not burdened by the Kleinian fallacy that specific verbalizable fantasies are present in earliest infancy" (Kohut 1977, p. 100).[2] This clarification appears legitimate and even helpful at first glance. However, a second look

---

[2] Despite this and many other theoretical fallacies, Klein's position is more secure in the analytic universe than that of Kohut. This point was made to me by my friend and colleague Thomas Wolman, M.D. "Kohut has affected the internal development of psychoanalysis but from the position of an outsider. Melanie Klein, on the other hand, maintained an analytic posture despite the wide theoretical gulf separating her from the mainstream psychoanalysis. Kohut will therefore go the way of Horney and Sullivan. The Kleinian system will never meet that fate but will exist (coexist) inside psychoanalysis. We can thus term Klein a 'disturbing insider' and Kohut a 'useful outsider' in the chamber of analytic dialogue" (personal communication, 1984).

reveals the magician's trick: a comparison with Klein and not with Fairbairn at this point helps Kohut establish the novelty of the theoretical assumption in question.

Possible Explanations of Kohut's Solipsism

Whatever form the historical solipsism may take, its presence remains strikingly obvious in the writings of Kohut and his followers. My demonstration of such disregard does not itself explain the reasons for this perplexing stance, but it does (and should) prompt a search for them. I can think of *five explanatory hypotheses*, but two can easily be rejected. The five are ignorance, arrogance, the one-sidedness of the new, political needs of psychoanalysis, and unknown personal factors. The *first* of these, ignorance, borders on the unthinkable; indeed, in the preface to his 1977 monograph, Kohut shows clear awareness of the overlaps between his theories and the works of others and even mentions various such comparisons that have been made. The *second* hypothesis, professional arrogance, is too simplistic and off-handed a dismissal of what appears to be a more complexly determined phenomenon. The *third* hypothesis invokes the temporary one-sidedness in thinking that frequently follows a new discovery. Freud (1916–1917) pointed to such a tendency when he stated that in the matters of scientific theory, "people are very fond of selecting one position of truth, putting it in place of the whole, and then discarding the rest, which is no less true, in favor of this one position." (p. 346)

In other words, the joy (an affect Kohut frequently refers to) of discovering the deep significance of the narcissistic sector of personality or of empathy may have transiently overcome customary scientific attention to thoroughness and caution. Perhaps. And perhaps that is what led Kohut to explain his lack of integration of his views with other related works by stating that his focus was not on "scholarly completeness" (1977). However, if this one-sidedness were in actuality temporary, then one would have seen an attempt in his later writings (Kohut 1979, 1980, 1982) at such integration. One does not find it there, nor does one see any major trend of that sort in the works of his followers.

The *fourth* explanation would demand that we view Kohut's "emergence" as a quasi-sociopolitical process within the psychoanalytic cosmos. It is known that at certain times in the history of a society someone with knowledge, drive, and personal charisma can give voice to its mute, unspoken, but pressing needs. Cooper (1983) implicitly suggests this when he says that in a slower phase of creativity and faced with a changing patient clientele, American psychoanalysis may have needed a stimulus to rejuvenate its creative potential, and that self psychology may have provided the much required nudge. From this perspective, then, Kohut's failure to mention others' contributions can be seen as a careful and deliberate literary device to assure a high profile and an aura of originality (and therefore promise) around his propositions. The "new language," and the hope it implicitly offers, then becomes both an answer to unmet needs within a profession and at the same time a potential search for a new audience.

The *fifth* and final explanation of Kohut's solipsism may involve idiosyncratic and personal matters that can only be understood (or even raised) in a future psychobiography of Kohut himself as an individual. As time allows a greater distance from the unsettling impact of this aloofness, we may gain a better understanding of it.

LINEAR DETERMINISM

In self psychology we are presented with an easy solution for the extraordinary complex problems of the roots and causes of human psychopathology: defective maternal (or paternal) empathy. Case after case in self psychology literature illustrates this position. Let us take a few examples from *The Restoration of the Self* (Kohut 1977). Mr. M's mother had "flawed empathy . . . [and] incapacity to tune in" (p. 9). Mr. U's mother was "oddly unempathic [and] emotionally shallow" (p. 55). Mr. W's mother was "highly unempathic" (p. 160), and Mr. I's mother was "highly unempathic" (p. 166). The same trend can be discerned in *The Psychology of the Self* (Goldberg 1978). Mr. E's mother had been "distant, preoccupied and exhausted" (p. 265). Mrs. R's mother was a "decidedly idiosyncratic self-centered woman" (p. 301), and Mr. B's mother was "chronically preoccupied with her own self" (p. 367). The self of Mr. Z's mother (Kohut 1979) displayed a "central hollowness" and a "psychotic core" (p. 15). The message is loud and clear. It is the lack of empathic responsiveness on the part of the parents, especially the mother, that is the main etiologic agent for narcissistic pathology. Indeed, Kohut (1977) proposes that the mothers of many of his patients have a "pathogenic personality disorder" (p. 189).[3] This single etiologic factor is relied upon to explain extremely complex sets of circumstances including narcissistic personality disorder, borderline conditions, perversions, delinquency, and addictions.

If one can escape the almost hypnotic influence of the repeated presentation of similar data, then one begins to raise serious questions about this single-minded and quite literally deterministic approach. Among the

---

[3] Wallerstein (1983) aptly compares this suggestion to the now disproven "overly simple conception of the schizophrenogenic mother" (p. 52).

questions that come to one's mind are the following: If the nature of the parental empathy toward the child is the sole determinant of the personality outcome, how is one to understand the phenomenon of mentally healthy and well-adjusted adults who as children were raised by severely disturbed parents (Anthony 1974)? And how is one to explain that not all children raised by the same mother develop similar character structures? Clearly, siblings of narcissistic individuals do not necessarily have similar psychostructural organizations. Therefore, even if one were to accept the etiologic role of the mother, it would seem more appropriate to speak of a pathogenically unempathic *attitude* that she especially directed toward *one* particular child—and that, too, perhaps during a *specific* developmental period—rather than positing the existence in her of a pathogenically unempathic personality disorder. The heuristic advantage that would result is that one would then question when the difficulty in empathy was most injurious and where it was coming from. Kohut and his followers attribute it solely to the mother's psychopathology, ignoring in the process the possibility that a "constitutional misfit" (Thomas and Chess 1980, 1984) of the mother and her infant may be contributing to the difficulties in meaningful empathic communication between them. Stein (1979) points out further omissions resulting from the exclusive emphasis upon the mother's side of the equation:

> The accidents of fate—from the meeting of ovum and sperm, the physiological condition of the mother (empathic or not) that affects the fetus and the newborn, access to nutrition, literal or cultural, the presence of siblings, early death of parents and others—none of these factors is given sufficient weight in Kohut's world of etiology. (p. 677)

Even in the realm of parental influence, self psychology does not seem to do justice to "the spectrum of mothering and fathering experiences by patients considered to have narcissistic disorders" (Rothstein 1980, pp. 430–431). Almost totally ignored are the roles that patients' gender, birth order, and special endowments or the lack thereof, parental overvaluation, and the child's regressive movements from the struggles of the oedipal phase may play in the genesis of narcissistic personality disorder. Further, in what appears to be an over-enthusiastic "deficiency perspective" (Rothstein 1980), Kohut and his followers overlook what did happen as against what was lacking in the childhood of these individuals.

In defense of Kohut, it should be acknowledged that a decisively unifactorial model of pathogenesis does exert a powerful, regressive pull on the theoretician's work ego. The intellectual comfort and the aesthetic elegance offered by such models are difficult to turn down. Indeed, in the field of physical medicine (admittedly, somewhat less so recently), such "economy" in the etiological pursuit has always been regarded as a theoretical virtue. Thus, Kohut has the sanction of legacy and is quite "traditional" in that regard. This also brings up a related second point that Kohut's critics must admit. Kohut is not alone in presenting an etiologic model that is environmentally based, unifactorial, and reductionistic, and in which the clinical theoretician tends to over-identify with the child as a victim. Such over-identification may, in part, be responsible for the poignancy that often characterizes the writings of the authors mentioned below. Theoretical narrowness is subtly present in some of Winnicott's works (1965). It is more clearly discernible in Guntrip's writings (1969, 1971) and Khan's essays, especially the more recent ones (Khan 1983). Laing (1960, 1964) had earlier championed this viewpoint, extending it to include conspiratorial motives in parents. One also sees the continuation of this tradition in the popular recent work of Alice Miller (1981), which suggests that narcissistic character pathology emanates from the child's being unempathically treated as a narcissistic extension of the parent. While Miller is well aware of intrapsychic factors, the flavor of the bad, unempathic mother permeates her work.

An important consequence of the linear, unifactorial mode of etiological thinking is the minimization of the conscious and unconscious fantasy elaboration of the child's perceptions of his environment. Patients' accounts of their childhood, including descriptions of their parents, are readily believed as factual, with little consideration of defensive compromises of memory and current perception. The paramount role that unconscious fantasy (Arlow 1969) plays in psychopathological formations thus fails to receive adequate attention.[4] For instance, in the case of Mr. M (Kohut 1977) the etiologic emphasis is upon the empathic failures of his adopted mother. The fantasies that Mr. M as a child may have elaborated about his natural mother, his abandonment by her, his adoption, and so forth, and the effects of these fantasies upon him, are not mentioned in the case report.

The reductionistic mode of thinking is not limited to etiological postulates alone. It pervades the self psychology view of the cross-sectional dynamics of psychopathology as well. Kohut's explanation (1980) of agoraphobia is one such instance. He makes it clear that in his view the agoraphobic's consciously felt need for a reassuring companion is the key to what lies in his psychic depths—namely, the continued search for a

---

[4] Kohut's overemphasis on the environmental factors is only one source of the minimization of the unconscious. Viewing the self as a supraordinate structure, and the resulting "humanistic holism" (Palombo 1978, p. 9), is another contributing factor. The effects of these and other aspects of Kohut's thought upon the concept of a dynamic unconscious have been discussed in greater detail by Palombo (1978), Rangell (1982), Richards (1982), and Cooper (1983), among others.

maternal self-object.[5] The repressed prostitution fantasy frequently associated with agoraphobia (Freud 1892–1899, p. 253, 1897 extract) may be present but is regarded as superficial, the result of disintegration products of an earlier lack of self-cohesion. Cooper (1983) points out that such reasoning

> leads to a clinical conclusion that the surface phenomena of the symptom . . . may be a clear guide to the individual's depth psychology, not requiring the detours of multiple wish-defense layers. . . . This view necessarily deemphasizes the repressed, distorted, pathological, sexual and aggressive fantasy. (p. 14)

The one-symptom/one-meaning tendency negates the concept of overdetermination and the "principle of multiple function" (Waelder 1930). This propensity also affects the manner in which the data of clinical process itself are interpreted. For instance, the buying of an expensive violin by Mr. M during the terminal phase of his analysis is explained by Kohut (1977) as being

> a form of psychoanalytic homework through which he tried to learn to express his exhibitionistic strivings in realistic yet gratifying ways. The patient's newly acquired structures, however, enabled him to enjoy the expression of his exhibitionistic strivings; in the fantasies that accompanied his playing he offered his grandiose self to the admiring view of multitudes which he experienced as "maternal," without being inhibited by the fear that he would suffer the crushing frustration of maternal disinterest, and without the even greater fear that he would become hypomanically overstimulated and thus experience the dissolution of his exhibiting self. The violin playing and the accompanying fantasies of admiring listening crowds were able to deal with the excess of his exhibitionistic needs that had become activated in the transference yet could not be fully absorbed within the psychoanalytic situation. The violin playing enabled the patient to persevere in the analytic work by lessening the psychic tensions to which the transference exposed him, and it made its own positive contribution to the goal of working through by creating provisional, temporarily useful structures in the sector of the creative employment of his narcissistic strivings. (pp. 38–39)

Mr. M's subsequent decision to sell the violin and dedicate himself to creative writing is explained by Kohut on the grounds that the patient's innate abilities were in that realm. Since Mr. M's father was also skilled in

---

[5] Helene Deutsch (1929) also regarded the involvement of a partner as the crucial determinant of the agoraphobic's malady. However, she felt that hostile and controlling fantasies were frequently hidden underneath the consciously experienced need for reassurance and libidinal attachment.

the sphere of words, Kohut believes that Mr. M's turning from music to writing clearly demonstrated that "the patient was turning from the mirroring mother to the idealized father" (p. 38).

> The analysis opened the road to an activity that permitted him joyful self-realization. His work as a writer enabled him to gratify his grandiose-exhibitionistic strivings to display himself to his mother, satisfy his need to merge with his idealized father, and enjoy the employment of the genuine talents he possessed. (p. 40)

The poetic appeal of these explanations is striking. They are perhaps accurate as well. However, the clinical material provided by Kohut lends itself to other, equally plausible explanations. It should be emphasized that the purpose of presenting alternate views of the material is not to question the correctness of Kohut's interpretations. It is only to point out their apparent failure to take into account any other possible meanings besides those pertaining to mirroring and idealizing needs.

With this caveat, and with the recognition that attributing additional (or alternate) meanings to someone else's clinical material is fraught with limitations and runs the risk of being "experience-distant," let us return to Mr. M's report. The material can surely be looked at in different ways. For instance, the buying and selling of the violin can also be seen as representing a struggle over phallic competitive strivings toward the analyst/father. Being admired by the "maternal" audience may have incestuous implications that would be simultaneously exciting and threatening. Kohut suggests that the patient's fear of hypomanic over-stimulation was related to a threatened dissolution of his exhibiting self. Perhaps. But it could *also* be related to a fear/wish of crushing the analyst. Giving up the violin could then be understood as a self-induced, preemptive oedipal defeat, a self-castration only to be denied by taking up creative writing. One also wonders whether Mr. M was somehow aware of Kohut's own interest in music and his publications ("creative writing") on the subject of music. Taking this perspective, the violin/creative writing episode may appear to have even deeper transference significance. The drive-defense constellation and its multidetermined, multilayered, and repetitive nature are obvious in this example. However, these alternative—or, most likely, additional—explanations are not considered by Kohut.

The strictly deterministic and linear approach inherent here is evident in all three spheres discussed above—the realm of etiological hypotheses, psychodynamic explanation of symptoms, and the understanding of the material in the clinical hour. In the first sphere that of etiology what is most striking about the unifactorial approach is the almost complete negation of the child's constitution.

DISREGARD OF CONSTITUTIONAL FACTORS

Reading the self psychology literature one is struck by the emphasis upon the impact of parental personalities on the growing child. Parallel and complementary to this emphasis is the implied disregard of constitutional factors. The omission is manifest in the self psychology view of how the self comes into being and also of how psychopathology originates, but I shall here briefly focus on how the topic of the origin of the self is treated in self psychology. The "nuclear self" (Kohut 1977) is reported to form during the earliest stages of neonatal life by the "deeply anchored responsiveness of the self-objects" (p. 100) to the newborn. Indeed, Kohut asserts that the person's psychological self has its virtual beginnings at the moment when the mother sees her baby for the first time. Thus, from the earliest period of infancy the major influence upon formation of the self is seen as emanating from the environment. No mention is made of constitutional factors. The child is viewed as a *tabula rasa*; the increasing evidence that neonates vary greatly in their inherent "temperament" (Thomas and Chess 1980, 1984) is negated. Kohut also ignores the effects of individual differences in "central and peripheral nervous system organization" (Lustman 1956) and "reactions to sensory stimuli" (Bergman and Escalona 1949) upon the elicitation and assimilation of maternal responsiveness (Greenspan 1981). He not only overlooks these subtle ways in which the infant's constitution contributes to the mothering experience but also minimizes the role of body itself as the foundation of the self. For example, he fails to speak of Mahler's relevant observations (1968) on the shift of cathexis in the neonate from the inside of the body to the sensoriperceptive rind of the ego and the role of this shift in "self boundary formation" (Mahler and McDevitt 1982). He does not take into account the role played in formation of boundaries of the body self by libidinization, through the earliest ministrations of the mother (Hoffer 1950), or later by hurts and bumps as the toddler aggressively comes up against the physical world (Mahler et al. 1975). That the importance of the integration of part-images of the body into a whole self-image is not recognized by Kohut is surprising, since many narcissistic and borderline individuals have subtle disturbances in the perception of their bodily selves (Bach 1977). Freud's dictum that "the ego is first and foremost a bodily ego" (1923) does not seem to apply to the self as postulated by Kohut and his followers.

Clearly there are two separate questions involved here. The first refers to whether one can hypothesize a rudimentary self from the earliest stages of infancy, and the second to what the origins are of this rudimentary self. The first, although admittedly a significant and much debated question, is not the one I am concerned with here. It is the second I have chosen to examine. Let us therefore return to Kohut's view that the beginning of the self is in the environment's recognition of it. This emphasis is not restricted to the early steps in the formation of the self. Events and developments in later childhood, as these affect consolidation of the self, are also described in predominantly environmental terms. The self is seen as bipolar in origin. At one pole are the *nuclear ambitions* of early childhood, and at the other are the *nuclear idealized goals* acquired in later childhood. The earlier constituents, Kohut suggests, are predominantly derived from the relation with the maternal self-object, while the constituents acquired later may come from parental figures of either sex. The two "poles" are approximately equivalent to the concepts of grandiose self and idealized parent image in Kohut's earlier (1971) terminology. In that framework, these protostructures were seen as being gradually internalized by the sequence of empathic gratification, phase-specific modulation, and nontraumatic disappointment. In the newer framework—that is, the framework of self psychology in its "broader sense"—the emphasis on internalization per se is less. The term itself occurs infrequently, and the process is described in vague phenomenological phrases of "selective inclusion and exclusion" (Kohut 1977, p. 183).[6] The intrapsychic and metapsychological correlates of these processes are not described anywhere. However, this bipolar "internalization" is viewed as leading to the cohesion and inner fullness of the self.

Curiously, a third element in the formation of the self is introduced at this stage. This element definitely seems to belong to the child's "internal environment" (Hoffer 1952). It refers to the "innate talents and abilities" (Kohut 1977) around which the self will be formed and in the uniquely personal bedrock of which the two halves of the self will be anchored. While this proposition appears appealing, it also leaves one with a peculiar theoretical paradox. If there are innate talents and abilities in a positive sense, then should there not be innate lack of talents, in the broadest sense of the word, and innate disabilities? Why do the latter find no mention in the formulations of self psychology? Also ignored is the influence that maturation of autonomous ego functions has on the self experience (Hartmann 1950). And no mention is made of the role special neonatal sensitivities and developmental lags play in influencing maternal responsiveness. The quality and usefulness of maternal care is seen

---

[6] As self psychology has moved from its "narrower" (1971) to its "broader" (1977) sense, its language has undergone a significant alteration. What were grandiose self, idealized parent imago, internalization, and narcissistic transferences have become nuclear goals, nuclear ambitions, selective inclusion, and self-object transference. Indeed, numerous such changes have occurred. One that is theoretically quite suggestive is reflected, as pointed out by Rothstein (1980), in the titles of the two Kohut monographs: *"Analysis* of the Self" (1971) has become *"Restoration* of the Self" (1977) (italics mine).

only as a function of the mother and as not a complex process involving two parties. In this regard Weil (1978) noted that "the experience of mothering in itself depends on the perceptual constellation and interplay of each individual child with his individual mother" (p. 468). It is therefore not surprising that Weil's concept (1970) of the "basic core" of the self is an inseparable amalgam of the given/constitutional and evoked/environmental constituents. This is in sharp contrast with Kohut's "nuclear self," which is practically all psyche and no soma. Indeed, in his last published paper Kohut (1982) emphasizes his theory's divorce from biology by declaring self psychology to be a "psychology through and through."[7]

Nowhere is the disregard of the body more apparent than in the manner in which the sex of the growing child is treated in self psychology. In all the discussions of the origins of the self, no mention is made of the role played by the "constitutionally pre-destined, gender-defined differences in the behavior of boys and girls" (Mahler et al. 1975, p. 224). The profound psychological consequences of the anatomical distinction between the sexes are completely ignored. Anatomy, far from being destiny, seems to play no part in it. Kohut's interpretation of the oedipus complex is similarly sanitized.[8] In his descriptions there is greater emphasis on the empathic or unempathic responses of the parents to the oedipal child than upon the child's own internal fantasy life during this phase. He also overemphasizes the "prehistory of the oedipus complex" (Freud 1925) at the cost of the oedipal phase proper. While it is well recognized that preoedipal development affects the oedipal phase at times, giving it an "irrevocable pregenital cast" (Fenichel 1945), and that a solidly established self is a prerequisite for the deep and genuinely triadic relationships characteristic of this phase, Kohut presents these as novel postulates. Characteristically, his emphasis remains on the interpersonal, environmental factors even in this context. The impact of sexual differences upon the separation–individuation processes (Mahler et al. 1975) is

---

[7] The disregard of biology is additionally apparent in Kohut's writings through his complete omission of the phylogenetic dimension, which was ever-present in Freud's conceptualizations.

[8] First, in Kohut's description of the oedipal phase there is little or no mention of urinary stream pleasure, literal phallic exhibitionism, female genitalia, infantile theories of childbirth, penis envy, primal scene, etc. Second, and perhaps more important, Kohut seems unable to recognize the genuinely triadic, as against dyadic, nature of relationships typical of this phase. Even the Odysseus myth, which Kohut proposes (1982) as the centerpiece of his theory and by which he wishes to replace the centrality of oedipus complex, is essentially a dyadic parable.

overlooked. He also does not take into account the "early genital phase" (Roiphe 1968) and its crucial influence on object relations, basic mood, fantasy life, and many other aspects of ego functioning (Galenson and Roiphe 1971, 1974, 1980). The genital schematization beginning in this phase and continuing through later phallic–oedipal epochs constitutes the basis for gender identity, an integral aspect of the self experience, but it finds no place in Kohut's formulation of the development of the self. How a depth psychology that puts self experience at the very center of its study can manage to avoid discussing issues of gender identity remains perplexing, to say the least.[9]

The neglect of sexual differences becomes even more disturbing if one remembers that approximately 90 percent of cases reported upon by Kohut and his followers are males. Yet no explanation is offered for such clustering. Observing the male preponderance among those with narcissistic characters in general, I have previously raised questions about it (Akhtar and Thomson 1982):

> Is this simply a reflection of the predominance of men currently undergoing psychoanalysis (Pulver 1978)? Is there a diagnostic bias involved? Are male children at greater risk of being treated as ambivalently special in our culture? Finally, is the predominance of men evidence that the development of narcissistic personality disorder is somehow intertwined with male psychosexual development? (p. 19)

The last question now acquires greater significance in view of the fact that while narcissistic personality disorder seems more common among males (Akhtar and Thomson 1982), borderline personality disorder has been demonstrated (Akhtar et al., 1986) to be more common among females. If one could eliminate the possible artifacts caused by diagnostic and referral biases, then this difference would suggest a significant impact of sex of the individual upon the nature of psychopathological formation. Since narcissistic and borderline conditions are regarded as belonging on a developmental (Mahler et al. 1972, 1975), dynamic (Kernberg 1970, 1975; Kohut 1971, 1977) and phenomenological (Adler 1981; Akhtar 1984a) continuum of severity, the sex-related difference in their incidence leads one to speculate that similarly traumatic preoedipal experiences have a more troubled outcome in the female than in the male child. Perhaps the experience of maleness and specifically the possession of a penis provides a tangible evidence of one's distinction from the

---

[9] In a different but overlapping context, Friedman (1980) remarks that "Kohut is much clearer about how someone is fulfilled by his career than about why he is satisfied by the way he makes love" (p. 408).

mother (Chassegeut-Smirgel 1970)[10] and is thus a greater reassurance against the ambivalent symbiotic pull during what Mahler and her colleagues (1975) have labeled the rapprochement subphase of separation–individuation process. Mahler has emphasized that this period is more troubled for the girl than for the boy and that it is the recognition of sexual difference that accounts for the variance. I suggest that the borderline versus narcissistic outcome of a rapprochement fixation is an exaggerated and pathologic counterpart of the normal difference in the rapprochement phase of the two sexes. While multiple earlier and later factors ultimately determine the phenotypal presentation, this situation is a firm reminder of how sex of the growing child can have profound influence on the nature of his/her self. By treating the sexual differences as nonexistent, therefore, the work of Kohut and his followers creates theoretical scotoma of alarming proportions.

THE POSTULATE OF CONFLICT-FREE PSYCHOPATHOLOGY

Intrapsychic conflict is central to the structural model of the mind, and psychoanalysis has prototypically been a psychology of conflict. In Ernst Kris's (1947) famous aphoristic definition, the subject matter of psychoanalysis is regarded as nothing but "human behavior viewed as conflict." Brenner (1976, 1982) provides a more current and more detailed statement of the same fundamental theme, and there remains a broad consensus among practicing psychoanalysts that the concept of conflict is basic to the understanding and treatment of psychopathology. The inevitability and even desirability of conflict in the maturation and development of the self are also themes that most analysts acquiesce in peacefully.

In contrast, self psychology proposes that the origins of the self are conflict-free and that certain kinds of psychopathology are not manifestations of intrapsychic conflict but of a state of psychological deficit. These "primary disturbances of the self" (Kohut and Wolf 1978) include psychoses, borderline states, narcissistic behavior disorders, and narcissistic personality disorders. The theory proposes that such conditions cannot be adequately understood by traditional psychoanalytic ways of thinking because they emphasize the existence of a conflict at the core of all psychopathology. Instead, self psychology holds that these conditions

---

[10] It is interesting to note that in Chasseguet-Smirgel's own work (1984) on perversions, almost all the patients reported upon are men. Not only this, even the historical and fictional examples (see for instance, "Perversion as exemplified by three Luciferian characters" in Chasseguet-Smirgel 1984, pp. 13–23) are restricted to males. The observation acquires greater relevance to the topic when one notices the not inconsiderable overlap (e.g., megalomania, striving for power, sadism, near-fusion of ego and ego-ideal, bypassing the oedipal dilemma, etc.) between her "perverse" character organization and what is being referred to here as narcissistic personality disorder.

betray a deficit, a defect, at the core of the self, and therefore can be understood, explained, and treated only by Kohutian methods. This stance has caused a major rupture in the historical continuity of the psychoanalytic emphasis upon conflict from Freud (1926) to Brenner (1982). It also leaves many phenomena unexplained and many questions unanswered. For instance, is there no inherent conflict between grandiose and idealizing aspirations? Do the grandiose beliefs about the self not come in conflict with the more realistic conscious and preconscious assessments of the self and its abilities? Does the patient not experience any conflict between his narcissistic wishes and the moral prohibitions that he acquires later? Kohut and Wolf (1978) state

> If it was the grandiose-exhibitionistic pole of a person's self that had been exposed to unempathic over-stimulation in childhood, then no healthy glow of enjoyment can be obtained by him from external success. On the contrary, since these people are subject to being flooded by unrealistic, archaic greatness fantasies which produce painful tension and anxiety, they will try to avoid situations in which they could become the center of attention. (p. 419)

Careful scrutiny of this particular example reveals the necessity for the concept of conflict. The expression "being flooded" itself implies an aspect of the mind that is the source of the flood and another psychic structure that is its potential victim. In other words, what is being flooded and from where? Is there no conflict between the two aspects, agencies, structures involved here? In another example, the same logical necessity of internal conflict applies to Kohut and Wolf's description of "contact-shunning personalities."

> These individuals avoid social contact and become isolated, not because they are disinterested in others, but, on the contrary, just because their need for them is so intense. (p. 422)

The phrase "on the contrary" mediates here between the need for others and their avoidance. Is this not a description of an internal conflict?[11] It is interesting to note at this point that a strikingly similar

---

[11] Clearly, clarifying attempts of this kind may be derided as phenomenological hair-splitting and as taking the word "conflict" too literally. Such attempts may appear to ignore the progressive movement of psychoanalytic thought in the direction of object-relations theory, in keeping with a greater understanding of the initial dyad and its many reverberations. As a consequence of such movement, there is a political conservative vs. progressive aspect to the conflict–deficit debate (see, for instance, the latter part of Greenspan's 1977 paper). "Conflict" here would stand for oedipal, neurotic conflict and not an internal psychic struggle alone, while "deficit" would imply preoedipal or dyadic and not exclude an intrapsychic struggle of forces. I wish to emphasize that my decision here to define the term "conflict" quite sharply is purposive and not based on ignorance of the unfortunate, political buzz-word significance of the term.

phenomenon was earlier described by Burnham et al. (1969) under the designation "need-fear dilemma," without renunciating the concept of intrapsychic conflict altogether.

How, then, in the face of such evidence, is self psychology able to negate the presence of conflict in such patients? One possible explanation may lie in the extremely narrow definition of the concept of "conflict" in the writings of self psychology. Almost exclusively (see for instance Kohut 1977, pp. 132, 260) an intrapsychic conflict is equated with a structural or intersystemic conflict. This is precisely where the problem arises. Clearly, two extreme positions have been taken in this regard. The first is that of Arlow and Brenner (1964), who attempt to explain all varieties of psychopathology by the structural conflict model. The second is that of Kohut (1977, 1982) and his followers, who claim—perhaps rightly—that the structural conflict model is not applicable to narcissistic pathology and throw out the entire conflict theory, in the proverbial manner of the baby with the bath water.

Reality lies in the middle. Not all intrapsychic conflict is structural or *intersystemic* conflict. It is also possible to identify an *intrasystemic conflict* (Freud A, 1965) between, for instance, "different instinctual tendencies (heterosexuality and homosexuality, activity and passivity, love and hate) or between conflicted ego impulses" (Wallerstein 1983, p. 36). And to the list of the intersystemic and intrasystemic, one should add the important category of *object relations conflict*. This kind of conflict involves a less differentiated psychic structure that is antecedent to id-ego-superego differentiation. Describing what he considers the crucial difference between a structural or intersystemic conflict and an object relations conflict, Dorpat (1976) writes that

> in a structural conflict, the subject experiences (or is capable of experiencing if some part of the conflict is unconscious) the opposing tendencies as aspects of himself. . . . In the object relations conflict, the subject experiences the conflict as being between his own wishes and his representations (e.g., introjects) of another person's values, prohibitions or injunctions. (pp. 869–870)

Dorpat places his concept of object relations conflict midway between Anna Freud's classes (1965) of "external" (interpersonal) and "internalized" (intersystemic) conflicts seen in children.

This manner of conceptualizing various types of intrapsychic conflicts is consonant with the hierarchical model proposed by Gedo and Goldberg (1973). Their design allows for a tripartite model at a higher developmental level and an object relations model at a lower developmental level. This view is also evident in Kernberg's (1970) hierarchy of character organization, and in Greenspan's (1977) correlation of "internal object constancy" (Mahler 1968) with structural conflicts and of the lack of such constancy with object relations conflicts.

Let us return now, with this enriched view of the concept of conflict, to Kohut's proposition that individuals with narcissistic pathology have only a psychological defect and no internal conflict. Such persons may indeed have few (or fewer) structural conflicts but a great many object relations conflicts. The "contact-shunning" narcissist, for instance, who feels the need of people and yet avoids them, is struggling with his own exhibitionistic wishes and his own inhibitions against them. However, he seems to feel it has something to do with people. This experiential distortion of an internal conflict, when observed by someone in a position of "concordant identification" (Racker 1957) can lead to a conclusion that the patient's mental suffering is conflict-free. The postulate of a deficit would then be the next logical step.

Needless to say, the conflict–deficit dichotomy, regarded as "puzzling and . . . fundamentally unhelpful" by Wallerstein (1981, p. 37), has serious implications. It has led to the creation of the reified psychological postulates of the "Tragic Man" and the "Guilty Man" (Kohut 1977). Here I am using these expressions in their "narrow" sense—that is, the "Tragic Man" refers to an individual with a psychological deficit who is struggling to maintain cohesion of his fragmenting self, and the "Guilty Man" refers to one battling with his prohibited sexual and aggressive longings. This manner of thinking leads to an artificial separation of preoedipal and oedipal development. As I have suggested elsewhere:

> The Tragic Man is no less "guilty" if one takes into account the paranoid distortions of parental objects under the influence of pregenital aggression, the superego precursors and the "guilt" over having taken too much from the mother and in the process depleted her. Similarly, the Guilty Man is no less tragic insofar as the sources of his guilt are his incestuous and patricidal fantasies (and not acts), wishes that emanated in him with the unfolding of a constitutional blueprint beyond his control and a family structure not of his choosing. What is more tragic than to punish oneself for one's own thoughts? The artificial dichotomy of the Tragic Man and the Guilty Man oversimplifies human experience, ignores genetic spirality, overlooks the "principle of multiple function" (Waelder 1930) and produces unnecessary and unfortunate duplicity in psychoanalytic technique. (Akhtar 1984a)

The conflict–deficit, Guilty Man–Tragic Man dichotomy also has significant bearing upon psychoanalytic views of child development, traumatic states, relationship of reality and fantasy, and so forth. Finally, the metaphors of Guilty Man and Tragic Man in their "broader sense," to paraphrase Kohut, have profound impact on the psychoanalytic view of the very nature of the man. That is a topic that is beyond the scope of the present essay, but it is important to keep in mind that such a dichotomy, whether in its narrow or broad sense, is fundamentally against the analytic mode of thinking. As Wallerstein comments:

> in the flow and flux of analytic clinical material we are always in the world of "both/and." We deal constantly, and in turn, both with the oedipal, where there is a coherent self, and the preoedipal, where they may not yet be; with defensive regressions and with developmental arrests; with defensive transferences and defensive resistances and with recreations of earlier traumatic and traumatized states. (1983, p. 31)

CONCLUSION

The self psychology of Heinz Kohut and his followers has many theoretical shortcomings. After briefly commenting upon Kohut's historical solipsism, I have discussed three such shortcomings of self psychology and their effects upon views of personality development and psychopathology. These three limitations of self psychology are 1) its tendency toward linear determinism, 2) its disregard of inborn, constitutional elements of the self, and 3) its postulate of a conflict-free, deficit-based model of psychopathology.

Nowhere in the entire corpus of self psychology are these shortcomings more obvious than in the Kohutian overemphasis on the impact of parental personalities on the growing child's psyche. Years ago Hartmann (1952) recognized that studies showing the impact of incomplete or empty relationships with the mother on ego development (e.g., Spitz 1945) were valuable but, with characteristic thoroughness, also indicated "the danger of overemphasizing and oversimplifying this side":

> That the ego needs, in order properly to function and to develop, a secure relation not only to the drives but also to the objects, is obviously true. But ego development and object relationships are correlated in more complex ways than some recent works would have us believe— which we could already expect on theoretical grounds. We do not know much about corrections of very early unsatisfactory situations through later maturational processes. It might also be that not only "poor" early object relations can be sometimes made up for by later ego development, but also that so-called "good" object relations may become a developmental handicap—probably, I should think, if and insofar as the child has not succeeded in utilizing them for the strengthening of his ego. (p. 15)

As is obvious, Hartmann's manner of conceptualization is inclusive. It takes into account the numerous forces that act upon ego development, whether they emanate from instinctual drives, inborn ego characteristics, or external reality. It pays attention to complex interplay between the mother and the child, between development and maturation, and between constitutional and environmental factors. Kohut's shortcoming is not that he lacks the richness and depth of Hartmann's thought. It is that he seems purposely to avoid it.

REFERENCES

Adler G: The borderline-narcissistic personality disorder continuum. Am J Psychiatry 1981; 138:46-50

Akhtar S: A self psychology by another name. . . . Contemporary Psychiatry 1982; 9:275-278

Akhtar S: Self psychology vs. mainstream psychoanalysis: and the winner is . . . .Contemporary Psychiatry 1984a; 3:113-117

Akhtar S: The syndrome of identity diffusion. Am J Psychiatry 1984b; 114:1381-1385

Akhtar S, Thomson JA: Overview: narcissistic personality disorder. Am J Psychiatry 1982; 139:12-20

Akhtar S, Doghramji K, Byrne JP: The demographic profile of borderline personality disorder. J Clin Psychiatry 1984; 47:196-198

Anthony EJ: The syndrome of the psychologically invulnerable child, in The Child and His Family: Children at Psychiatric Risk, vol. 3. Edited by Anthony EJ, Koupernik C. New York, John Wiley & Sons, 1974

Arlow JA: Unconscious fantasy and disturbances of conscious experience. Psychoanal Q 1969; 38:1-27

Arlow JA, Brenner C: Psychoanalytic Concepts and the Structural Theory. New York, International Universities Press, 1964

Bach S: On the narcissistic state of consciousness. Int J of Psychoanal 1977; 58:209-233

Bergman P, Escalona SK: Unusual sensitivities in very young children. Psychoanal Study Child 1949; 314:333-352

Blum HP: Theories of the self and psychoanalytic concepts: discussion. J Am Psychoanal Assoc 1982; 30:959-978

Brazelton TB: Neonatal assessment, in The Course of Life: Psychoanalytic Contributions Toward Understanding Human Development, vol. I. Edited by Greenspan SI, Pollock GH. Washington, DC, U.S. Government Printing Office, 1981

Brenner C: Psychoanalytic Technique and Psychic Conflict. New York, International Universities Press, 1976

Brenner C: The Mind in Conflict. New York, International Universities Press, 1982

Burnham D, Gibson R, Gladstone A: Schizophrenia and the Need–Fear Dilemma. New York, International Universities Press, 1969

Chasseguet-Smirgel J: Female Sexuality. Ann Arbor, MI, The University of Michigan Press, 1970

Chasseguet-Smirgel J: Creativity and Perversion. New York, W. W. Norton, 1984

Cooper AM: The place of self psychology in the history of depth psychology, in The Future of Psychoanalysis. Edited by Goldberg A. New York, International Universities Press, 1983

Deutsch H: The genesis of agoraphobia. Int J Psychoanal 1929; 10:51-69

Dorpat T: Structural conflict and object relations conflict. J Am Psychoanal Assoc 1976; 25:855-874

Emde R, Graensbauer T, Harmon R: Emotional Expression in Infancy: A Biobehavorial Study. New York, International Universities Press, 1976

Fairbairn WRD: An Object Relations Theory of the Personality. New York, Basic Books, 1952

Fairbairn WRD: Synopsis of an object relations theory of the personality. Int J Psychoanal 1963; 44:224-225

Fenichel O: The Psychoanalytic Theory of Neurosis. New York, Norton, 1945

Friedman L: Kohut: a book review essay. Psychoanal Q 1980; 49:393-422.

Freud A: Normality and Pathology in Childhood: The Writings of Anna Freud, vol 6. New York, International Universities Press, 1965

Freud S: Extracts from the Fliess Papers (1892-1899). Complete Psychological Works, Standard Edition, vol 1. Translated and edited by Strachey J. London, Hogarth Press, 1966

Freud S: Introductory lectures on psycho-analysis, part 3 (1916-1917), in Complete Psychological Works, Standard Edition, vol. 16. Translated and edited by Strachey J. London, Hogarth Press, 1963

Freud S: The ego and the id (1923), in Complete Psychological Works, Standard Edition, vol. 19. Translated and edited by Strachey J. London, Hogarth Press, 1961

Freud S: Some psychical consequences of the anatomical distinction between the sexes (1925), in Complete Psychological Works, Standard Edition, vol. 19. Translated and edited by Strachey J. London, Hogarth Press, 1961

Freud S: Inhibitions, symptoms and anxiety (1926), in Complete Psychological Works, Standard Edition, vol. 20. London, Hogarth Press, 1959

Galenson E, Roiphe H: The impact of early sexual discovery on mood, defensive organization and symbolization. Psychoanal Study Child 1971; 26:196-216

Galenson E, Roiphe H: The emergence of genital awareness during the second year of life, in Sex Differences in Behavior. Edited by Friedman RC, Richart RM, Van de Wiele RL. New York, John Wiley & Sons, 1974

Galenson E, Roiphe H: The preoedipal development of the boy. J Am Psychoanal Assoc 1980; 28:805-827

Gedo JE, Goldberg A: Models of the Mind. Chicago, University of Chicago Press, 1973

Goldberg A: The Psychology of the Self. New York, International Universities Press, 1978

Goldberg A: On the nature of the "misfit," in The Future of Psychoanalysis. Edited by Goldberg A. New York, International Universities Press, 1983

Greenspan SI: The oedipal–preoedipal dilemma: a reformulation in the light of object relations theory. International Review of Psychoanalysis 1977:4:381-391

Greenspan SI, Lourie RS: Developmental structuralist approach to the classification of adaptive and pathologic personality organizations: infancy and early childhood. Am J Psychiatry 1981; 138:725-735

Guntrip H: Schizoid Phenomena, Object Relations and the Self. New York, International Universities Press, 1969

Guntrip H: Psychoanalytic Theory, Therapy and the Self. New York, Basic Books, 1971

Hartmann H: The mutual influences in the development of ego and id. Psychoanal Study Child 1952; 7:9-30

Hartmann H: Comments on the psychoanalytic theory of the ego (1950), in Essays on Ego Psychology. New York, International Universities Press, 1964

Hoffer W: Development of the body ego. Psychoanal Study Child 1950; 5:18-24

Hoffer W: The mutual influences in the development of ego and id. Psychoanal Study Child 1952; 7:31-50

Jacobson E: The Self and the Object World. New York, International Universities Press, 1964

Kernberg OF: Borderline personality organization. J Am Psychoanal Assoc 1967; 15:641-685

Kernberg OF: A psychoanalytic classification of character pathology. J Am Psychoanal Assoc 1970; 18:800-822

Kernberg OF: Further contributions to the treatment of narcissistic personalities. Int J Psychoanal 1974; 55:215-240

Kernberg OF: Borderline Conditions and Pathological Narcissism. New York, Jason Aronson, 1975

Kernberg OF: Object Relations Theory and Clinical Psychoanalysis. New York, Jason Aronson, 1976

Kernberg OF: Self, ego, affects and drives. J Am Psychoanal Assoc 1982; 30:893-918

Khan MMR: Hidden Selves. New York, International Universities Press, 1983

Kohut H: The Analysis of the Self. New York, International Universities Press, 1971

Kohut H: Thoughts on narcissism and narcissistic rage. Psychoanal Study Child 1972; 27:360-400

Kohut H: The Restoration of the Self. New York, International Universities Press, 1977

Kohut H: The two analyses of Mr. Z. Int J Psychoanal 1979; 60:3-27

Kohut H: Summarizing reflections, in Advances in Self Psychology. Edited by Goldberg A. New York, International Universities Press, 1980

Kohut H: Introspection, empathy and the semi-circle of mental health. Int J Psychoanal 1982; 63:395-407

Kohut H, Wolf ES: The disorders of the self and their treatment: an outline. Int J Psychoanal 1978; 59:413-425

Kris E: The nature of psychoanalytic propositions and their validation (1947), in Selected Papers. New Haven, Yale University Press, 1975

Laing RD: The Divided Self. London, Tavistock, 1960

Laing RD, Esterson A: Sanity, Madness and the Family. London, Tavistock, 1964

Lustman SL: Rudiments of the ego. Psychoanal Study Child 1956; 11:89-98

Mahler MS: On Human Symbiosis and the Vicissitudes of Individuation. New York, International Universities Press, 1968

Mahler MS: A study of the separation–individuation process and its possible application to borderline phenomena in the psychoanalytic situation. Psychoanal Study Child 1972; 26:403-424

Mahler MS, McDevitt JB: Thoughts on the emergence of the sense of self with particular emphasis on the body self. J Am Psychoanal Assoc 1982; 30:827-848

Mahler MS, Pine F, Bergman A: The Psychological Birth of the Human Infant. New York, Basic Books, 1975

Miller A: The Prisoners of Childhood. New York, Basic Books, 1981

Pulver SE: Survey of psychoanalytic practice 1976: some trends and implications. J Am Psychoanal Assoc 1978; 26:615-631

Racker H: The meanings and uses of countertransference. Psychoanal Q 1957; 26:303-357

Rangell L: The self in psychoanalytic theory. J Am Psychoanal Assoc 1982; 30:863-892

Reich A: Narcissistic object choice in women. J Am Psychoanal Assoc 1953; 1:22-44

Reich A: Pathologic forms of self-esteem regulation. Psychoanal Study Child 1960; 15:215-232

Richards AD: The superordinate self in psychoanalytic theory and in the self psychologies. J Am Psychoanal Assoc 1982; 30:939-957

Robbins M: Current controversy in object relations theory as outgrowth of a schism between Klein and Fairbairn. Int J Psychoanal 1980; 61:477-492

Roiphe H: On an early genital phase: with an addendum on genesis. Psychoanal Study Child 1968; 23:348-365

Rothstein A: Toward a critique of the psychology of the self. Psychoanal Q 1980; 49:423-455

Segel NP: Narcissism and adaptation to iniquity. Int J Psychoanal 1981; 62:465-476

Spitz RA: Hospitalization: an inquiry into the genesis of psychiatric conditions in early childhood. Psychoanal Study Child 1945; 1

Stein MR: Review of The Restoration of the Self. J Am Psychoanal Assoc 1979; 27:665-680

Stern DN: A microanalysis of mother–infant interaction: behavior regulating social contact between a mother and her 3½ month old twins, in Infant Psychiatry. Edited by Rexford E, Sanders L, Shapiro T. New Haven, Yale University Press, 1976

Thomas A, Chess S: Temperament and Development. New York, Brunner/Mazel, 1980a

Thomas A, Chess S: The Dynamics of Psychological Development. New York, Brunner/Mazel, 1980b

Thomas A, Chess S: Genesis and evolution of behavioral disorders: from infancy to adult life. Am J Psychiatry 1984; 141:1-9

Thomas A, Chess S, Birch HG, et al: Behavioral Individuality in Early Childhood. New York, New York University Press, 1963

Thomas A, Chess S, Birch HG: Temperament and Behavior Disorders in Children. New York, New York University Press, 1968

Ticho EA: The alternate schools and the self. J Am Psychoanal Assoc 1982; 30:849-862

Treurniet N: Psychoanalysis and self psychology: a metapsychological essay with a clinical illustration. J Am Psychoanal Assoc 1983; 31:59-100

Volkan VD: Primitive Internalized Object Relations. New York, International Universities Press, 1976

Volkan VD: Narcissistic personality disorder, in Critical Problems in Psychiatry. Edited by Cavenar JO, Jr, Brodie HKH. Philadelphia, Lippincott, 1982

Waelder R: The principle of multiple function: observations on overdetermination. Psychoanal Q 1930; 5:45-62

Wallerstein RS: The bipolar self: discussion of alternative perspectives. J Am Psychoanal 1981; 29:337-394

Wallerstein RS: Self psychology and "classical" psychoanalytic psychology: the nature of their relationship, in The Future of Psychoanalysis. Edited by Goldberg A. New York, International Universities Press, 1983

Weil AP: The basic core. Psychoanal Study Child 1970; 25:442-460

Weil AP: Maturational variations and genetic dynamic issues. J Am Psychoanal Assoc 1978; 26:461-491

Winnicott D: Transitional objects and transitional phenomena. Int J Psychoanal 1953; 34:89-97

Winnicott D: The Maturational Process and the Facilitating Environment. London, Hogarth Press, 1965

Winnicott D: The mirror-role of the mother and family in child development, in The Predicament of the Family: A Psychoanalytical Symposium. Edited by Lomas P. London, Hogarth Press, 1967

Winnicott D: Playing and Reality. New York, Penguin Books, 1971

CHAPTER 14

On the Theory of Psychoanalytic Technique: A Critique of Some New Points of View

Arnold D. Richards, M.D.

In this presentation I will consider the current status of the theory of psychoanalytic technique. To this end, I will borrow Martin Bergmann's useful distinction (personal communication 1981) between "extenders" and "modifiers" of traditional psychoanalytic theory. Extenders, according to Bergmann, extend the theoretical and/or technical reach of analysis to new areas without forsaking basic classical principles; modifiers, on the other hand, offer radical reconceptualizations discontinuous with the psychoanalytic theory developed by Freud. I will first review the work of Heinz Kohut, whose approach to psychoanalytic technique revolves around the use of empathy to detect and chart the emergent course of "selfobject" transferences. I will try to show that Kohut should be considered a "modifier" with respect to the technical implications of his work. I will then turn to contributions of two recent "extenders" of the traditional theory of technique, Merton Gill and Anton Kris.

The juxtaposition of Kris and Gill with Kohut is instructive because it brings into focus the difference between theorists who amplify and then "extend" selected constituents of psychoanalytic technique and theorists whose "modifying" technical prescriptions disturb the ensemble of constituents compromising classical technique. We shall see that Kris and Gill are most helpful when their technical proposals are accepted not as additions to classical theory but as perceptive elaborations of those constituents of classical technique to which they have accorded preeminence. Analogously, Kohut's radical modification of the analyst's technical enterprise is instructive because it highlights what cannot be dispensed with if a theory of technique is to remain "psychoanalytic." My conclusion will be cautionary: classical theory of technique is an interlocking body of precepts and assumptions that *collectively* constitute the psychoanalytic method of treatment. Extenders who accord superordinate technical status to a single precept or assumption do so at the risk of downplaying aspects of technique equally integral to the psychoanalytic process. Modifiers who offer new technical precepts on the basis of therapeutic or philosophical "visions" that depart from Freud's basic approach end up with a "psychoanalysis" that is basically different in its way of thinking and of treating from the psychoanalysis bequeathed us by Freud.

HEINZ KOHUT AND THE TECHNICAL IMPLICATIONS OF SELF PSYCHOLOGY

My intention here is to comment primarily on the technical implications of self psychology rather than to offer a critique of the self-psychological theory of therapy per se (see Friedman 1980). To this end, I must assume that my readers are familiar with the essential planks of Kohut's theory of therapy—the notions of selfobject transference, of "archaic" and "mature" selfobjects, of "optimal frustration," and of "transmuting internalization." The following remarks are based primarily on a reading of Kohut's later works, from *The Restoration of the Self* (1977) through his posthumously published *How Does Analysis Cure?* (1984), supplemented by the contributions of Basch (1984a, 1984b, 1984c), one of Kohut's most forceful and articulate proponents.

Kohut's central stress on a selfobject transference as the royal road to the induction of an analytic process has technical implications that in my judgment place him beyond the pale of the "extenders" and securely in the camp of the "modifiers" of traditional psychoanalytic theory. Kohut's transmutation of Freud's notion of transference posits a new clinical attentiveness to contentless mental states that consign psychic conflict— and the "insight" through which such conflict is mediated and resolved— to a decidedly secondary status. Although Kohut's proponents, notably Basch, maintain that he remains within the mainstream of classical psychoanalysis by virtue of his retention and enlargement of the transference concept, in my view Kohut's notion of transference is so different from the classical position that the approach becomes a new technique as well as a "new view of man." I refer both to the concepts that Kohut invokes in speaking of the "mobilization" of a transference and the technical strategies that follow from this conceptual recasting. Consider this passage from the beginning of *How Does Analysis Cure?*: "In the analysis of narcissistic personality disturbances all existing defects in the self become spontaneously mobilized, as selfobject, narcissistic transferences" (p. 4). Transference, we see at once, represents for Kohut the mobilization of an archaic need corresponding to a "self" deficit: we might refer to it in shorthand as a mobilized self deficit.

The technical implications of a therapeutic focus upon the phenomenology and dynamics of "selfobject" transference follow from the fact that the latter is not offered as a species of transference in Freud's sense but as the clinical capstone of a new theory of motivation, a "selfobject theory of motivation" (Basch 1984a). As Basch has observed, Kohut's self psychology represents a "single theory of development organized around the maturation of the self that encompassed or transcended Freud's instinct theory" (1984a, p. 15). This theory differentiates analysands suffering from "overstimulation and premature sexual excitement"—an ostensibly trivial category subsuming rarely seen psychoneurotic patients— from analysands who "as children [have] been understimulated rather than overstimulated," who "instead of defending themselves against an instinctual overload are struggling with an inability to deal appropriately with their emotional needs" (p. 10).

The consequence of this diagnostic dichotomization of patients is a major modification of psychoanalytic theory and the technical precepts deriving from it. We are presented with a new class of psychopathology to be radically differentiated from the types of pathology for which traditional analysis is deemed adequate and for which self psychology is proposed as a complex and internally consistent alternative. Freud's psychoanalysis is antithetical to such an "either/or" approach (see Wallerstein 1983); in its commitment to overdetermination and the status of developmental deficit in intrapsychic conflict as interactive variables, it remains securely wedded to an embracing "both/and" approach. To argue, as Basch does, that instinctual "conflict is only one of the many forms of developmental failure with which analysis must be prepared to deal" (p. 12) is to propose a dichotomy with negative technical implications; traditional psychoanalysis becomes a psychology concerned with conflict, whereas self psychology becomes a psychology concerned with arrested development. Yet, as I will try to show, traditional analysis as a conflict theory has more to say about development than self psychology as a theory of developmental arrest has to say about psychic conflict.

Elsewhere (Richards 1982), I have attempted to support this conclusion with clinical data. Reporting on the analytic treatment of a male patient with prominent hypochondriacal symptoms, I questioned Kohut's claim (1977, pp. 105–161) that the clinical explanation of hypochondriasis can best be undertaken from the vantage point of a contentless "disintegration anxiety" displaced onto the body. For Kohut, that is, hypochondriacal worries about physical defects are "replicas of the anxieties of childhood and [the] need for the attention of the missing selfobject" (1977, p. 161). Yet in my case the analysis illuminated the specific conflicts— oedipal and preoedipal—underlying the patient's hypochondriacal symptoms. These symptoms embodied compromise formations that preserved the childhood relationship with an intrusive mother at the same time that they warded off and expressed in displaced fashion the castration anxiety connected with the maternal identification and with the passive and feminine negative oedipal trend. The clinical report provided the analytic data on which this dynamic formulation was based. My paper's central thesis regarding hypochondriasis was that "the symptom is meaningful in terms of conflict, content, and genesis, rather than merely indicative of a general failure to develop a cohesive or stable self-representation in response to his mother's general failure of empathy" (Richards 1982, p. 333).

Basch (1984a) contends that "the reformulation of psychoanalytic theory and practice sparked by Kohut's work now represents the mainstream of psychoanalysis" (p. 16). The implication is that the reformulations of self psychology are continuous with traditional psychoanalytic theory and practice.

Gail Reed in a recent paper (1987) argues that self psychology and traditional analysis use "different rules of interpretation." This is to say that whereas self psychology and traditional analysis go about gathering their psychological data in the same way, the theoretical framework through which these data are ordered is radically different (see also Stepansky 1983). According to Reed, self-psychological rules of interpretation include three primary elements: 1) the translation of surface elements into hidden elements according to the dictates of the theory of the self; 2) the positing of relationships between these elements and actions of these elements as undisguised aspects of the "self theory"; and 3) the equation of the hidden content of the interpretation with an "aspect of the self or rather with the narrative of its deficient genesis." "According to the theory of therapeutic action," Reed continues, "the restoration of the self occurs because of the restoration of meaning: the analyst's empathic understanding provides that which unempathic parents could not, thus paving the way for structure building" (pp. 430–431). She then goes on to highlight the distinction between the interpretive approach mandated by this theory of therapy and the interpretive approach intrinsic to traditional psychoanalysis:

> Interpretations of this [self-psychological] nature do not require that the patient provide particular verbal connections (as opposed to accounts of manifest history) between the surface meaning and the meaning to be restored; self theory does not account for verbal transformations, for the transformation of dream thought into pictorial representation, for instance. Thus associations and selfstate dreams are irrelevant. Rather it is the theory of the self that provides these connections. Restoration of meaning depends upon a prior belief on the part of an interpreter that there is a specific translation of elements to be made. (p. 431)

Reed's critique calls into question the claim that self psychology remains psychoanalysis by virtue of its reliance on the category of transference. With respect to the selfobject transference, Reed observes that "the manifest transference behavior of the patient is interpreted the same way as the patient's verbal productions," that is, according to the rules of interpretation that differ radically from those of traditional psychoanalysis. Moreover, even to the extent that self-psychological diagnoses *are* based on transference configurations, these diagnoses, as they emerge in the clinical self-psychological literature (e.g., Goldberg 1978), appear to be premature. The fact that early in analysis an analysand presents a phase of positive transference in which the analyst is idealized does not establish without question the basic structure of the analysand's psychopathology; the same can be said of analysands who early present a configuration that can be labeled, at the manifest level, a "mirror" transference.

Interpretations framed in terms of such manifest transference constellations tend toward a constricting circularity that undercuts the open-endedness of traditional psychoanalytic inquiry: the premature detection of a selfobject transference serves to confirm the analyst's original assumption that the patient's disturbance is "narcissistic" while at the same time it discourages the exploration of the presenting psychopathology from the standpoint of intrapsychic conflict. Friedman (1980) has commented perceptively on the built-in circularity inherent in the "homeostatic explanations" that follow from Kohut's elevation of the self to the status of superordinate structure (pp. 405–406). Elsewhere he observes that the sort of theory revolving around the putative expression—transferential or otherwise—of a need for structure per se is one that

> would not account for the conflict, repression, defenses, and resistances
> exhibited by narcissistic patients. In practice the analyst would find
> himself trying to help the patient integrate into his personality a need
> that is supposed to be a wholehearted quest for integration itself. Such a
> proposition can scarcely be formulated, let alone argued. (p. 402)

Elsewhere I have attempted to demonstrate the clinical problems consequent on such an approach by examining in detail several self-psychological case histories revolving around the emergence of a presumably conflict-free selfobject transference (Richards 1982, 1983). In brief, I believe that the self-psychological tendency to take such manifest transference configurations as prefigured structures with a predictable pattern of unfolding works against an elucidation of the conflicts, drive-related and otherwise, that routinely underlie such configurations. By resting content with these "idealizing" or "mirroring" constellations as interpretive endpoints, self psychologists miss the "polyvalence of words" by which classical analysis "challenges us to listen to the patient" (Reed 1987). Technically, self psychology "modifies" traditional psychoanalysis by veering away from an investigative methodology (Horowitz 1978) that "throws us forever back on a patient's associations" (p. 27).

By way of exemplifying this point, I wish to review critically one of the case presentations found in Goldberg's *The Psychology of the Self* (1978). All of the analyses reported in this collection were conducted by Kohut's coworkers; the volume was prepared with Kohut's collaboration.

Mr. I, a 25-year-old industrial engineer, single, complained of an inability to perform adequately on his new job and of having no relationships with women. Feeling overly attached to his family, he described his mother as blatantly seductive and mentioned incestuous wishes he felt toward his sister. In the opening phase of treatment with a female analyst, Mr. I's need to recount his nightly sexual exploits in detail was interpreted as a need "to bask in the analyst's admiration of his sexual exploits and to keep his analytic experience completely under his control in fear of overstimulation" (p. 23). This need was in turn taken to indicate a "mirror transference," a designation that labels the patient's manifest behavior toward the analyst without exploring the possible unconscious purposes, "resistance value," and adaptational gain of such "mirroring" behavior. On one occasion early in the analysis Mr. I met the analyst outside the office, felt enormously stimulated, and had "recurrent dreams of a highly incestuous flavor." This response was taken as a sign of the type of narcissistic disturbance corresponding to the emergence of the "selfobject" transference the analyst had already identified. But might not other explanations have emerged had the analyst not framed all her interpretations from the standpoint of the patient's "mirror transference"? Associations obtained in a more open-ended fashion might have illuminated a whole range of oedipal derivatives, showing how the incident in question related, for example, to primal scene observations or to seductive experiences in early childhood. The fact that this analyst was inattentive to the seductive significance of her analysand's presenting behavior may well have resulted in the incident outside the office. Could Mr. I's need to report his sexual exploits in detail have been an attempt to seduce the analyst, perhaps defensively, to avoid being seduced and abused himself?

Ascription to the patient of an "idealizing transference" during the middle phase of treatment had a comparatively restrictive effect on the analyst's attentiveness to clinical issues unrelated to the patient's self state. During this phase of the analysis, for example, the analyst alludes to the patient's subtle depreciative attitudes toward the analyst but fails to consider the possibility that such feelings may have masked significant negative transference. For example, we are informed that one day Mr. I noticed the analyst's name among the signatories of an ad in the local newspaper endorsing a candidate for political office. The patient became infuriated because this political activity reminded him of his father, who was intolerant of every political opinion that differed from his own. The analyst commented that

> Mr. I's rage at the analyst for her "thoughtless political action"
> highlighted and brought more clearly to the fore how much he needed
> the analyst as a reliable external source of tension regulation. His
> fear that the analyst would leave him unprotected against rising
> exhibitionistic tension (because he himself could not control his) had its
> roots in Mr. I's traumatic experiences with his parents. (p. 24)

In fixing solely on the economic issue of tension regulation, the analyst may well have overlooked the vicissitudes of the patient's rage and aggression, possible guilt over aggressive wishes, and fear of retaliation. This oversight is significant, as it was at this very point in the analysis that the patient described to the analyst a fantasy in the shower in which he was furious at his father and wished him dead.

The analyst's selective inattention to the genetic meaning of Mr. I's aggression during this stage of treatment is suggestive of certain unexplored problems that run through the entire case report. Mr. I was viewed as a patient unable to maintain adequately his narcissistic equilibrium—that is, he was unable to modulate his inner tension and avoid feelings of overstimulation or emptiness. His "intense, addiction-like" (p. 18) attachment to the analyst was therefore viewed only as an attempt to deal with these issues of over- and understimulation. In accordance with this clinical orientation, the genetic fact that Mr. I was exposed to open parental nudity in childhood was interpreted only from the standpoint of "excessive overstimulation," impinging deleteriously on a single "narcissistic" developmental line. The question of how this potentially traumatic exposure became internalized—for example, how it entered into unconscious fantasies that helped shape the analysand's representational world—falls beyond the parameters of self-psychological inquiry. Comparably, the clinical focus on Mr. I's missing psychic structure led the analyst to view emerging oral- and anal-incorporative fantasies as archaic attempts to acquire such psychic structure. These fantasies were not approached as mental productions with intrinsically meaningful content.

Throughout, the basic idea is that as the "self" heals, and as psychic structure is built up through transmuting internalization, the drives somehow take care of themselves. This simplifies but also constricts the investigative field, as the need to explore the content of disturbing archaic fantasies is eliminated. Psychic resistance to the unfolding of childhood sexuality is given equally short shrift. The possibility remains that the positive feelings Mr. I felt toward the analyst during treatment flowed not only from the analyst's supportive "selfobject" functioning but also from the patient's relief and gratitude that unpleasant subjects entailing resistances were left unexplored in the analysis.

I have, I think, demonstrated that self-psychological analysis relying on the primacy of selfobject transferences is technically disjunct from traditional analysis. I now wish to turn briefly to a complementary dimension of the self-psychological stress on contentless mental states in the guise of selfobject transferences: the reevaluation of empathy as the methodological centerpiece of psychoanalytic technique.

In his "Reflections" on *advances* in self psychology, Kohut (1980) writes as follows:

> I do not believe that assigning a central role to empathy . . . as the requisite observational tool of psychoanalysis can endanger the scientific status of psychoanalysis. . . . Since a psychology of complex mental states is unthinkable without empathy, the only question one can legitimately

ask is whether a psychology of complex mental states can ever be
scientific. If we express our conviction that it can, we have in the same
breath acknowledged our acceptance of empathy—an operation which
indeed is not just a valuable tool of the psychology of complex mental
states, but defines its essence and determines the content of its field.
(p. 482)

Now few analysts would question the claim that empathic comprehension of the patient is an implicit premise of successful clinical work. But
empathy cannot on this basis constitute a defining feature of analysis as
an empirical method for obtaining data within the psychoanalytic situation. Empathically obtained data, as Stepansky (1983) has observed, need
not be "psychoanalytic" data. He questions whether it makes sense to
characterize a "neutral" empathic operation as "scientific," given the fact
that a scientific research tradition such as psychoanalysis cannot be
adequately defined "without commenting systematically on the ontology
underlying the particular ordering principles, the theories that organize
data and provide the basis for deductive explanation." Research tradi-
tions, he argues, cannot be defined solely on the basis of the precision
with which they "obtain" the data that "fall within their respective
domains" (1983, p. 67).

In my "Self Theory, Conflict Theory, and the Problem of Hypochondriasis" (1981), I have tried to show that self psychology can make empathy the primary constituent of psychoanalytic technique only by assign-
ing superordinate conceptual status to self states. We have then a
technical precept masking a fundamental modification of theory: just as
clinical preoccupation with a genre of selfobject transference directs our
attention away from the drive-related conflicts that underlie such manifest configurations, so the methodological primacy of empathy in com-
prehending "contentless states of the self" leads us away from strategies
that aim at decoding unconscious fantasy systems and the conflicts they
contain.

Kohut, to be sure, repeatedly maintains that empathy is a value-free
operation "employed only for data-gathering" (1980, p. 483). But his
distinction between prior "empathic" comprehension and subsequent
theoretical explanation is countered by the fact that analytic understanding per se presumes a language of discourse in categories of explanation. Thus for Kohut it follows that the "understanding" of complex
mental states to which the analyst gains empathic access is an understanding framed in the language of self psychology and revolving around
primitive mirroring needs, feelings of fragmentation and cohesion, and so
forth. In short, when Kohut asserts that empathy is "an instrument for
the acquisition of objective knowledge about the inner life of another
person" (p. 485), this claim is suffused with his own value-laden pre-

suppositions about the nature of that "inner life"—that is, the explanatory categories through which it can best be understood. Ultimately then, the methodological primacy of empathy, like the interpretive primacy of selfobject transferences, is in the service of a holistic approach that prematurely frames explanations in terms of the whole person. It attends to self states holistically conceived at the expense of details both of thought and behavior and of lower order adaptive functions (Palombo 1980). Insofar as this orientation encourages the analyst to accept an absence of content and, more specifically, an absence of unconscious conflict in the clinical data at hand, it results in a significant modification of traditional analysis.

KOHUT: MODIFIER PAR EXCELLENCE

In arguing that in its technical implications self psychology departs sufficiently from traditional analysis to constitute a "modification," I am simply echoing Kohut's own verdict in his later writings. In his "Reflections on Advances in Self Psychology," he referred to himself as "a devoted investigator who scans the psychological field with a *new* instrument of observation" (1980, p. 476, italics mine). He went on to stress the "unbridgeable obstacle" between his work and that of other analytic investigators (e.g., Otto Kernberg and Margaret Mahler) in terms of the "basically different outlook regarding the scientific evaluation of the nature of man and the significance of his unrolling life" (p. 478). He then presents the specifically self-psychological outlook on the nature of man: "Self psychology does not see the essence of man's development as a move from dependence to independence, from merger to autonomy, or even as a move from nonself to self"; rather, self psychology takes as its *sine qua non* "man's need for selfobjects throughout the whole span of his life" (p. 479).

On the basis of this orientation Kohut predicated as the subject matter of self psychology the investigation of "the sequence of self-selfobject relationships that occur throughout life." The theory of psychopathology that followed from this program has a one-sided focus. Selfobjects, for Kohut, exist for the idealizing and mirroring functions they provide, and it is their failure to provide these functions adequately that is centrally implicated in the development of "illness." Kohut's formulation contains an important truth, to be sure, but it is noteworthy for its focus on the external milieu at the expense of an unconscious fantasy world in dynamic equilibrium with the significant figures of the environment. The self-psychological viewpoint for Kohut stands in radical opposition to the "maturation morality" that typifies traditional analysis. In basing both his theory of development and his theory of therapy on a continuing need for selfobjects throughout life (they represent our psychological "oxygen"), Kohut leaves little room for issues of autonomy and independence, issues that remain central to the therapeutic task in traditional analysis. Moreover, the preeminent place accorded the selfobject function of objects "skews the object world along a single dimension, throwing out the window the wealth of data generated by the psychoanalytic method." Classical analysis does not, as Kohut and Basch (1984a, 1984b) maintain, reduce to a unidimensional, drive-taming focus on oedipal conflicts. Rather it aims at delineating a world of unconscious fantasy that involves wishes, fears, and calamities specific to all levels of development, psychosexual and otherwise. The dynamic meaning of this world is as rich and varied as the infinite combinations and permutations of the elements that constitute it (e.g., parental constellation, sibling constellation, aggressive and libidinal feelings, trauma, injury, loss, separation, etc.).

As against all this, Kohut holds forth with a distinctive technique, one in which the "introspective, empathic observational mode" (Ornstein 1982) is the technical posture required to make contact with "the experiencing total self" of the patient, the "self" which is implicated in the contentless mental states or deficit states viewed as central to psychopathology. But by emphasizing empathic comprehension and contentless self states, Kohut only highlights the discontinuity between his developmental assumptions and theory of psychopathology and the developmental assumptions and theory of psychopathology central to traditional psychoanalysis. The technical enshrinement of empathy then shifts the analytic focus from intrapsychic reality to functional deficits attributable to the patient's environment—for example, to a lack of parental empathy in early childhood. The result then is a restrictive therapeutic focus that reduces to a dramatically secondary role those very issues that are intrinsic to *analytic* investigation. One cannot consider Kohut an extender rather than a modifier when it is his own judgment that the difference between the traditional outlook and his self-selfobject point of view are of such magnitude that to effect an integration "we would have to demand from either the other schools of thought or from self psychology the relinquishment of the central value system that determines the content of scientific observation and the significance assigned to the data" (1980, p. 48).

ANTON KRIS AND THE FREE ASSOCIATION METHOD

Anton Kris's *Free Association: Method and Process* (1982) is a book with lots of sensible clinical advice and helpful operational distinctions to guide analysts in their everyday work. Kris, a technical "extender," puts forth the method of free association as a "central point of reference" for conceptualizing the participation of both analyst and analysand in the analytic process. For Kris, analytic treatment aims at enabling the patient to complete associational sequences by helping him recognize and overcome the forces impeding such expression. Free association is primary while symptom reduction, development and resolution of the transference, and insight are secondary—that is, they follow from the analytically restored ability to associate freely. Kris urges the analyst to work primarily to facilitate the patient's ability to free associate; in fact, he goes so far as to argue that the analyst does not analyze the patient. Rather he ascribes "such functions to the method of free association. To analyze, in that sense, is an intransitive verb referring to the psychoanalyst's participation in that method" (1982, pp. 29–30).

Kris takes pains to enlarge his view by cataloguing the multiple *aims* of free association, but his position remains somewhat reductionistic nonetheless. To the extent that he focuses on the patient's ability to associate freely as a sign of health, his technical stance tends toward cultivation of "the good analysand." We may well question whether the proper goal of analytic treatment is to render the patient a good analysand in the eyes of the analyst.

One technical consequence of Kris's approach is a truncated perspective on transference. He elaborates his view on the relationship between free association and transference, proposing on the one hand that "transference establishes a human relationship whose aims are confined to promoting the patient's free associations in the service of a therapeutic objective" (pp. 61–62); on the other hand, he includes among the organizing principles of transference "a tendency to disrupt the agreement for analysis, to reject the constraints of verbal free association, to affirm the misperceptions of the analyst as reality, to redress old injuries, and to seek gratification rather than reexperience old frustrations" (pp. 61–62). It follows then that Kris sees transference as routinely tending to derail free association. But is it absolutely necessary for a patient to associate freely in order for the transference to develop? I think not, though certainly there are aspects of transference that will not come to the fore if free association is impeded. A more balanced position would hold that free association promotes the elucidation of transference, even as transference may impede the progress of free association.

Kris's stress on free association as the technical raison d'être of psychoanalysis constricts the view of the analyst's role in the analytic process. Kris stresses, for example, that the analyst "has no rights of authority," adding that restricting the analyst's role to the facilitation of free association tends to "diminish common errors of unintentional authoritarianism" (p. 22). He is aware of the fact that the patient frequently tends to view the analyst as an authority—in Kohut's terms, to idealize him. But he proposes that such feelings enter the analytic process only to the extent that they impede the flow of free associations.

There is wisdom in these caveats regarding analyst authoritarianism, to be sure, but they overlook the authority that follows naturally from the analyst's therapeutic identity. Analyst as authoritative expert versus analyst as nonauthoritarian guide in the free association process—both are integral to the analyst's identity. It is impossible to resolve the dichotomy by appealing to one "role" over the other. To argue that the analyst's perceived expertise and status as a therapeutic specialist have no relevance to the analytic process is hardly tenable.

Similar reservations must be made with regard to Kris's discussion of the desirability of answering questions in analysis. Consistent with his concern regarding authoritarianism, he submits that "the responsibility of the analyst to warn patients of impending dangers is based not upon the authority of the analyst or upon some superior understanding of the world. It derives from the analyst's function in the free association method" (p. 28). According to Kris, in instances where the analyst must make unilateral decisions owing to the patient's limited capacity to exercise judgment, "the limits of applicability of the free association method have already been breached" (p. 29). True enough. But what is the technical yield of this proviso? It is difficult to codify analytic rules to cover such contingencies. We all occasionally relate to our patients' information based on our knowledge; such communications may or may not figure in the analytic process. The only "rule" that governs such noninterpretive interventions is that we be aware of what we are doing and remain alert to the potential consequences, positive or negative, of such activity.

Kris's attempt to elaborate a theory of technique around the method of free association has an avowedly antitheoretical edge. Recoiling from an intellectual climate that has focused on rival "models of the mind" and has recently placed "deficit psychology" in opposition to conflict psychology, Kris seeks to remove us from theoretical controversy and return us to basic process issues. He is explicit about this intent, informing us at the outset that he is focusing on "initial formulations in the analytic process relatively free of theories of the mind" (1982, p. 1). Kris's position is that we cannot make adequate use of higher order theories until we have developed initial formulations of the psychoanalytic process in terms of method (pp. ix, xi, 33, 103–105). In an article, "The Analyst's Conceptual Freedom and the Method of Free Association" (1983), Kris advocates a "conceptual freedom," which he equates with a "sort of eclecticism within the realm of psychoanalytic theory" (p. 407). He contends that theory limits observation insofar as it "promote[s] moving from the theory to the associations rather than in the opposite direction" (pp. 407–408). Kris's bugbear in all this is the sort of "premature closure" that short-circuits an attentive investigation of the clinical data; such closure epitomizes what he considers the "misapplication of theory."

What Kris overlooks in his otherwise sensible remarks is that a theory of technique nonetheless assumes a theory of the psychoanalytic process and, ultimately, a theory of cure. Even his operational stress on the analysand's ability to associate freely makes such an assumption: in asserting that the "method of free association serves the therapeutic aim of promoting continuities (of thought, affect, memory, sense of self, and so on) whereas psychopathology is characterized by corresponding discontinuities" (p. 408), Kris is implicitly developing a theory of therapeutic action and cure around a continuity–discontinuity axis. However, such a "theory" is insufficiently comprehensive—and insufficiently *psychoanalytic*—to replace the traditional theory. A fully adequate theory must contain the defining characteristics of the analytic process; these include the infantile neurosis, the transference neurosis, and working through. It must also range beyond strictly operational concepts and include, for example, a principle of repetition (distinct from the repetition compulsion linked by Freud to the death instinct and considered to be beyond the pleasure principle) to account for the efficacy of analysis as a treatment modality.

MERTON GILL AND THE CENTRALITY OF TRANSFERENCE

Merton Gill's recent contribution to the theory of technique parallels Kris's in making one element of the therapeutic process technically superordinate (Gill 1979, 1982; Gill and Hoffman 1982). Whereas Kris focuses on the therapeutic gains that follow from the patient's restored ability to associate freely, Gill centers the therapeutic action of analysis on the cultivation, exploration, and eventual resolution of the "here-and-now" transference. Analysis of the transference, he contends, is "the heart of psychoanalytic technique." Offering a definition of transference that encompasses virtually all aspects of the analyst–analysand interaction, he distinguishes between "conscious appropriate elements of the person's way of relating as manifestations of transference" and "inappropriate unconscious elements" (p. 10). He adds that the "unobjectionable" roots of transference cannot be excluded from clinical scrutiny, thereby taking issue with analysts who, like Zetzel (1956) and Greenson (1965), consider the "therapeutic" or "working" alliance exempt from analytic scrutiny. Likewise he rejects Stone's view (1961) of the "mature transference" as a configuration to be partially gratified rather than analyzed. Gill's perspective on transference interpretation is broad. It includes 1) interpretations of resistance to the awareness of transference and 2) interpretations of resistance to the resolution of transference. It is in regard to the first category in particular that he developed his thesis of the centrality of transference analysis to analytic technique. By resistance to the awareness of transference Gill is referring to associations containing implicit allusions to the transference that the analysand cannot or will not recognize. He believes that such latently transferential associations are ubiquitous in analysis; if the analyst is to do his job right, he must spare no effort in deciphering their hidden transferential meanings.

Gill's proposition that the patient's presenting neurosis can invariably be translated into a transference neurosis has important technical implications. He seems to recommend that relatively little analytic attention be directed to the systematic recovering of memories, contending that if resistance to the awareness of transference is overcome and the ensuing resistance to the resolution of the transference is worked through, the relevant childhood memories will automatically achieve consciousness. For Gill then, as for Strachey (1934), only transference interpretations are "mutative." Gill does not, however, seem to share Strachey's view of the centrality of superego shift in this process (Etchegoyen 1983). Gill contests the importance of extratransference interpretations in the analytic process. He believes that neurosis "can *always* be transformed into transference, provided the analyst does what is clinically necessary to facilitate the expansion of the transference in the analytic situation" (p. 59).

Gill's technical prescriptions, which proceed from his claim that analysis reduces to transference interpretation, represent, I believe, a skewed perspective on the theory of therapy and on the theory of cure. The integral relationship between the recovery of childhood memories and the development of transference underscores this point. The recovery of early memories facilitates both the unfolding of the transference and the patient's understanding of its nature. This is common analytic experience. And it is equally true that the experience of the here-and-now transference leads to the recovery of memories central to the analysand's psychopathology. The analyst, we might say, from both inside and outside, is simultaneously participating in the here-and-now interaction and providing interpretations from his "observer" vantage point; he is not simply a participant observer but at one and the same time a participant *and* an observer. In Gill's view of technique it is the complex interdependent nature of the analyst's *multiple* orientations that is sometimes obscured.

I would offer a similar criticism of Gill's repeated insistence that the translation of the presenting neurosis into a transference is the aim of analysis and as such is central to its therapeutic efficacy. As a theoretical commentary on one dimension of the analytic process, Gill's position is unassailable. But it overlooks the fact that as therapists we are continually dealing with a "means-end" problem that calls for flexible clinical judgment. The goal of psychoanalytic treatment is insight that will enable the analysand to achieve significant personality change on behalf of enhanced creativity and productivity along with more satisfactory adaptation in human relationships. Analysis of the transference is a central means to this end certainly, but it is not equivalent to this end: the goal of analysis is not reducible to the analysand's "resolved" relationship with the analyst.

Given the different needs of different analysands, it is not always the case that resistance to the awareness of transference must be rigorously pursued, sought out, and "dogged" by the analyst to the exclusion of other analytic tasks. It cannot be said that anything short of this aggressive approach constitutes "underplaying" resistance to the awareness of the transference. Rather than turning every stone to see if some hidden transference meaning might lie beneath it, the analyst must retain a cautious, open-minded flexibility in the methods he adopts to effect the translation of the presenting neurosis into its transference analogue. It is possible to pursue the here-and-now transference so rigorously that the genetic roots of transference conflicts in infantile sexuality and aggression may get lost in the transferential shuffle. Clinical judgment is required to determine whether analytic interventions should focus more on primary childhood objects or more on relationships to these objects as mediated by the transference. This basic fact of clinical life is obscured by the preeminence Gill attributes to transference interpretations in each and every analysis.

Both the strengths and the weaknesses of Gill's technical focus on the here-and-now transference are highlighted in volume 2 of *The Analysis of Transference* (1982). Here Gill and his collaborator Hoffman, by way of validating the technical strategies proffered in volume 1, present and offer commentary on the transcripts of nine therapeutic sessions. It should be noted at the outset that only six of these sessions come from analyses, and one of these was with a patient seen sitting up. The remaining three patients were seen in therapy once a week. Of five sessions conducted by therapists attempting to apply Gill's point of view, three involved the once-a-week therapy patients and one involved the analytic patient who did not use the couch. In sum, then, Gill presents us with four "bad" analytic sessions, one "good" analytic session, one "good" analytic session in which the patient was seen sitting up, and three "good" psychotherapy sessions. He does not tell us how he arrived at this selection of sessions, or why he elected to analyze the sessions in vacuo that is, without the benefit of any historical background or clinical data from earlier or later sessions. It is particularly regrettable that we have but one "good" analytic case conducted on the couch. To test these proposals with adequate rigor would require more adequate clinical data, perhaps a combination of longitudinal case studies with verbatim transcripts of pivotal sessions.

As a result of these methodological problems, Gill and Hoffman are more persuasive in criticizing sessions evincing faulty technique than in demonstrating the unquestioned primacy of here-and-now transference interpretation in those they deem successful. In their discussion of Patient B, for example, they have little difficulty demonstrating the inappropriateness of a penis meaning arbitrarily imputed to the patient's dream associations by the analyst. More perceptively, they point to the analyst's failure to appreciate the import of an interaction at the analyst's door as the session began: the patient expressed her perception of the analyst as impatient and critical on opening the door. Rather than probing the meaning of this perception in terms of issues, say, of initiative and self-assertion, the analyst permitted the session to begin with a four-minute silence.

In the case of Patient C, Gill and Hoffman criticize the similarly forced imputation of castration meaning on the productions of a woman patient. When this patient responded angrily to the interpretation, adding that she wished to knock all the analyst's books off the wall, the analyst responded in turn that this was really a wish to knock his penis off. Gill and Hoffman deem this remark "an almost unbelievably pat interpretation that exemplifies our point. Instead of finding out what she means by wanting to knock down his books, the analyst uses what she has said to reiterate his fixed conviction . . . which she has just characterized as unhelpful" (p. 58). Interestingly, this patient proceeded to relate books and reading to compensatory feelings for not having a penis; thus, as Gill subsequently acknowledges, the session may well provide an example of a correct interpretation proceeding from faulty technique. Gill's point is that the analyst had in any event missed the fact that the patient experienced him as an unreasonable dictator and that this perception was based on the patient's actual experience of the analyst; indeed, he seemed to foist interpretations on the patient without due concern for either the evidence or her feelings.

In the case of Patient D, Gill and Hoffman discuss a session in which the patient responded to the analyst's interpretation with the remark, "That's obvious now." They point to the analyst's failure to analyze this comment as a "significant and common flaw" (p. 86). Their insistence that analysts attend to the pseudocompliant aspects of such seemingly facile acceptance of interpretations is certainly a useful technical reminder, but there is no way of determining whether their inference about Patient D is correct on the basis of the transcript of this single session.

Had the patient's "That's obvious now" generated relevant memories of associations, or a modulation of the character trait being explored, it might well have betokened a deepening of the analytic process and a working through of the patient's comprehension of the issues.

It is with respect to Patient A that Gill and Hoffman provide examples of what they mean by inferring latent transference meaning from the overt productions of the patient. To give but one example: the patient tells an involved story about her cat and the ASPCA. This agency delayed in treating the cat for an illness, and the animal subsequently died. The authors comment that "the cat died because they fooled around instead of operating. The latent meaning may be that the analyst's silence is doing nothing and the analysis may die. She may be growing increasingly angry at his inactivity" (p. 19).

Now this interpretation is surely one possibility, but is it the only one? How can the analyst know this to be so? The only technical dictum that follows from clinical data of this sort is that the analyst must "listen" to the patient's productions and attempt to "read" unconscious meanings and themes in them. These meanings and themes invariably pertain to wishes and fantasies, which, to be sure, may include transference wishes and fantasies. But the analyst can hardly assume that such wishes and fantasies are necessarily limited to the patient's reactions to the analyst in the here and now. In many cases the discernment of unconscious meanings will proceed from the analyst's sense of what has transpired in recent sessions, from his understanding of the latent content of a series of dreams—indeed, from his cumulative knowledge of the entire analysis to that point. The analyst's imputation of unconscious meaning proceeds from a complex process of "knowing" that must take into account the patient's achieved level of cognitive, intuitive, and empathic functioning. This presupposes an ongoing attentiveness to a whole host of nonverbal cues, bodily movements, and additional data processed by what is sometimes called the "analytic instrument." When the analyst, on the basis of this material, undertakes to communicate his inference of unconscious meaning to the patient via an interpretation, he must synthesize knowledge from a variety of sources, judge the adequacy and persuasive force of the evidence for a connection between current productions and latent meaning, and make a further judgment as to the patient's readiness to assimilate the interpretation.

I would like to comment briefly on the theoretical basis of Gill's position regarding analysis of the transference. In a recent article, "The Point of View of Psychoanalysis: Energy Discharge or Person" (1983), Gill proposes that the basic integrative viewpoint of analysis should be the "relationship between people, not the discharge of energy" (pp. 524–525). Denying the need for both viewpoints, he insists that the interrelational perspective "must subsume the data which lead to the energy discharge point of view" (p. 528).

Gill believes that the point of view of the person obliges us to "reach a conception of transference and countertransference different from the prevailing one" (p. 544). He equates this prevailing view with a false dichotomy between transference and countertransference—understood as distortions of reality—and reality itself. Gill maintains, on the other hand, that

> transference is distinguished from nontransference not by using a distortion of reality but by the rigidity with which the person maintains his view of reality as shown in his relative obliviousness to existing external circumstances and changes in circumstances and to alternative modes of relating to others, which in turn have the potential of evoking different kinds of responses and new forms of interpersonal experience. The person in the grip of a transference is blind to such potential. (p. 544)

It follows for Gill that the aim of analysis is to make patterns of interpersonal interactions as explicit as possible; this aim defines psychoanalysis. If psychopathology is understood in terms of interpersonal relations, then explicating maladaptive interactional patterns will have "the most far-reaching and stable beneficial influence on the patient's patterns of interaction" (p. 545). Thus, "the patient's experience of a relationship should be [the analyst's] primary goal" (p. 545). The therapist's task is to look for "disguised references by the patient to his experience of his relationship with the therapist in the here and now" and to explicate this relationship "in the spirit of seeing the plausibility of the patient's experience" (p. 545).

Thus Gill returns to the here and now as the central medium of psychoanalytic exchange. "Only after the patient's experience has been explored from this point of view will [the analyst] raise questions about possible other interpretations of the ongoing interaction with the goal of elucidating the patient's transference contribution to his experience" (p. 546). Exploration of the here and now invariably precedes exploration of the analysand's past, and the latter should be explored "with the same perspective which the therapist uses in his examination of the here-and-now interaction with himself, that is, that the past also took place in an interpersonal context" (p. 548).

One can readily agree that the past took place in an "interpersonal" context (childhood is, after all, our first "interpersonal" experience) without accepting Gill's conclusion that the analyst who embraces his approach will conduct analyses in a manner different from the prevalent approach. I think he means that an interpersonal focus on "persons" results in a technique that focuses more on the therapist as participant than as observer, more on the present than the past, and more on the plausibility of the patient's experience than its distortions. Gill believes that in contradistinction to this approach the "prevalent conception of free association and regression will in time lead to the relatively direct expression of bodily urges, little related to interpersonal reaction whether with others in the past or with the therapist in the present" (p. 545).

The problem with Gill's conclusion is that it is based on a false dichotomy between the viewpoint of the "person" and a traditional viewpoint that he, without sufficient justification, reduces to "energy discharge." It is true, as Gill stresses, that "psychological man exists only in an interpersonal context" (p. 526), but I do not believe that psychoanalytic ego psychology, with its reliance on the structural theory and its model of conflict, reduces to an energy discharge model pure and simple. Structural theory has, I believe, explanatory richness in excess of what Gill imputes to it; it includes concepts relating to bodily process, psychological wish, and object relations in dynamic interrelation. This is particularly true of the structural viewpoint on conflict, which, with its concepts of compromise formation, encompassing drive, defense, and superego contributions, goes far beyond an energy discharge model.

Gill's position is somewhat puzzling to me since it was Gill himself who, with Rapaport, clarified 25 years ago that the energic viewpoint is but one constituent of psychoanalytic metapsychology (Rapaport and Gill 1959). It follows then that a theory of technique deriving from structural theory and encompassing the multiple viewpoints of metapsychology (Brenner 1975) is more adequate to the interpersonal requirements of analytic work than Gill would have us believe. It is true that the theory proposes that free association and regression will lead to a greater expression of bodily urges, but only in the sense that the interpersonal relationships of early childhood are organized more purely along drive-related lines. Traditional theory does not thereby forsake the insight that such bodily urges are organized and gain expression in terms of interpersonal interactions. Drive and object can never be severed, whether in everyday life or in the analytic transference. The problem with Gill's approach, both its underpinnings and its operational implications, is that an excessive focus on the here and now of the analyst-analysand relationship, particularly to the extent that it involves a more interactive, back-and-forth discussion, may impede the process of free association. It may specifically forestall regression and mitigate against the revival of conflictual interpersonal interactions, both as they occurred in childhood and as they permeate the here-and-now transference.

GILL AND KRIS: SKEWED DISCOURSE

The problem with the technical strategies of both Kris and Gill is that they skew the therapeutic process along a single dimension. For Gill the patient speaks and the analyst thinks, "What is the patient trying to say about me and the analytic situation?" As I have observed, the aggressive pursuit of transference meaning may actually interfere with the analytic process, impeding the analyst's "hovering" attention and thereby limiting his ability to attend to the range of unconscious meanings embedded in the analysand's productions. The result may well be a tendency to respond to the patient's productions in stereotypical ways. This is not to say that there is no value in Gill's contribution: transference fantasies and attitudes pertaining to the here-and-now analyst–analysand interaction are indeed important and may even warrant a certain priority in our interpretive strategies. They cannot, however, comprise the entire analytic endeavor.

The same may be said of Kris's emphasis on strategies that facilitate the analysand's capacity to associate freely. This capacity is central to the induction of an analytic process but is not the sole criterion by which to assess analytic cure. Yet Kris seems to equate the operational primacy of the free association method with the psychoanalytic theory of therapy, ascribing to free association per se "the therapeutic functions of promot-[ing] continuities and . . . increas[ing] the freedom of association" (1982, p. 71). There is some truth to this ascription, but those functions hardly exhaust the therapeutic action of analysis. We are all familiar with situations in which the patient does not associate freely but nevertheless manages to communicate a central pathological constellation to the analyst via transference manifestations, symptoms, enactments, and so forth. We also know patients who, though they relate to their analysts everything that comes to mind, accomplish virtually nothing in their analytic work. They travesty analysis by saying "everything that comes to mind" while thereby hiding central issues from analytic scrutiny.

The problem for both Gill and Kris is that in according superordinate significance to a single dimension of the theory of therapy they obscure the interrelation of the various factors propelling analysis forward. The psychoanalytic theory of cure includes conceptually integrated principles that transcend Kris's strictly operational perspective: the infantile neurosis, the transference neurosis, the repetition principle, working through, and the curative potential of insight mediated by interpretation. These elements are mobilized in the analytic situation by employing the method of free association, but the theory of cure cannot be *defined* in terms of what is simply a methodological prerequisite. Similarly, the theory of cure transcends the notion of the resolved transference relationship. Ultimately, transference analysis must be absorbed in the broader attempt to uncover and understand the unconscious wishes and fantasies that emerge in childhood and (via the repetition principle) continue to affect the patient's current life adjustment. Optimally, the self-knowledge at which the analysand arrives at the conclusion of a successful analysis incorporates, even as it transcends, an understanding of the dynamics underlying the analytic interaction.

CONCLUSION

The perspective of the extender links the evolution of present-day theory and technique to the progressive enrichment of psychoanalytic theory via the sequential unfolding of instinct theory, economic, genetic, dynamic, and structural viewpoints, and finally, ego psychology (Rangell 1982). There is an integral connection between technique and the multiple viewpoints of classical theory (Fenichel 1941). These viewpoints lead to a conflict psychology enriched by an ego-psychological emphasis on the analysis of defenses. Analysis is in essence a conflict theory; analysts who agree with this principle are extenders rather than modifiers. Theoretical innovations that preserve analysis as a psychology of conflict and analytic technique as the means for decoding and interpreting conflict are not modifications. Psychoanalytic technique can be refined and expanded in response to conflicts that fall within the analyst's purview. As Rangell has observed, while ego psychology has significantly enhanced the theory of therapy by putting the analysis of defenses on a par with analysis of drive derivatives, the concepts of defenses and resistances are entirely compatible with the definition of analysis as a conflict psychology. Hartmann proposed fairly important changes in the theory of mental functioning without advocating significant alterations in technique (Richards 1984).

Self psychology is a modification because it embodies the conviction that analysis must expand beyond the boundaries of conflict theory. It arises out of Kohut's belief that the terminology, concepts, and interpretive strategies intrinsic to conflict theory are inadequate to meet the needs of patients suffering from deficit states. From these theoretical principles self psychology has generated a distinctive technique, one in which the "introspective, empathic observational mode" (Ornstein 1982) is the technical posture required to make contact with the "experiencing total self" of the patient, the "self" that is implicated in the contentless mental states or deficit states viewed as central to psychopathology. The analytic focus is shifted from intrapsychic reality to functional deficits attributable to the patient's environment. Empathic comprehension of the patient is an implicit premise of successful clinical work but is not a *defining feature* of analysis as an empirical method for obtaining data within the analytic situation. Empathically obtained data, in other words, are not exhaustive of psychoanalytic data. At best, the theoretical stress on empathy sensitizes us anew to a single precondition for the successful application of analytic technique; but it does not add to our understanding of technique per se, and it can hardly be said to constitute it.

Since both Gill and Kris consider psychoanalysis a conflict theory, they are, in the terms we have adopted, extenders rather than modifiers. However, Gill's recent emphasis on the dichotomy between person and energic drive and his opting for the person and the interpersonal may lead eventually to a theory of the mode of action of psychoanalysis that crosses the subtle line between the extender's shift in emphasis to the more radical rupture of the modifier. Similarly, Kris's distinction between conflicts of defense and conflicts of ambivalence may foreshadow a theoretical rupture of a different sort; for now, however, the main problem with his approach is its unidimensional focus and its possible blinding effects if applied too rigorously in actual analytic work.

Finally then, this chapter is based on the appreciation of psychoanalysis as a conflict psychology and all that this implies for the theory of technique. Kohut's self psychology is an alternate metapsychology with technical correlates and a therapeutic strategy different from those of psychoanalysis and as such should be judged in its own right (Greene 1984). Gill and Kris, on the other hand, in their attempts to reduce psychoanalytic theory of technique in the name of analytic rigor to a single one of its manifold aspects, risk an outcome in which such reductions may become superordinate theories in their own right.

REFERENCES

Basch MF: The selfobject theory of motivation and the history of psychoanalysis, in Kohut's Legacy: Contributions to Self Psychology. Edited by Stepansky PE, Goldberg A. Hillsdale, NJ, Analytic Press, 1984a
Basch MF: Selfobjects and selfobject transference: theoretical implications, in Kohut's Legacy: Contributions to Self Psychology. Edited by Stepansky PE, Goldberg A. Hillsdale, NJ, Analytic Press, 1984b
Basch MF: Selfobjects, development, and psychotherapy, in Kohut's Legacy: Contributions to Self Psychology. Edited by Stepansky PE, Goldberg A. Hillsdale, NJ, Analytic Press, 1984c
Brenner C: Affects and psychic conflict. Psychoanal Q 1975; 44:5-28
Etchegoyen RH: Fifty years after the mutative interpretation. Int J Psychoanal 1983; 64:445-459

Fenichel O: Problems of Psychoanalytic Technique. Albany, NY, Psycho-analytic Quarterly Inc, 1941

Friedman L: Kohut: a book review essay. Psychoanal Q 1980; 49:393-422

Gill M: The analysis of the transference. J Am Psychoanal Assoc 1979; 27 (Suppl):263-288

Gill M: Analysis of Transference, Vol. I: Theory and Technique. New York, International Universities Press, 1982

Gill M: The point of view of psychoanalysis: energy discharge or person? Psychoanalysis and Contemporary Thought 1983; 6:523-551

Gill M, Hoffman IZ: Analysis of Transference, Vol. II: Studies of Nine Audio-Recorded Psychoanalytic Sessions. New York, International Universities Press, 1982

Goldberg A: The Psychology of the Self: A Casebook. Written with the collaboration of Kohut H, edited by Goldberg A. New York, International Universities Press, 1978

Greene MA: The self psychology of Heinz Kohut. Bull Menninger Clin 1984; 48:37-53

Greenson R: The problem of working through, in Drives, Affects, Behavior, vol. 2. Edited by Schur M. New York, International Universities Press, 1965

Horowitz M: New York Psychoanalytic Society Meeting, Summary. Bull Assoc Psychoanalytic Med 1978; 17:43-47

Kohut H: The Restoration of the Self. New York, International Universities Press, 1977

Kohut H: Reflections on advances in self psychology, in Advances in Self Psychology. Edited by Goldberg A. New York, International Universities Press, 1980

Kohut H: How Does Analysis Cure? Edited by Goldberg A, Stepansky PE. Chicago, University of Chicago Press, 1984

Kris A: Free Association: Method and Process. New Haven, Yale University Press, 1982

Kris A: The analyst's conceptual freedom and the method of free association. Int J Psychoanal 1983; 64:407-411

Ornstein PH: On the psychoanalytic psychotherapy of primary self pathology, in Psychiatry Update 1982: The American Psychiatric Association Annual Review, Vol. 1. Edited by Grinspoon L. Washington, DC, American Psychiatric Press, 1982

Palombo SR: The archaic adaptive ego, in The Course of Life, Vol. III: Adulthood and the Aging Process. Edited by Greenspan SI, Pollock GH. Washington, DC, U.S. Government Printing Office, 1980

Rapaport D, Gill M: The points of view and assumptions of metapsychology. Int J Psychoanal 1959; 40:153-162

Reed G: Rules of clinical understanding in classical psychoanalysis and in self psychology: a comparison. J Am Psychoanal Assoc 1987; 35:421-446

Richards AD: Self theory, conflict theory, and the problem of hypochondriasis. Psychoanal Study Child 1981; 36:319-337

Richards AD: The superordinate self in psychoanalytic theory and the self psychologies. J Am Psychoanal Assoc 1982: 30:939-957

Stepansky P: Perspectives on dissent: Adler, Kohut, and the idea of a psychoanalytic research tradition, in The Annual of Psychoanalysis, Vol. II. Edited by the Chicago Institute for Psychoanalysis. New York, International Universities Press, 1983

Stone L: The Psychoanalytic Situation: An Examination of Its Development and Essential Nature. New York, International Universities Press, 1961

Strachey J: The nature of the therapeutic action of psychoanalysis. Int J Psychoanal 1934; 15:127-159

Wallerstein RS: Self psychological and "classical" psychoanalytic psychology: the nature of their relationship, in The Future of Psychoanalysis. Edited by Goldberg A. New York, International Universities Press, 1983

Zetzel ER: The concept of transference. Int J Psychoanal 1956; 37:369-376

INDEX